But grow in the grace and knowledge of our Lord and Savior Jesus Christ. To Him be the glory both now and forever. Amen.

—

2 PETER 3:18 NKJV

Once a Day
EVERY DAY...

FOR A
WOMAN
of
GRACE

Once a Day

EVERY DAY...

FOR A

WOMAN

of

GRACE

FREEMAN-SMITH

365 DAILY DEVOTIONS

INTRODUCTION

Being a godly woman in today's world can be a daunting task. Never have expectations been higher, never have distractions been so plentiful, and never have demands been greater. Thankfully, God stands ready, willing, and able to help us in every facet of our lives if we ask Him. But it's important to remember that the best way to ask God for His wisdom and His strength is to ask Him often.

Sometimes, when it seems that we have too many things to do and too few hours in which to do them, we may be tempted to rush through the day with little or no time for prayer and meditation; when we do so, we suffer because of our mistaken priorities. But, when we set aside time each day for God, we open ourselves to His love, His wisdom, and His strength.

The fabric of daily life is woven together with the threads of habit, and no habit is more important than that of consistent prayer and daily devotion to our Creator. And this book is intended to help. This text contains 365 chapters, one for each day of the year. During the next 12 months, please try this experiment: read a chapter each day. If you're already committed to a daily worship time, this book will enrich that experience. If you are not, the simple act of giving God a few minutes each morning will change the direction and the quality of your life.

This text addresses topics of particular interest to you, a Christian woman living in an uncertain world. If you take the time to meditate upon these devotional readings, you will be reminded of God's love, of His Son, and of His promises. May these pages be a blessing to you, and may you, in turn, be a blessing to those whom God has seen fit to place along your path.

READ THE BIBLE IN A YEAR

Reading the Bible from cover to cover in 365 days is a worthy goal for every Christian, including you. If you complete the suggested Bible readings found on each page of this book, you will, in 365 days, finish both the Old and New Testaments.

Each day provides yet another opportunity to study God's Word, to follow His path, and to reacquaint yourself with His promises. When you do these things, you will be richly blessed. So take the time to read His Word once a day, every day. No exceptions.

A GIFT BEYOND COMPREHENSION

Therefore, since we receive a kingdom which cannot be shaken, let us show gratitude, by which we may offer to God an acceptable service with reverence and awe....

Hebrews 12:28 NASB

The grace of God overflows from His heart. And if we open our hearts to Him, we receive His grace, and we are blessed with joy, abundance, peace, and eternal life.

The familiar words of Ephesians 2:8 make God's promise perfectly clear: "For by grace you have been saved through faith, and that not of yourselves; it is the gift of God" (NKJV). In other words, we are saved, not by our actions, but by God's mercy. We are saved, not because of our good deeds, but because of our faith in Christ.

God's grace is the ultimate gift, a gift beyond comprehension and beyond compare. And because it is the ultimate gift, we owe God the ultimate in thanksgiving.

God's grace is indeed a gift from the heart—God's heart. And as believers, we must accept God's precious gift thankfully, humbly, and, immediately—today is never too soon because tomorrow may be too late.

— A PRAYER —

Lord, You have saved me by Your grace. Keep me mindful that Your grace is a gift that I can accept but cannot earn. I praise You for that priceless gift, today and forever. Let me share the good news of Your grace with a world that desperately needs Your healing touch. Amen

PUTTING GOD FIRST

Thou shalt have no other gods before me.

Exodus 20:3 KJV

One of the quickest ways to improve your day and your life—and the surest way—is to do it with God as your partner. When you put God first in every aspect of your life, you'll be comforted by the knowledge that His wisdom is the ultimate wisdom and that His plans are the right plans for you. When you put God first, your outlook will change, your priorities will change, and your behaviors will change. And, when you put Him first, you'll experience the genuine peace and lasting comfort that only He can give.

In the book of Exodus, God instructs us to place no gods before Him. Does God rule your heart? Make certain that the honest answer to this question is a resounding yes. And then prepare yourself for the cascade of spiritual and emotional blessings that are sure to follow.

Our God is so wonderfully good, and lovely, and blessed in every way that the mere fact of belonging to Him is enough for an untellable fullness of joy!

Hannah Whitall Smith

— A PRAYER —

Dear Lord, Your love is eternal and Your laws are everlasting. When I obey Your commandments, I am blessed. Today, I invite You to reign over every corner of my heart. I will have faith in You, Father. I will sense Your presence; I will accept Your love; I will trust Your will; and I will praise You for the Savior of my life: Your Son Jesus. Amen

SEEKING GOD

But seek first the kingdom of God and His righteousness, and all these things shall be added to you.

Matthew 6:33 NKJV

The familiar words of Matthew 6 remind us that, as believers, we must seek God and His kingdom. And when we seek Him with our hearts open and our prayers lifted, we need not look far: God is with us always.

Sometimes, however, in the crush of our daily duties, God may seem far away, but He is not. God is everywhere we have ever been and everywhere we will ever go. He is with us night and day; He knows our thoughts and our prayers. And, when we earnestly seek Him, we will find Him because He is here, waiting patiently for us to reach out to Him.

Today, let us reach out to the Giver of all blessings. Let us turn to Him for guidance and for strength. Today, may we, who have been given so much, seek God and invite Him into every aspect of our lives. And, let us remember that no matter our circumstances, God never leaves us; He is here . . . always right here.

I am convinced beyond a shadow of any doubt that the most valuable pursuit we can embark upon is to know God.

Kay Arthur

— A PRAYER —

How comforting it is, Dear Lord, to know that if I seek You, I will find You. You are with me, Father, every step that I take. Let me reach out to You, and let me praise You for revealing Your Word, Your way, and Your love. Amen

ACCEPTING CHRIST

Yet we know that no one is justified by the works of the law but by faith in Jesus Christ. And we have believed in Christ Jesus, so that we might be justified by faith in Christ and not by the works of the law, because by the works of the law no human being will be justified.

Galatians 2:16 HCSB

God's love for you is deeper and more profound than you can imagine. God's love for you is so great that He sent His only Son to this earth to die for your sins and to offer you the priceless gift of eternal life. Now, you must decide whether or not to accept God's gift. Will you ignore it or embrace it? Will you return it or neglect it? Will you accept Christ, or will you turn from Him?

Your decision to accept Christ is the pivotal decision of your life. It is a decision that you cannot ignore. It is a decision that is yours and yours alone. It is a decision with profound consequences, both earthly and eternal. Accept God's gift: Accept Christ today.

Today, some of the hardest groups of people to reach are not the Jews but those who have gone to church all their lives, are familiar with the Gospel story, converse using spiritual cliches, and sing the traditional hymns of faith from memory, yet have never truly placed their faith in Jesus Christ.

Anne Graham Lotz

— A PRAYER —

Father, You gave Your Son that I might have life eternal. Thank You for this priceless gift and for the joy I feel in my heart when I give You my thoughts, my prayers, my praise, and my life. Amen

TALKING TO THE FATHER

You do not have, because you do not ask God.

James 4:2 NIV

Sometimes, amid the demands and the frustrations of everyday life, we forget to slow ourselves down long enough to talk with God. Instead of turning our thoughts and prayers to Him, we rely upon our own resources. Instead of praying for strength and courage, we seek to manufacture it within ourselves. Instead of asking God for guidance, we depend only upon our own limited wisdom. The results of such behaviors are unfortunate and, on occasion, tragic.

Are you in need? Ask God to sustain you. Are you troubled? Take your worries to Him in prayer. Are you weary? Seek God's strength. In all things great and small, seek God's wisdom and His grace. He hears your prayers, and He will answer. All you must do is ask.

When will we realize that we're not troubling God with our questions and concerns? His heart is open to hear us—his touch nearer than our next thought—as if no one in the world existed but us. Our very personal God wants to hear from us personally.

Gigi Graham Tchividjian

— A PRAYER —

Lord, when I have questions or fears, let me turn to You. When I am weak, let me seek Your strength. When I am discouraged, Father, keep me mindful of Your love and Your grace. In all things, let me seek Your will and Your way, Dear Lord, today and forever. Amen

THE POWER OF PRAYER

Be anxious for nothing, but in everything by prayer and supplication with thanksgiving let your requests be made known to God.

Philippians 4:6 NASB

"The power of prayer": these words are so familiar, yet sometimes we forget what they mean. Prayer is a powerful tool for communicating with our Creator; it is an opportunity to commune with the Giver of all things good. Prayer helps us find strength for today and hope for the future. Prayer is not a thing to be taken lightly or to be used infrequently.

Is prayer an integral part of your daily life, or is it a hit-or-miss habit? Do you "pray without ceasing," or is your prayer life an afterthought?

The quality of your spiritual life will be in direct proportion to the quality of your prayer life. Prayer changes things, and it changes you. Today, instead of worrying about your next decision, ask God to lead the way. Don't limit your prayers to meals or to bedtime. Pray constantly about things great and small. God is listening, and He wants to hear from you now.

— A PRAYER —

Dear Lord, make me a person whose constant prayers are pleasing to You. Let me come to You often with concerns both great and small. I trust in the power of prayer, Father, because prayer changes things and it changes me. In the quiet moments of the day, I will open my heart to You. I know that You are with me always and that You always hear my prayers. So I will pray and be thankful. Amen

HE IS LOVE

God is love, and the one who remains in love remains in God, and God remains in him.

1 John 4:16 HCSB

God is love. It's a sweeping statement, a profoundly important description of what God is and how God works. God's love is perfect. When we open our hearts to His perfect love, we are touched by the Creator's hand, and we are transformed.

Barbara Johnson observed, "We cannot protect ourselves from trouble, but we can dance through the puddles of life with a rainbow smile, twirling the only umbrella we need—the umbrella of God's love."

And the English mystical writer Juliana of Norwich noted, "We are so preciously loved by God that we cannot even comprehend it. No created being can ever know how much and how sweetly and tenderly God loves them."

So today, even if you can only carve out a few quiet moments, offer sincere prayers of thanksgiving to your Father. Thank Him for His blessings and His love.

Even before God created the heavens and the earth, He knew you and me, and He chose us! You and I were born because it was God's good pleasure.

Kay Arthur

— A PRAYER —

God, You are love. I love You, Lord, and as I love You more, I am able to love my family and friends more. Let me be Your loving servant, Heavenly Father, today and throughout eternity. Amen

YOUR SPIRITUAL JOURNEY

Consider it pure joy, my brothers, whenever you face trials of many kinds, because you know that the testing of your faith develops perseverance. Perseverance must finish its work so that you may be mature and complete, not lacking anything.

James 1:2-4 NIV

The journey toward spiritual maturity lasts a lifetime. As Christians, we can and should continue to grow in the love and the knowledge of our Savior as long as we live. Norman Vincent Peale had the following advice for believers of all ages: "Ask the God who made you to keep remaking you." That advice, of course, is perfectly sound, but often ignored.

When we cease to grow, either emotionally or spiritually, we do ourselves a profound disservice. But, if we study God's Word, if we obey His commandments, and if we live in the center of His will, we will not be "stagnant" believers; we will, instead, be growing Christians . . . and that's exactly what God wants for our lives.

One of the marks of Spiritual maturity is a consistent, Spirit-controlled life.

Vonette Bright

— A PRAYER —

Dear Lord, help me become the woman I can be and should be. Guide me along a path of Your choosing, and let me follow in the footsteps of Your Son, today and every day. Amen

HE OVERCOMES THE WORLD

God wanted everyone, not just Jews, to know this rich and glorious secret inside and out, regardless of their background, regardless of their religious standing. The mystery in a nutshell is just this: Christ is in you, therefore you can look forward to sharing in God's glory. It's that simple. That is the substance of our Message.

Colossians 1:27 MSG

There are few sadder sights on earth than the sight of a person who has lost all hope. In difficult times, hope can be elusive, but Christians need never lose it. After all, God is good; His love endures; He has promised His children the gift of eternal life.

If you find yourself falling into the spiritual traps of worry and discouragement, consider the words of Jesus. It was Christ who promised, "In the world you will have tribulation; but be of good cheer, I have overcome the world" (John 16:33 NKJV). This world is, indeed, a place of trials and tribulations, but as believers, we are secure. God has promised us peace, joy, and eternal life. And, of course, God always keeps His promises.

No other religion, no other philosophy promises new bodies, hearts, and minds. Only in the Gospel of Christ do hurting people find such incredible hope.

Joni Eareckson Tada

— A PRAYER —

Today, Dear Lord, I will live in hope. If I become discouraged, I will turn to You. If I grow weary, I will seek strength in You. In every aspect of my life, I will trust You. You are my Father, Lord, and I place my hope and my faith in You. Amen

JUDGE NOT

Therefore you are inexcusable, O man, whoever you are who judge, for in whatever you judge another you condemn yourself; for you who judge practice the same things.

Romans 2:1 NKJV

The warning of Matthew 7:1 is clear: "Judge not, that ye be not judged" (KJV). Yet even the most devoted Christians may fall prey to a powerful yet subtle temptation: the temptation to judge others. But as obedient followers of Christ, we are commanded to refrain from such behavior.

As Jesus came upon a young woman who had been condemned by the Pharisees, He spoke not only to the crowd that was gathered there, but also to all generations when He warned, "He that is without sin among you, let him first cast a stone at her" (John 8:7 KJV). Christ's message is clear, and it applies not only to the Pharisees of ancient times, but also to us.

Don't judge other people more harshly than you want God to judge you.

Marie T. Freeman

— A PRAYER —

Dear Lord, sometimes I am quick to judge others. But, You have commanded me not to judge. Keep me mindful, Father, that when I judge others, I am living outside of Your will for my life. You have forgiven me, Lord. Let me forgive others, let me love them, and let me help them . . . without judging them. Amen

THE WISDOM OF MODERATION

Patience is better than power, and controlling one's temper, than capturing a city.

Proverbs 16:32 HCSB

Moderation and wisdom are traveling companions. If we are wise, we must learn to temper our appetites, our desires, and our impulses. When we do, we are blessed, in part, because God has created a world in which temperance is rewarded and intemperance is inevitably punished.

Would you like to improve your life? Then harness your appetites and restrain your impulses. Moderation is difficult, of course; it is especially difficult in a prosperous society such as ours. But the rewards of moderation are numerous and long-lasting. Claim those rewards today.

No one can force you to moderate your appetites. The decision to live temperately (and wisely) is yours and yours alone. And so are the consequences.

To many, total abstinence is easier than perfect moderation.

St. Augustine

— A PRAYER —

Dear Lord, give me the wisdom to be moderate and self-disciplined. Let me strive to do Your will here on earth, and as I do, let me find contentment and balance. Let me be a disciplined believer, Father, today and every day. Amen

EXCITED ABOUT THE OPPORTUNITIES

May the God of hope fill you with all joy and peace as you trust in him, so that you may overflow with hope by the power of the Holy Spirit.

Romans 15:13 NIV

Are you excited about the opportunities of today and thrilled by the possibilities of tomorrow? Do you confidently expect God to lead you to a place of abundance, peace, and joy? And, when your days on earth are over, do you expect to receive the priceless gift of eternal life? If you trust God's promises, and if you have welcomed God's Son into your heart, then you believe that your future is intensely and eternally bright.

Today, as you prepare to meet the duties of everyday life, pause and consider God's promises. And then think for a moment about the wonderful future that awaits all believers, including you. God has promised that your future is secure. Trust that promise, and celebrate the life of abundance and eternal joy that is now yours through Christ.

God specializes in things fresh and firsthand. His plans for you this year may outshine those of the past. He's prepared to fill your days with reasons to give Him praise.

Joni Eareckson Tada

— A PRAYER —

Lord, as I take the next steps on my life's journey, let me take them with You. Whatever this day may bring, I thank You for the opportunity to live abundantly. Let me lean upon You, Father— and trust You—this day and forever. Amen

PEACE AND HIS WORD

*Those who love Your law have great peace, and nothing causes them
to stumble.*

Psalm 119:165 NASB

Do you seek God's peace? Then study His Word. God's Word
is unlike any other book. The Bible is a roadmap for life here on
earth and for life eternal.

The words of Matthew 4:4 remind us that, "Man shall not
live by bread alone but by every word that proceedeth out of the
mouth of God" (KJV). As believers, we must study the Bible and
meditate upon its meaning for our lives. Otherwise, we deprive
ourselves of a priceless gift from our Creator.

Warren Wiersbe observed, "When the child of God looks
into the Word of God, he sees the Son of God. And, he is transformed by the Spirit of God to share in the glory of God." God's
Holy Word is, indeed, a transforming, life-changing, one-of-a-
kind treasure. And, a passing acquaintance with the Good Book
is insufficient for Christians who seek to obey God's Word and to
understand His will.

Peace is the deepest thing a human personality can know; it is
almighty.

Oswald Chambers

— A PRAYER —

Dear Lord, I pray for peace in the world and peace within my
soul. You are the Giver of all things good, Father, and You give
me peace when I draw close to You. Help me to trust Your will,
to follow Your commands, and to accept Your peace, today and
forever. Amen

TOO BUSY

Don't burn out; keep yourselves fueled and aflame. Be alert servants of the Master, cheerfully expectant. Don't quit in hard times; pray all the harder.

Romans 12:11-12 MSG

Has the busy pace of life robbed you of the peace of mind that should be yours as a result of your relationship with Jesus Christ? If so, you are simply too busy for your own good. Through His Son Jesus, God offers you a peace that passes human understanding, but He won't force His peace upon you; in order to experience it, you must slow down long enough to sense His presence and His love.

Today, as a gift to yourself, to your family, and to the world, slow down and claim the inner peace that is your spiritual birth-right: the peace of Jesus Christ. When you ask, it will be given to you.

Often our lives are strangled by things that don't ultimately matter.

Grady Nutt

— A PRAYER —

Dear Lord, when the quickening pace of life leaves me with little time for worship or for praise, help me to reorder my priorities. When the demands of the day leave me distracted and discouraged, let me turn to Jesus for the peace that only He can give. And then, when I have accepted the spiritual abundance that is mine through Christ, let me share His message and His love with all who cross my path. Amen

WHEN IT'S HARD TO BE CHEERFUL

Be of good comfort, be of one mind, live in peace; and the God of love and peace will be with you.

2 Corinthians 13:11 NKJV

On some days, as every woman knows, it's hard to be cheerful. Sometimes, as the demands of the world increase and our energy sags, we feel less like cheering up and more like tearing up. But even in our darkest hours, we can turn to God, and He will give us comfort.

Few things in life are more sad, or, for that matter, more absurd, than a grumpy Christian. Christ promises us lives of abundance and joy, but He does not force His joy upon us. We must claim His joy for ourselves, and when we do, Jesus, in turn, fills our spirits with His power and His love.

When we earnestly commit ourselves to the Savior of mankind, when we place Jesus at the center of our lives and trust Him as our personal Savior, He will transform us, not just for today, but for all eternity. Then we, as God's children, can share Christ's joy and His message with a world that needs both.

— A PRAYER —

Lord, You care for me, You love me, and You have given me the priceless gift of eternal life through Your Son Jesus. Because of You, Lord, I have every reason to live each day with celebration and hope. Help me to face this day with a spirit of optimism and thanksgiving so that I may lift the spirits of those I meet as I share the Good News of Your Son. And, let me focus my thoughts on You and Your incomparable gifts today and forever. Amen

LIVING COURAGEOUSLY

Do not fear, for I am with you; do not be afraid, for I am your God. I will strengthen you; I will help you; I will hold on to you with My righteous right hand.

Isaiah 41:10 HCSB

Christian women have every reason to live courageously. After all, the final battle has already been won on the cross at Calvary. But even dedicated followers of Christ may find their courage tested by the inevitable disappointments and fears that visit the lives of believers and non-believers alike.

When you find yourself worried about the challenges of today or the uncertainties of tomorrow, you must ask yourself whether or not you are ready to place your concerns and your life in God's all-powerful, all-knowing, all-loving hands. If the answer to that question is yes—as it should be—then you can draw courage today from the source of strength that never fails: your Heavenly Father.

If a person fears God, he or she has no reason to fear anything else. On the other hand, if a person does not fear God, then fear becomes a way of life.

Beth Moore

— A PRAYER —

Dear Lord, sometimes I face challenges that leave me worried and afraid. When I am fearful, let me seek Your strength. When I am anxious, give me faith. Keep me mindful, Lord, that You are my God. With You by my side, Lord, I have nothing to fear today, tomorrow, or forever. Amen

FAITH ABOVE FEELINGS

The righteous will live by his faith.

Habakkuk 2:4 NIV

The Bible teaches that we should live by faith. Yet sometimes, despite our best intentions, negative feelings can rob us of the peace and abundance that would otherwise be ours through Christ. When anger or anxiety separates us from the spiritual blessings that God has in store, we must rethink our priorities and renew our faith. And we must place faith above feelings. Human emotions are highly variable, decidedly unpredictable, and often unreliable. Our emotions are like the weather, only far more fickle. So we must learn to live by faith, not by the ups and downs of our own emotional roller coasters.

Sometime during this day, you will probably be gripped by a strong negative emotion. Distrust it. Reign it in. Test it. And turn it over to God. Your emotions will inevitably change; God will not. So trust Him completely as you watch your feelings slowly evaporate into thin air—which, of course, they will.

We need to be able to make decisions based on what we know rather than on what we feel.

Joyce Meyer

— A PRAYER —

Heavenly Father, You are my strength and my refuge. As I journey through this day, I will encounter events that cause me emotional distress. Lord, when I am troubled, let me turn to You. Keep me steady, Lord, and in those difficult moments, renew a right spirit inside my heart. Amen

NO EXCUSES

Let us live in a right way . . . clothe yourselves with the Lord Jesus Christ and forget about satisfying your sinful self.

Romans 13:13-14 NCV

Excuses are everywhere . . . excellence is not. Whether you're a stay-at-home mom or a corporate CEO, your work is a picture book of your priorities. So whatever your job description, it's up to you, and no one else, to become masterful at your craft. It's up to you to do your job right, and to do it right now.

Because we humans are such creative excuse-makers, all of the best excuses have already been taken—we've heard them all before.

So if you're wasting your time trying to concoct a new and improved excuse, don't bother. It's impossible. A far better strategy is this: do the work now. Then, let your excellent work speak loudly and convincingly for itself.

We need to stop focusing on our lacks and stop giving out excuses and start looking at and listening to Jesus.

Anne Graham Lotz

— A PRAYER —

Heavenly Father, how easy it is to make excuses. But, I want to be a woman who accomplishes important work for You. Help me, Father, to strive for excellence, not excuses. Amen

FOLLOWING CHRIST

But whoever keeps His word, truly in him the love of God is perfected. This is how we know we are in Him: the one who says he remains in Him should walk just as He walked.

1 John 2:5-6 HCSB

Each day, as we awaken from sleep, we are confronted with countless opportunities to serve God and to follow in the footsteps of His Son. When we do, our Heavenly Father guides our steps and blesses our endeavors.

As citizens of a fast-changing world, we face challenges that sometimes leave us feeling overworked, overcommitted, and overwhelmed. But God has different plans for us. He intends that we slow down long enough to praise Him and to glorify His Son. When we do, He lifts our spirits and enriches our lives.

Today provides a glorious opportunity to place yourself in the service of the One who is the Giver of all blessings. May you seek His will, may you trust His word, and may you walk in the footsteps of His Son.

Jesus never asks us to give Him what we don't have. But He does demand that we give Him all we do have if we want to be a part of what He wishes to do in the lives of those around us!

Anne Graham Lotz

— A PRAYER —

Dear Jesus, my life has been changed forever by Your love and sacrifice. Today I will praise You, I will honor You, and I will walk with You. Amen

THE COMMANDMENT TO BE GENEROUS

Freely you have received, freely give.

Matthew 10:8 NKJV

God's Word commands us to be generous, compassionate servants to those who need our support. As believers, we have been richly blessed by our Creator. We, in turn, are called to share our gifts, our possessions, our testimonies, and our talents.

Concentration camp survivor Corrie ten Boom correctly observed, "The measure of a life is not its duration but its donation." These words remind us that the quality of our lives is determined not by what we are able to take from others, but instead by what we are able to share with others.

The thread of generosity is woven into the very fabric of Christ's teachings. If we are to be disciples of Christ, we, too, must be cheerful, generous, courageous givers. Our Savior expects no less from us. And He deserves no less.

God does not need our money. But, you and I need the experience of giving it.

James Dobson

— A PRAYER —

Dear Lord, Your Word tells me that it is more blessed to give than to receive. Make me a faithful steward of the gifts You have given me, and let me share those gifts generously with others, today and every day that I live. Amen

YOUR PRIMARY OBLIGATION

His divine power has given us everything we need for life and godliness through our knowledge of him who called us by his own glory and goodness.

2 Peter 1:3 NIV

When God created you, He equipped you with an assortment of talents and abilities that are uniquely yours. It's up to you to discover those talents and to use them, but the world may encourage you to do otherwise. At times, society will attempt to pigeonhole you, to standardize you, and to make you fit into a particular, preformed mold. Perhaps God has other plans.

At times, because you're an imperfect human being, you may become so wrapped up in meeting society's expectations that you fail to focus on God's expectations.

Who will you try to please today: God or society? Your primary obligation is not to please imperfect men and women. Your obligation is to strive diligently to meet the expectations of an all-knowing and perfect God. Period.

You will get untold flak for prioritizing God's revealed and present will for your life over man's . . . but, boy, is it worth it.

Beth Moore

— A PRAYER —

Dear Lord, today I will honor You with my thoughts, my actions, and my prayers. I will seek to please You, and I will strive to serve You. Your blessings are as limitless as Your love. And because I have been so richly blessed, I will worship You, Father, with thanksgiving in my heart and praise on my lips, this day and forever. Amen

PRAYER CHANGES THINGS AND YOU

And everything—whatever you ask in prayer, believing—you will receive.

Matthew 21:22 HCSB

Is prayer an integral part of your daily life, or is it a hit-or-miss habit? Do you "pray without ceasing," or is your prayer life an afterthought? As you consider the role that prayer currently plays in your life—and the role that you think it should play—remember that the quality of your spiritual life is inevitably related to the quality of your prayer life.

Prayer changes things and it changes you. So today, instead of turning things over in your mind, turn them over to God in prayer. Instead of worrying about your next decision, pray about it. Don't limit your prayers to meals or to bedtime. Pray often about things great and small. God is listening, and He wants to hear from you.

The more a man bows his knee before God, the straighter he stands before men.

Anonymous

— A PRAYER —

O Lord, my Creator, conform me to Your image. Create in me a clean heart, a new heart that reflects Your love for me. When I need to change, change me, Lord, and make me new. Amen

YOUR BIBLE AND HIS PURPOSE

The words of the Lord are pure words, like silver tried in a furnace.

Psalm 12:6 NKJV

Are you sincerely seeking to discover God's will and follow it? If so, study His Word and obey His commandments. The words of Matthew 4:4 remind us that, "Man shall not live by bread alone, but by every word that proceeds from the mouth of God" (NKJV). As believers, we must study the Bible and meditate upon its meaning for our lives. Otherwise, we deprive ourselves of a priceless gift from our Creator.

Jonathan Edwards advised, "Be assiduous in reading the Holy Scriptures. This is the fountain whence all knowledge in divinity must be derived. Therefore let not this treasure lie by you neglected." God's Holy Word is a priceless treasure, and a passing acquaintance with it is insufficient for Christians who seek to obey God's Word and to understand His will. After all, man (or woman) does not live by bread alone . . .

Victory is the result of Christ's life lived out in the believer. It is important to see that victory, not defeat, is God's purpose for His children.

Corrie ten Boom

— A PRAYER —

Dear Lord, You are the Creator of the universe, and I know that Your plan for my life is grander than I can imagine. Let Your purposes be my purposes, and let me trust in the assurance of Your promises. Amen

THE FUTILITY OF WORRY

Worry is a heavy load, but a kind word cheers you up.

Proverbs 12:25 NCV

"Worry does not empty tomorrow of its sorrow; it empties today of its strength." So writes Corrie ten Boom, a woman who survived a Nazi concentration camp during World War II. And while our own situations cannot be compared to Corrie's, we still worry about countless matters both great and small. Even though we are Christians who have been given the assurance of salvation—even though we are Christians who have received the promise of God's love and protection—we find ourselves fretting over the countless details of everyday life. Jesus understood our concerns when He spoke the reassuring words found in Matthew 6:25: "Therefore I tell you, do not worry about your life . . ." (NIV).

As you consider the promises of Jesus, remember that God still sits in His heaven and you are His beloved child. And you are protected.

Since the Lord is your shepherd, what are you worried about?

Marie T. Freeman

— A PRAYER —

Lord, sometimes, I can't seem to help myself: I worry. Even though I know to put my trust in You, I still become anxious about the future. Give me the wisdom to trust in You, Father, and give me the courage to live a life of faith, not a life of fear. Amen

THE FOUNDATIONS OF FRIENDSHIP

Therefore, putting away lying, "Let each one of you speak truth with his neighbor," for we are members of one another.

Ephesians 4:25 NKJV

Lasting friendships are built upon a foundation of honesty and trust. It has been said on many occasions that honesty is the best policy. For believers, it is far more important to note that honesty is God's policy. And if we are to be servants worthy of our Savior, Jesus Christ, we must be honest and forthright in all our communications with others.

Sometimes, honesty is difficult; sometimes, honesty is painful; sometimes, honesty makes us feel uncomfortable. Despite these temporary feelings of discomfort, we must make honesty the hallmark of all our relationships; otherwise, we invite needless suffering into our own lives and into the lives of those we love.

Sometime soon, perhaps even today, you will be tempted to bend the truth or perhaps even to break it. Resist that temptation. Truth is God's way . . . and it must be your way, too.

The single most important element in any human relationship is honesty—with oneself, with God, and with others.

Catherine Marshall

— A PRAYER —

Lord, You are a God of truth; let me be a woman of truth. Sometimes speaking the truth is difficult, but when I am weak or fearful, Lord, give me the strength to speak words that are worthy of the One who created me, so that others might see Your eternal truth reflected in my words and my deeds. Amen

BEYOND JEALOUSY

Where jealousy and selfishness are, there will be confusion and every kind of evil.

James 3:14 NCV

Are you too wise to be consumed with feelings of jealousy? Hopefully so. After all, Jesus clearly taught us to love our neighbors, not to envy them. But sometimes, despite our best intentions, we fall prey to feelings of resentfulness, jealousy, bitterness, and envy. Why? Because we are human, and because we live in a world that places great importance on material possessions (possessions which, by the way, are totally unimportant to God).

The next time you feel pangs of envy invading your thoughts, remind yourself of two things: 1. Envy is a sin, and 2. God has already showered you with so many blessings that if you're a thoughtful, thankful believer, you have no right to ever be envious of any other person on earth.

What God asks, does, or requires of others is not my business; it is His.

Kay Arthur

— A PRAYER —

Dear Lord, deliver me from the needless pain of envy. You have given me countless blessings. Let me be thankful for the gifts I have received, and let me never be resentful of the gifts You have given others. Amen

PREPARING FOR ETERNITY

These things I have written to you who believe in the name of the Son of God, that you may know that you have eternal life.

1 John 5:13 NKJV

God has given you the gift of life. How will you use that gift? Will you allow God's Son to reign over your heart? And will you treat each day as a precious treasure from your Heavenly Father? You should, and, hopefully, you will.

Every day that we live, we should be preparing to die. If we seek to live purposeful, productive lives, we will be ever mindful that our time here on earth is limited, and we will conduct ourselves accordingly.

Life is a glorious opportunity, but it is also shockingly brief. We must serve God each day as if it were our last day. When we do, we prepare ourselves for the inevitable end of life here on earth, and for the victory that is certain to follow.

It ought to be the business of every day to prepare for our last day.

Matthew Henry

— A PRAYER —

Lord, You have given me the gift of eternal love; let me share that gift with the world. Help me, Father, to show kindness to those who cross my path, and let me show tenderness and unfailing love to my family and friends. Make me generous with words of encouragement and praise. And, help me always to reflect the love that Christ Jesus gave me so that through me, others might find Him. Amen

AT PEACE WITH THE PAST

Abundant peace belongs to those who love Your instruction; nothing makes them stumble.

Psalm 119:165 HCSB

Peace and bitterness are mutually exclusive. So, if you are mired in the quicksand of regret, it's time to plan your escape. How can you do so? By accepting the past.

The world holds few if any rewards for those who remain angrily focused upon the injustices of yesterday. Still, the act of forgiveness is difficult for all but the most saintly men and women. Being frail, fallible, imperfect human beings, most of us are quick to anger, quick to blame, slow to forgive, and even slower to forget. Yet as Christians, we are commanded to forgive others, just as we, too, have been forgiven.

If you have not yet made peace with the past, it's now time to declare an end to all hostilities. When you do so, you can then learn to live quite contentedly in a much more appropriate time period: this one.

We can't just put our pasts behind us. We've got to put our pasts in front of God.

Beth Moore

— A PRAYER —

Dear Lord, help me accept the past, help me enjoy the present, and help me plan for the future. While I am doing these things, help me to trust You more and more . . . this day and every day. Amen

THE NEED TO PERSEVERE

You need to persevere so that when you have done the will of God, you will receive what he has promised.

Hebrews 10:36 NIV

If you've led a perfect life with absolutely no foul ups, blunders, mistakes, or flops, you can skip this chapter. But if you're like the rest of us, you know that occasional disappointments and failures are an inevitable part of life. These setbacks are simply the price of growing up and learning about life. But even when you experience bitter disappointments, you must never lose faith.

When we encounter the inevitable difficulties of life-here-on-earth, God stands ready to protect us. And, while we are waiting for God's plans to unfold, we can be comforted in the knowledge that our Creator can overcome any obstacle, even if we cannot.

Just remember, every flower that ever bloomed had to go through a whole lot of dirt to get there!

Barbara Johnson

— A PRAYER —

Lord, when life is difficult, I am tempted to abandon hope in the future. But You are my God, and I can draw strength from You. When I am exhausted, You energize me. When I am afraid, You give me courage. You are with me, Father, in good times and in bad times. I will persevere in the work that You have placed before me, and I will trust in You forever. Amen

PRAISING HIS MARVELOUS WORKS

Enter into His gates with thanksgiving, and into His courts with praise. Be thankful to Him, and bless His name. For the Lord is good; His mercy is everlasting, and His truth endures to all generations.

Psalm 100:4-5 NKJV

In the Hebrew version of the Old Testament, the title of the book of Psalm is translated "hymns of praise," and with good reason. Much of the book is a breathtakingly beautiful celebration of God's power, God's love, and God's creation. The psalmist writes, "Let everything that breathes praise the Lord. Hallelujah!" (150:6 HCSB).

As Christians, we should continually praise God for all that He has done and all that He will do. His works are marvelous, His gifts are beyond understanding, and His love endures forever.

Do you sincerely desire to be a worthy servant of the One who has given you eternal love and eternal life? Then praise Him. And don't just praise Him on Sunday morning. Praise Him all day long, every day, for as long as you live . . . and then for all eternity.

Preoccupy my thoughts with your praise beginning today.

Joni Eareckson Tada

— A PRAYER —

Lord, let me give thanksgiving and praise to You. And, let me share the joyous news of Jesus Christ with a world that needs His transformation and His salvation. Amen

TRUSTING HIS PRIORITIES

When people do not accept divine guidance, they run wild. But whoever obeys the law is happy.

Proverbs 29:18 NLT

Have you asked God to help prioritize your day, or are you muddling along without His help? Have you asked Him for guidance and for the courage to do the things that need to be done, or are you seeking guidance only from the person in the mirror? If you're genuinely consulting God, then you're continually inviting your Creator to reveal Himself in a variety of ways. And if you wish to be a thoughtful, productive follower of Christ, you must do no less.

When you allow God to reign over your heart, He will honor you with blessings that are simply too numerous to count. So, as you plan for the day ahead, make God's will your ultimate priority. When you do, your daily to-do list will take care of itself.

Great relief and satisfaction can come from seeking God's priorities for us in each season, discerning what is "best" in the midst of many noble opportunities, and pouring our most excellent energies into those things.

Beth Moore

— A PRAYER —

Dear Lord, today is a new day. Help me finish the important tasks first, even if they are unpleasant. Don't let me put off until tomorrow what I should do today. Amen

RENEWAL AND CELEBRATION

Then the One seated on the throne said, "Look! I am making everything new."

Revelation 21:5 HCSB

Each new day offers countless opportunities to celebrate life and to serve God's children. But each day also offers countless opportunities to fall prey to the countless distractions of our difficult age.

Consider this day a new beginning. Consider it a fresh start, a renewed opportunity to serve your friends and family with willing hands and a loving heart.

Gigi Graham Tchividjian spoke for women everywhere when she observed, "How much of our lives are, well, so daily. How often our hours are filled with the mundane, seemingly unimportant things that have to be done, whether at home or work. These very 'daily' tasks could—and should—become a celebration."

Make your life a celebration. After all, your talents are unique, as are your opportunities. So the best time to really live—and really celebrate—is now.

— A PRAYER —

Lord, I am an imperfect woman. Because my faith is limited, I may become overwhelmed by the demands of the day. When I feel tired or discouraged, renew my strength. When I am worried, let me turn my thoughts and my prayers to you. Let me trust Your promises, Dear Lord, and let me accept Your unending love, now and forever. Amen

GREATNESS ACCORDING TO GOD

So then, men ought to regard us as servants of Christ and as those entrusted with the secret things of God. Now it is required that those who have been given a trust must prove faithful.

1 Corinthians 4:1-2 NIV

How do you achieve greatness in the eyes of God? By making yourself a humble servant. Of course, being a fallible human being, you may feel the temptation to build yourself up in the eyes of your neighbors. Resist that temptation. Instead, serve your neighbors quietly and without fanfare. Find a need and fill it . . . humbly. Lend a helping hand and share a word of kindness . . . anonymously. Take the time to minister to those in need.

Then, when you have done your best to serve your neighbors and to serve your God, you can rest comfortably knowing that in the eyes of your Heavenly Father, you have achieved greatness. And God's eyes, after all, are the only ones that really count.

So many times we say that we can't serve God because we aren't whatever is needed. We're not talented enough or smart enough or whatever. But if you are in covenant with Jesus Christ, He is responsible for covering your weaknesses, for being your strength.

Kay Arthur

— A PRAYER —

Dear Lord, in weak moments, I try to build myself up by placing myself ahead of others. But You want me to be a humble servant to those who need my encouragement, my help, and my love. Today, I will do my best to follow in the footsteps of Your Son Jesus by serving others humbly, faithfully, and lovingly. Amen

YOUR JOURNEY CONTINUES

I've told you these things for a purpose: that my joy might be your joy, and your joy wholly mature.

John 15:11 MSG

Complete spiritual maturity is never achieved in a day or in a year or even in a lifetime. The journey toward spiritual maturity is an ongoing process that continues, day by day, throughout every stage of life. Every stage of life has its opportunities and its challenges, and if we're wise, we continue to seek God's guidance as each new chapter of life unfolds. Norman Vincent Peale advised: "Ask the God who made you to keep remaking you." That counsel is perfectly sound, but easy to ignore.

When we cease to grow, either emotionally or spiritually, we do ourselves a profound disservice. But, if we focus our thoughts—and attune our hearts—to the will of God, we will make each day another stage in the spiritual journey . . . and that's precisely what God intends for us to do.

If all struggles and sufferings were eliminated, the spirit would no more reach maturity than would the child.

Elisabeth Elliot

— A PRAYER —

Heavenly Father, I want to grow closer to You each day. I know that obedience to Your will strengthens my relationship with You, so help me to follow Your commandments and obey Your Word today and always. Amen

HE PRESERVES US

He'll wipe every tear from their eyes. Death is gone for good—tears gone, crying gone, pain gone—all the first order of things gone.

Revelation 21:4 MSG

Women of every generation have experienced adversity, and this generation is no different. But, today's women face challenges that previous generations could have scarcely imagined. Thankfully, although the world continues to change, God's love remains constant. And, He remains ready to comfort us and strengthen us whenever we turn to Him.

God's Word promises, "The Lord is near to all who call upon Him, to all who call upon Him in truth. He will fulfill the desire of those who fear Him; He also will hear their cry and save them. The Lord preserves all who love Him" (Psalm 145:18-20). This comforting passage reminds us that when we are troubled, we should call upon God, and in time, He will heal us. And until He does, we may be comforted in the knowledge that we never suffer alone.

The love of God exists in its strongest and purest form in the very midst of suffering and tragedy.

Suzanne Dale Ezell

— A PRAYER —

Dear Lord, Your Word promises that You will not give us more than we can bear; You have promised to give us rest from our sorrows and deliverance from our pain. Today, Father, I pray for those who suffer and for those who mourn. And I thank You for sustaining us in our days of sorrow. May we trust You always and praise You forever. Amen

TOO BUSY TO GIVE THANKS?

Enter into His gates with thanksgiving, and into His courts with praise. Be thankful to Him, and bless His name. For the Lord is good; His mercy is everlasting, and His truth endures to all generations.

Psalm 100:4-5 NKJV

Life has a way of constantly coming at us. Days, hours, and moments are filled with urgent demands requiring our immediate attention.

When the demands of life leave us rushing from place to place with scarcely a moment to spare, we may fail to pause and thank our Creator for His gifts. But, whenever we neglect to give proper thanks to the Father, we suffer because of our misplaced priorities.

Today, make a special effort to give thanks to the Creator for His blessings. His love for you is eternal, as are His gifts. And it's never too soon—or too late—to offer Him thanks.

One reason why we don't thank God for his answer to our prayer is that frequently we don't recognize them as being answers to our prayers. We just take his bountiful supply or dramatic action for granted when it comes.

Evelyn Christenson

— A PRAYER —

Dear Lord, sometimes, amid the demands of the day, I lose perspective, and I fail to give thanks for Your blessings and for Your love. Today, help me to count those blessings, and let me give thanks to You, Father, for Your love, for Your grace, for Your blessings, and for Your Son. Amen

WHAT'S REALLY IMPORTANT

Anyone trusting in his riches will fall, but the righteous will flourish like foliage.

Proverbs 11:28 HCSB

In the demanding world in which we live, financial prosperity can be a good thing, but spiritual prosperity is profoundly more important. Yet our society leads us to believe otherwise. The world glorifies material possessions, personal fame, and physical beauty above all else; these things, of course, are totally unimportant to God. God sees the human heart, and that's what is important to Him.

As you establish your priorities for the coming day, remember this: The world will do everything it can to convince you that "things" are important. The world will tempt you to value fortune above faith and possessions above peace. God, on the other hand, will try to convince you that your relationship with Him is all-important. Trust God.

Why is love of gold more potent than love of souls?

Lottie Moon

— A PRAYER —

Heavenly Father, when I focus intently upon You, I am blessed. When I focus too intently on the acquisition of material possessions, I am troubled. Make my priorities pleasing to You, Father, and make me a worthy servant of Your Son. Amen

THE PEACE THAT PASSES ALL UNDERSTANDING

Peace, peace to you, and peace to your helpers! For your God helps you.

1 Chronicles 12:18 NKJV

Through His Son, God offers a "peace that passes all understanding," but He does not force His peace upon us. God's peace is a blessing that we, as children of a loving Father, must claim for ourselves . . . but sometimes we are slow to do so. Why? Because we are fallible human beings with limited understanding and limited faith.

Have you found the lasting peace that can be yours through Jesus, or are you still rushing after the illusion of "peace and happiness" that the world promises but cannot deliver?

Today, as a gift to yourself, to your family, and to your friends, claim the inner peace that is your spiritual birthright: the peace of Jesus Christ. It is offered freely; it has been paid for in full; it is yours for the asking. So ask. And then share.

That peace, which has been described and which believers enjoy, is a participation of the peace which their glorious Lord and Master himself enjoys.

Jonathan Edwards

— A PRAYER —

The world talks about peace, but only You, Lord, can give a perfect and lasting peace. True peace comes through the Prince of Peace, and sometimes His peace passes all understanding. Help me to accept His peace—and share it—this day and forever. Amen

TOO MUCH STUFF?

Let your conduct be without covetousness; be content with such things as you have. For He Himself has said, "I will never leave you nor forsake you."

Hebrews 13:5 NKJV

Martin Luther observed, "Many things I have tried to grasp and have lost. That which I have placed in God's hands I still have." His words apply to all of us. Our earthly riches are transitory; our spiritual riches are not.

Do you often find yourself focusing on your material possessions instead of your spiritual ones? If so, it's time to slow yourself down and reorder your priorities. And it's time to focus on more important matters: the spiritual riches that are yours though Christ Jesus.

He who dies with the most toys . . . still dies.

Anonymous

— A PRAYER —

Dear Lord, all I have belongs to You. When I leave this world I take nothing with me. Help me to value my relationship with You—and my relationships with others—more than I value my material possessions. Amen

PLEASING GOD

But neither exile nor homecoming is the main thing. Cheerfully pleasing God is the main thing, and that's what we aim to do, regardless of our conditions.

2 Corinthians 5:9 MSG

Sometimes, because you're an imperfect human being, you may become so wrapped up in meeting society's expectations that you fail to focus on God's expectations. To do so is a mistake of major proportions—don't make it. Instead, seek God's guidance as you focus your energies on becoming the best "you" that you can possibly be. And, when it comes to matters of conscience, seek approval not from your peers, but from your Creator.

Who will you try to please today: God or man? Your primary obligation is not to please imperfect men and women. Your obligation is to strive diligently to meet the expectations of an all-knowing and perfect God. Trust Him always. Love Him always. Praise Him always. And seek to please Him. Always.

Don't be addicted to approval. Follow your heart. Do what you believe God is telling you to do, and stand firm in Him and Him alone.

Joyce Meyer

— A PRAYER —

Dear Lord, thank You for all the blessings You have given me. Today and every day I will do my best to please You by thinking good thoughts and doing good deeds. Amen

SPEECH AND THE GOLDEN RULE

A good man out of the good treasure of his heart brings forth good things, and an evil man out of the evil treasure brings forth evil things.

Matthew 12:35 NKJV

The words of Matthew 7:12 are clear: "In everything, do to others what you would have them do to you, for this sums up the Law and the Prophets" (NIV). This commandment is, indeed, the Golden Rule for Christians of every generation. And if we are to observe the Golden Rule, we must be careful to speak words of encouragement, hope, and truth to all who cross our paths.

Sometimes, when we feel uplifted and secure, it is easy to speak kind words. Other times, when we are discouraged or tired, we can scarcely summon the energy to uplift ourselves, much less anyone else. But, God's commandment is clear: we must observe the Golden Rule "in everything."

God intends that we speak words of kindness, wisdom, and truth, no matter our circumstances, no matter our emotions. When we do, we share a priceless gift with the world, and we give glory to the One who gave His life for us. As believers, we must do no less.

— A PRAYER —

Lord, You have warned me that I will be judged by the words I speak. And, You have commanded me to choose my words carefully so that I might be a source of encouragement and hope to all whom I meet. Keep me mindful, Lord, that I have influence on many people . . . make me an influence for good. And may the words that I speak today be worthy of the One who has saved me forever. Amen

TOUCHED BY THE SAVIOR

And when the woman saw that she was not hid, she came trembling, and falling down before him, she declared unto him before all the people for what cause she had touched him, and how she was healed immediately. And he said unto her, Daughter, be of good comfort: thy faith hath made thee whole; go in peace.

Luke 8:47-48 KJV

Until we have been touched by the Savior, we can never be completely whole. Until we have placed our hearts and our lives firmly in the hands of the living Christ, we are incomplete. Until we come to know Jesus, we long for a sense of peace that continues to elude us no matter how diligently we search.

It is only through God that we discover genuine peace. We can search far and wide for worldly substitutes, but when we seek peace apart from God, we will find neither peace nor God.

As believers, we are invited to accept the "peace that passes all understanding" (Philippians 4:7 NIV). That peace, of course, is God's peace. Let us accept His peace, and let us share it today, tomorrow, and every day that we live.

Whoever you are, whatever your condition or circumstance, whatever your past or problem, Jesus can restore you to wholeness.

Anne Graham Lotz

— A PRAYER —

Dear Lord, when I am broken, make me whole. You sent Your perfect Son to save imperfect people like me. I will welcome the Prince of Peace into my heart today, tomorrow, and forever. Amen

ACCEPTING HIS ABUNDANCE

Live in me. Make your home in me just as I do in you. In the same way that a branch can't bear grapes by itself but only by being joined to the vine, you can't bear fruit unless you are joined with me. I am the Vine, you are the branches. When you're joined with me and I with you, the relation intimate and organic, the harvest is sure to be abundant.

John 15:4-5 MSG

Are you the kind of woman who accepts God's spiritual abundance without reservation? If so, you are availing yourself of the peace and the joy that He has promised. Do you sincerely seek the riches that our Savior offers to those who give themselves to Him? Then follow Him. When you do, you will receive the love and the abundance that Jesus offers to those who follow Him.

Seek first the salvation that is available through a personal, passionate relationship with Christ, and then claim the joy, the peace, and the spiritual abundance that the Shepherd offers His sheep.

If you want purpose and meaning and satisfaction and fulfillment and peace and hope and joy and abundant life that lasts forever, look to Jesus.

Anne Graham Lotz

— A PRAYER —

Thank You, Father, for the abundant life that is mine through Christ Jesus. Guide me according to Your will, and help me to be a worthy servant in all that I say and do. Give me courage, Lord, to claim the gifts You have promised—and give me the wisdom to share those gifts, today and every day. Amen

HE HEALS
THE BROKENHEARTED

Blessed is a man who endures trials, because when he passes the test he will receive the crown of life that He has promised to those who love Him.

James 1:12 HCSB

Adversity of some kind has plagued women of every generation. Today's women face challenges that previous generations could have not imagined. Thankfully, no matter how the world continues to change, one thing remains constant—God's love. And, He remains ready to comfort us and strengthen us whenever we turn to Him.

If you are like most women, it is simply a fact of life: from time to time, you worry. You worry about health, about finances, about safety, about relationships, about family, and about countless other challenges of life, some great and some small. Where is the best place to take your worries? Take them to God. Take your troubles to Him, and your fears and your sorrows. Seek protection from the One who cannot be moved.

Jesus Christ is not a security from storms. He is perfect security in storms.

Kathy Troccoli

— A PRAYER —

Dear Heavenly Father, when I am troubled, You heal me. When I am afraid, You protect me. When I am discouraged, You lift me up. During the difficult days of my life, I will trust You. And whatever my circumstances, Lord, I thank You for Your blessings, for Your love, and for Your Son. Amen

ACTIONS AND BELIEFS

If the way you live isn't consistent with what you believe, then it's wrong.

Romans 14:23 MSG

We must do our best to make sure that our actions are accurate reflections of our beliefs. Our theology must be demonstrated, not only by our words but, more importantly, by our actions. In short, we should be practical women, quick to act upon the beliefs that we hold most dear.

We may proclaim our beliefs to our hearts' content, but our proclamations will mean nothing—to others or to ourselves—unless we accompany our words with deeds that match. The sermons that we live are far more compelling than the ones we preach.

Like it or not, your life is an accurate reflection of your creed. If this fact gives you cause for concern, don't bother talking about the changes that you intend to make—make them. Now.

You cannot spell God or Gospel until you first spell "go."

Anonymous

— A PRAYER —

Heavenly Father, I believe in You, and I believe in Your Word. Help me to live in such a way that my actions validate my beliefs—and let the glory be Yours forever. Amen

FAITH OR FEAR?

Even when I go through the darkest valley, I fear [no] danger, for You are with me.

Psalm 23:4 HCSB

Although God has guided us through our struggles and troubles many times before, it is easy for us to lose hope whenever we face adversity, uncertainty, or unwelcome changes.

The next time you find yourself facing a fear-provoking situation, remember that the One who calmed the wind and the waves is also your personal Savior. Then ask yourself which is stronger: your faith or your fear. The answer should be obvious. So, when the storm clouds form overhead and you find yourself being tossed on the stormy seas of life, remember this: Wherever you are, God is there, too. And, because He cares for you, you are protected.

With God, it isn't who you were that matters; it's who you are becoming.

Liz Curtis Higgs

— A PRAYER —

Dear Lord, I will open my heart to You. I will take my concerns, my fears, my plans, and my hopes to You in prayer. And, then, I will trust the answers that You give. You are my loving Father, and I will accept Your will for my life today and every day that I live. Amen

TRUSTING YOUR CONSCIENCE

Let us come near to God with a sincere heart and a sure faith, because we have been made free from a guilty conscience, and our bodies have been washed with pure water.

Hebrews 10:22 NCV

It has been said that character is what we are when nobody is watching. How true. When we do things that we know aren't right, we try to hide them from our families and friends. But even then, God is watching.

Few things in life torment us more than a guilty conscience. And, few things in life provide more contentment than the knowledge that we are obeying the conscience that God has placed in our hearts.

If you sincerely want to create the best possible life for yourself and your loved ones, never forsake your conscience. And remember this: when you walk with God, your character will take care of itself . . . and you won't need to look over your shoulder to see who, besides God, is watching.

God desires that we become spiritually healthy enough through faith to have a conscience that rightly interprets the work of the Holy Spirit.

Beth Moore

— A PRAYER —

Dear Lord, You speak to me through the Bible, through the words of others, and through that still, small voice within. Through my conscience, You reveal Your will for my life. Show me Your plan for this day, Heavenly Father, and let me share the Good News of Your Son. Amen

THE IMPORTANCE OF DISCIPLINE

For God has not given us a spirit of fear and timidity, but of power, love, and self-discipline. So you must never be ashamed to tell others about our Lord.

2 Timothy 1:7-8 NLT

Wise women understand the importance of discipline. In Proverbs 28:19, the message is clear: "Those who work their land will have plenty of food, but the ones who chase empty dreams instead will end up poor" (NCV).

If we work diligently and faithfully, we can expect a bountiful harvest. But we must never expect the harvest to precede the labor.

Poet Mary Frances Butts advised, "Build a little fence of trust around today. Fill each space with loving work, and therein stay." And her words still apply.

Thoughtful women understand that God doesn't reward laziness or misbehavior. To the contrary, God expects His children (of all ages) to lead disciplined lives . . . and when they do, He rewards them.

The alternative to discipline is disaster.

Vance Havner

— A PRAYER —

Lord, I want to be a disciplined believer. Let me use my time wisely, and let me teach others by the faithfulness of my conduct, today and every day. Amen

ENTHUSIASM NOW

Do your work with enthusiasm. Work as if you were serving the Lord, not as if you were serving only men and women.

Ephesians 6:7 NCV

Do you see each day as a glorious opportunity to serve God and to do His will? Are you enthused about life, or do you struggle through each day giving scarcely a thought to God's blessings? Are you constantly praising God for His gifts, and are you sharing His Good News with the world? And are you excited about the possibilities for service that God has placed before you, whether at home, at work, at church, or at school? You should be.

You are the recipient of Christ's sacrificial love. Accept it enthusiastically and share it fervently. Jesus deserves your enthusiasm; the world deserves it; and you deserve the experience of sharing it.

Enthusiasm, like the flu, is contagious—we get it from one another.

Barbara Johnson

— A PRAYER —

Dear Lord, the Christian life is a glorious adventure—let me share my excitement with others. Let me be an enthusiastic believer, Father, and let me share my enthusiasm today and every day. Amen

LIVING IN A FEAR-BASED WORLD

I sought the Lord, and He answered me and delivered me from all my fears.

Psalm 34:4 HCSB

We live in a fear-based world, a world where bad news travels at light speed and good news doesn't. These are troubled times, times when we have legitimate fears for the future of our nation, our world, and our families. But as Christians, we have every reason to live courageously. After all, the ultimate battle has already been fought and won on that faraway cross at Calvary.

Perhaps you, like countless other believers, have found your courage tested by the anxieties and fears that are an inevitable part of life. If so, God wants to have a little chat with you. The next time you find your courage tested to the limit, God wants to remind you that He is not just near, He is here.

Your Heavenly Father is your Protector and your Deliverer. Call upon Him in your hour of need, and be comforted. Whatever your challenge, whatever your trouble, God can handle it.

People who focus on their fears don't grow. They become paralyzed.

John Maxwell

— A PRAYER —

Dear Lord, when I am fearful, keep me mindful that You are my protector and my salvation. Thank You, Father, for a perfect love that casts out fear. Because of You, I can live courageously and faithfully this day and every day. Amen

FORGIVENESS DAY BY DAY

See that no one renders evil for evil to anyone, but always pursue what is good both for yourselves and for all.

1 Thessalonians 5:15 NKJV

If we could forgive other people "once and for all," life would be so much simpler, but it doesn't seem to work that way. Forgiveness is seldom a "one-time" decision; usually, forgiveness is a much more gradual process.

If you're trapped in the emotional quicksand of bitterness, it's time to schedule a daily conference with God. When you visit with the Father, you should ask Him specifically to lift the burdens of the past from your heart.

Each new day is a gift from God, but if your heart is filled with anger or regret, you simply won't be able to enjoy God's blessings. So, if you're struggling to forgive someone who has hurt you, do the right thing: spend a few quiet moments each morning thanking God for His gifts and asking Him to heal your broken heart. He can heal you—and He will heal you—if you don't grow tired of asking for His help.

God forgets the past. Imitate him.

Max Lucado

— A PRAYER —

Dear Lord, today I will choose to forgive those who have hurt me. I will empty my heart of bitterness and fill it with love. I will obey Your Word by offering love and mercy to others, just as You have offered mercy and love to me. Amen

HEEDING HIS CALL

I urge you to live a life worthy of the calling you have received.

Ephesians 4:1 NIV

It is terribly important that you heed God's calling by discovering and developing your talents and your spiritual gifts. If you seek to make a difference—and if you seek to bear eternal fruit—you must discover your gifts and begin using them for the glory of God.

Every believer has at least one gift. In John 15:16, Jesus says, "You did not choose Me, but I chose you and appointed you that you should go and bear fruit, and that your fruit should remain, that whatever you ask the Father in My name He may give you." Have you found your special calling? If not, keep searching and keep praying until you find it. God has important work for you to do, and the time to begin that work is now.

If God has called you, do not spend time looking over your shoulder to see who is following you.

Corrie ten Boom

— A PRAYER —

Heavenly Father, You have called me, and I acknowledge that calling. In these quiet moments before this busy day unfolds, I come to You. I will study Your Word and seek Your guidance. Give me the wisdom to know Your will for my life and the courage to follow wherever You may lead me, today and forever. Amen

HIS PROMISES TO YOU

This is my comfort in my affliction: Your promise has given me life.

Psalm 119:50 HCSB

God's promises are found in a book like no other: the Holy Bible. The Bible is a roadmap for life here on earth and for life eternal. As Christians, we are called upon to trust its promises, to follow its commandments, and to share its Good News.

As believers, we must study the Bible daily and meditate upon its meaning for our lives. Otherwise, we deprive ourselves of a priceless gift from our Creator. God's Holy Word is, indeed, a transforming, life-changing, one-of-a-kind treasure. And, a passing acquaintance with the Good Book is insufficient for Christians who seek to obey God's Word and to understand His will.

God has made promises to mankind and to you. God's promises never fail and they never grow old. You must trust those promises and share them with your family, with your friends, and with the world.

We have ample evidence that the Lord is able to guide. The promises cover every imaginable situation. All we need to do is to take the hand he stretches out.

Elisabeth Elliot

— A PRAYER —

Dear God, the Bible contains many promises. Let me trust Your promises, and let me live according to Your Holy Word, not just for today, but forever. Amen

TRUSTING HIS TIMING

Therefore humble yourselves under the mighty hand of God, that He may exalt you in due time.

1 Peter 5:6 NKJV

If you sincerely seek to be a woman of faith, then you must learn to trust God's timing. You will be sorely tempted, however, to do otherwise. Because you are a fallible human being, you are impatient for things to happen. But, God knows better.

God has created a world that unfolds according to His own timetable, not ours . . . thank goodness! We mortals might make a terrible mess of things. God does not.

God's plan does not always happen in the way that we would like or at the time of our own choosing. Our task—as believing Christians who trust in a benevolent, all-knowing Father—is to wait patiently for God to reveal Himself. And reveal Himself He will. Always. But until God's perfect plan is made known, we must walk in faith and never lose hope. And we must continue to trust Him. Always.

Will not the Lord's time be better than your time?

C. H. Spurgeon

— A PRAYER —

Dear Lord, Your wisdom is infinite, and the timing of Your heavenly plan is perfect. You have a plan for my life that is grander than I can imagine. When I am impatient, remind me that You are never early or late. You are always on time, Father, so let me trust in You. Amen

HE CHANGES YOU

I'm baptizing you here in the river, turning your old life in for a kingdom life. His baptism—a holy baptism by the Holy Spirit—will change you from the inside out.

Mark 1:8 MSG

God has the power to transform your life if you invite Him to do so. Your decision is straightforward: whether or not to allow the Father's transforming power to work in you and through you. God stands at the door and waits; all you must do is knock. When you do, God always answers.

Sometimes, the demands of daily life may drain you of strength or rob you of the joy that is rightfully yours in Christ. But even on your darkest day, you may be comforted by the knowledge that God has the power to renew your spirit and your life.

Are you in need of a new beginning? If so, turn your heart toward God in prayer. Are you weak or worried? Take the time—or, more accurately, make the time—to delve deeply into God's Holy Word. Are you spiritually depleted? Call upon fellow believers to support you, and call upon Christ to renew your sense of joy and thanksgiving. When you do, you'll discover that the Creator of the universe is in the business of making all things new—including you.

— A PRAYER —

Dear Lord, You sent Your Son to this earth that we might have the gift of eternal life. Thank You, Father, for that priceless gift. Help me to share the wondrous message of Jesus with others so that they, too, might accept Him as their Savior. And, let me praise You always for the new life You have given me, a life that is both abundant and eternal. Amen

WHERE TO TAKE YOUR CONCERNS

Be anxious for nothing, but in everything by prayer and supplication with thanksgiving let your requests be made known to God.

Philippians 4:6 NASB

If you are like most women, it is simply a fact of life: from time to time, you worry. You worry about health, about finances, about safety, about relationships, about family, and about countless other challenges of life, some great and some small. Where is the best place to take your worries? Take them to God. Take your troubles to Him, and your fears, and your sorrows.

Barbara Johnson correctly observed, "Worry is the senseless process of cluttering up tomorrow's opportunities with leftover problems from today." So if you'd like to make the most out of this day (and every one hereafter), turn your worries over to a Power greater than yourself . . . and spend your valuable time and energy solving the problems you can fix . . . while trusting God to do the rest.

We are not called to be burden-bearers, but cross-bearers and light-bearers. We must cast our burdens on the Lord.

Corrie ten Boom

— A PRAYER —

Lord, You understand my worries and my fears, and You forgive me when I am weak. When my faith begins to waver, help me to trust You more. Then, with Your Holy Word on my lips and with the love of Your Son in my heart, let me live courageously, faithfully, prayerfully, and thankfully today and every day. Amen

OVERCOMING THE WORLD

Whatever has been born of God conquers the world. This is the victory that has conquered the world: our faith.

1 John 5:4 HCSB

All of us face times of adversity. On occasion, we all must endure the disappointments and tragedies that befall believers and nonbelievers alike. The reassuring words of 1 John 5:4 remind us that when we accept God's grace, we overcome the passing hardships of this world by relying upon His strength, His love, and His promise of eternal life.

When we face the inevitable difficulties of life-here-on-earth, God stands ready to protect us. Our responsibility, of course, is to ask Him for protection. When we call upon Him in heartfelt prayer, He will answer—in His own time and according to His own plan—and He will heal us. And while we are waiting for God's plans to unfold and for His healing touch to restore us, we can be comforted in the knowledge that our Creator can overcome any obstacle, even if we cannot. Let us take God at His word, and let us trust Him.

— A PRAYER —

Dear Heavenly Father, You are my strength and my protector. When I am troubled, You comfort me. When I am discouraged, You lift me up. When I am afraid, You deliver me. Let me turn to You, Lord, when I am weak. In times of adversity, let me trust Your plan and Your will for my life. Your love is infinite, as is Your wisdom. Whatever my circumstances, Dear Lord, let me always give the praise, and the thanks, and the glory to You. Amen

ASKING FOR WISDOM

If any of you lack wisdom, let him ask of God, that giveth to all men liberally, and upbraideth not; and it shall be given him.

James 1:5 KJV

How often do you ask God for His help and His wisdom? Occasionally? Intermittently? Whenever you experience a crisis? Hopefully not. Hopefully, you've acquired the habit of asking for God's assistance early and often. And hopefully, you have learned to seek His guidance in every aspect of your life.

The Bible promises that God will guide you if you let Him. Your job is to let Him. But sometimes, you will be tempted to do otherwise. Sometimes, you'll be tempted to go along with the crowd; other times, you'll be tempted to do things your way, not God's way. When you feel those temptations, resist them.

God stands at the door and waits. When you knock, He opens. When you ask, He answers. Your task, of course, is to seek His guidance prayerfully, confidently, and often.

God will help us become the people we are meant to be, if only we will ask Him.

Hannah Whitall Smith

— A PRAYER —

I seek wisdom, Lord, not as the world gives, but as You give. Lead me in Your ways and teach me from Your Word so that, in time, my wisdom might glorify Your kingdom and Your Son. Amen

EACH DAY A GIFT

Shout with joy to the LORD, O earth! Worship the LORD with gladness. Come before him, singing with joy.

Psalm 100:1-2 NLT

Life should never be taken for granted. Each day is a priceless gift from God and should be treated as such.

Hannah Whitall Smith observed, "How changed our lives would be if we could only fly through the days on wings of surrender and trust!" And Clement of Alexandria noted, "All our life is a celebration for us; we are convinced, in fact, that God is always everywhere. We sing while we work . . . we pray while we carry out all life's other occupations." These words remind us that this day is God's creation, a gift to be treasured and savored.

Today, let us celebrate life with smiles on our faces and kind words on our lips. After all, this is God's day, and He has given us clear instructions for its use. We are commanded to rejoice and be glad. So, with no further ado, let the celebration begin . . .

The highest and most desirable state of the soul is to praise God in celebration for being alive.

Luci Swindoll

— A PRAYER —

Dear Lord, You have given me so many reasons to celebrate. Today, let me choose an attitude of cheerfulness. Let me be a joyful Christian, Lord, quick to laugh and slow to anger. And, let me share Your goodness with my family, my friends, and my neighbors, this day and every day. Amen

CARING FOR OUR CHILDREN

And he took a child, and set him in the midst of them: and when he had taken him in his arms, he said unto them, whosoever shall receive one of such children in my name, receiveth me; and whosoever shall receive me, receiveth not me, but him that sent me.

Mark 9:36-37 KJV

Have you hugged a child lately? If so, you've experienced one of life's great pleasures. Every child is a priceless gift from the Creator. And when we share love and affection with our children, we—and they—are blessed beyond measure.

As parents, friends of parents, aunts, and grandmothers, we understand the critical importance of raising our children with love, with discipline, and with God. It's a tall order and a profoundly important responsibility . . . but with God's help, we can do it.

Every child deserves the presence of caring adults who serve as godly role models. May we, as concerned adults, behave ourselves—and raise our children—accordingly.

Children are the hands by which we take hold of heaven.

Henry Ward Beecher

— A PRAYER —

Lord, when I have the glorious opportunity to care for children, let me love them, care for them, nurture them, teach them, and lead them to You. When I am weary, give me strength. When I am frustrated, give me patience. And, let my words and deeds always demonstrate to Your blessed children the love that I feel for them . . . and for You. Amen

COURTESY MATTERS

Be hospitable to one another without grumbling.

1 Peter 4:9 NKJV

Did Christ instruct us in matters of etiquette and courtesy? Of course He did. Christ's instructions are clear: "In everything, therefore, treat people the same way you want them to treat you, for this is the Law and the Prophets" (Matthew 7:12 NASB). Jesus did not say, "In some things, treat people as you wish to be treated." And, He did not say, "From time to time, treat others with kindness." Christ said that we should treat others as we wish to be treated in every aspect of our daily lives. This, of course, is a tall order indeed, but as Christians, we are commanded to do our best.

Today, be a little kinder than necessary to family members, friends, and total strangers. And, as you consider all the things that Christ has done in your life, honor Him with your words and with your deeds.

Courtesy is contagious.

Marie T. Freeman

— A PRAYER —

Guide me, Lord, to treat all those I meet with courtesy and respect. You have created each person in Your own image; let me honor those who cross my path with the dignity that You have bestowed upon them. We are all Your children, Lord; let me show kindness to all. Amen

ENCOURAGING WORDS FOR FAMILY AND FRIENDS

No rotten talk should come from your mouth, but only what is good for the building up of someone in need, in order to give grace to those who hear.

Ephesians 4:29 HCSB

Life is a team sport, and all of us need occasional pats on the back from our teammates. As Christians, we are called upon to spread the Good News of Christ, and we are also called to spread a message of encouragement and hope to the world.

Whether you realize it or not, many people with whom you come in contact every day are in desperate need of a smile or an encouraging word. The world can be a difficult place, and countless friends and family members may be troubled by the challenges of everyday life. Since you don't always know who needs our help, the best strategy is to try to encourage all the people who cross your path. So today, be a world-class source of encouragement to everyone you meet. Never has the need been greater.

— A PRAYER —

Dear Heavenly Father, because I am Your child, I am blessed. You have loved me eternally, cared for me faithfully, and saved me through the gift of Your Son Jesus. Just as You have lifted me up, Lord, let me lift up others in a spirit of encouragement and optimism and hope. And, if I can help a fellow traveler, even in a small way, Dear Lord, may the glory be Yours. Amen

FAITH FOR THE FUTURE

For we walk by faith, not by sight.

2 Corinthians 5:7 NKJV

The first element of a successful life is faith: faith in God, faith in His Son, and faith in His promises. If we place our lives in God's hands, our faith is rewarded in ways that we—as human beings with clouded vision and limited understanding—can scarcely comprehend. But, if we seek to rely solely upon our own resources, or if we seek earthly success outside the boundaries of God's commandments, we reap a bitter harvest for ourselves and for our loved ones.

Do you desire the abundance and success that God has promised? Then trust Him today and every day that you live. Trust Him with every aspect of your life. Trust His promises, and trust in the saving grace of His only begotten Son. Then, when you have entrusted your future to the Giver of all things good, rest assured that your future is secure, not only for today, but also for all eternity.

Never be afraid to trust an unknown future to a known God.

Corrie ten Boom

— A PRAYER —

Dear Lord, help me to be a woman of faith. Help me to remember that You are always near and that You can overcome any challenge. With Your love and Your power, Lord, I can live courageously and faithfully today and every day. Amen

WHICH PATH?

In all your ways acknowledge Him, and He shall direct your paths.

Proverbs 3:6 NKJV

God's love for you is deeper and more profound than you can imagine. God's love for you is so great that He sent His only Son to this earth to die for your sins and to offer you the priceless gift of eternal life. Now, you must decide whether or not to accept God's gift. Will you ignore it or embrace it? Will you return it or neglect it? Will you accept Christ's love and build a lifelong relationship with Him, or will you turn away from Him and take a different path?

Your decision to allow Christ to reign over your heart is the pivotal decision of your life. It is a decision that you cannot ignore. It is a decision that is yours and yours alone. Accept God's gift now: allow His Son to preside over your heart, your thoughts, and your life, starting this very instant.

The love life of the Christian is a crucial battleground. There, if nowhere else, it will be determined who is Lord: the world, the self, and the devil—or the Lord Christ.

Elisabeth Elliot

— A PRAYER —

Dear Lord, You sent Your Son so that I might have abundant life and eternal life. Thank You, Father, for my Savior, Christ Jesus. I will follow Him, honor Him, and share His Good News, this day and every day. Amen

WHAT'S YOUR GRADE?

The greatest among you must be a servant. But those who exalt themselves will be humbled, and those who humble themselves will be exalted.

Matthew 23:11-12 NKJV

God's heart overflows with generosity and mercy. And as believers in a loving God, we must, to the best of our abilities, imitate our Heavenly Father. Because God has been so incredibly generous with us, we, in turn must be generous with others.

Jesus has much to teach us about generosity. He teaches that the most esteemed men and women are not the self-congratulatory leaders of society but are, instead, the humblest of servants.

If you were being graded on generosity, how would you score? Would you earn "A"s in philanthropy and humility? Hopefully so. But if your grades could stand a little improvement, today is the perfect day to begin.

Today, you may feel the urge to hoard your blessings. Don't do it. Instead, give generously to your neighbors, and do so without fanfare. Find a need and fill it . . . humbly. Lend a helping hand and share a word of kindness . . . anonymously. This is God's way.

It is the duty of every Christian to be Christ to his neighbor.

Martin Luther

— A PRAYER —

Lord, there can be no delight in keeping Your blessings for myself. True joy is found in sharing what I have with others. Make me a generous, loving, humble woman, Dear Lord, as I follow the example of Your Son. Amen

EMBRACING GOD'S LOVE

We love Him because He first loved us.

1 John 4:19 NKJV

As a woman, you know the profound love that you hold in your heart for your own family and friends. As a child of God, you can only imagine the infinite love that your Heavenly Father holds for you.

God made you in His own image and gave you salvation through the person of His Son Jesus Christ. And now, precisely because you are a wondrous creation treasured by God, a question presents itself: What will you do in response to the Creator's love? Will you ignore it or embrace it? Will you return it or neglect it? That decision, of course, is yours and yours alone.

When you embrace God's love, your life's purpose is forever changed. When you embrace God's love, you feel differently about yourself, your neighbors, your family, and your world. More importantly, you share God's message—and His love—with them.

Your Heavenly Father—a God of infinite love and mercy—is waiting to embrace you with open arms. Accept His love today and forever.

There is no pit so deep that God's love is not deeper still.

Corrie ten Boom

— A PRAYER —

Dear God, You are love. You love me, Father, and I love You. As I love You more, Lord, I am also able to love my family and friends more. I will be Your loving servant, Heavenly Father, today and throughout eternity. Amen

HE HAS A PLAN FOR YOU

You will show me the path of life; in Your presence is fullness of joy; at Your right hand are pleasures forevermore.

Psalm 16:11 NKJV

God has a plan for your life. He understands that plan as thoroughly and completely as He knows you. And, if you seek God's will earnestly and prayerfully, He will make His plans known to you in His own time and in His own way.

If you sincerely seek to live in accordance with God's will for your life, you will live in accordance with His commandments. You will study God's Word, and you will be watchful for His signs.

Sometimes, God's plans seem unmistakably clear to you. But other times, He may lead you through the wilderness before He directs you to the Promised Land. So be patient and keep seeking His will for your life. When you do, you'll be amazed at the marvelous things that an all-powerful, all-knowing God can do.

Don't put a question mark where God put a period.

Anonymous

— A PRAYER —

Dear Lord, I am Your creation, and You created me for a reason. Give me the wisdom to follow Your direction for my life's journey. Let me do Your work here on earth by seeking Your will and living it, knowing that when I trust in You, Father, I am eternally blessed. Amen

BEYOND THE DAILY GRIND

Come to Me, all you who are weary and burdened, and I will give you rest. Take My yoke upon you and learn from Me, because I am gentle and humble in heart, and you will find rest for your souls. For My yoke is easy and My burden is light.

Matthew 11:28-30 HCSB

Even the most inspired women can, from time to time, find themselves running on empty. Why? Because the inevitable demands of daily life can drain us of our strength and rob us of the joy that is rightfully ours in Christ. Thankfully, God stands ready to renew our spirits, even on the darkest of days. God's Word is clear: When we genuinely lift our hearts and prayers to Him, He renews our strength.

Are you seeking a renewed sense purpose? Turn your heart toward God in prayer. Are you weak or worried? Take the time to delve deeply into God's Holy Word. Are you spiritually depleted? Call upon fellow believers to support you, and call upon Christ to renew your spirit and your life. When you do, you'll discover that the Creator of the universe stands always ready and always able to create a new sense of wonderment and joy in you.

Surrender your mind to the Lord at the beginning of each day.

Warren Wiersbe

— A PRAYER —

Dear Lord, You can make all things new. I am a new creature in Christ Jesus, and when I fall short in my commitment, You can renew my effort and my enthusiasm. When I am weak or worried, restore my strength, Lord, for my own sake and for the sake of Your kingdom. Amen

STILL GROWING

When I was a child, I spoke like a child, I thought like a child, I reasoned like a child. When I became a man, I put aside childish things.

1 Corinthians 13:11 HCSB

If we are to grow as women, we need both knowledge and wisdom. Knowledge is found in textbooks. Wisdom, on the other hand, is found through experience, through years of trial and error, and through careful attention to the Word of God. Knowledge is an important building block in a well-lived life, and it pays rich dividends both personally and professionally. But, wisdom is even more important because it refashions not only our minds, but also our hearts.

When it comes to your faith, God doesn't intend for you to stand still. He wants you to keep growing as a woman and as a spiritual being. No matter how "grown-up" you may be, you still have growing to do. And the more you grow, the more beautiful you become, inside and out.

I do not know how the Spirit of Christ performs it, but He brings us choices through which we constantly change, fresh and new, into His likeness.

Joni Eareckson Tada

— A PRAYER —

Dear Lord, help me become the person I can be and should be. Help me correct my shortcomings and overcome my obstacles. Show me the path of Your choosing, and let me follow in the footsteps of Your Son, today and every day. Amen

THE SELF-FULFILLING PROPHECY

But as for me, I will hope continually, and will praise You yet more and more.

Psalm 71:14 NASB

The self-fulfilling prophecy is alive, well, and living at your house. If you trust God and have faith for the future, your optimistic beliefs will give you direction and motivation. That's one reason that you should never lose hope, but certainly not the only reason. The primary reason that you, as a believer, should never lose hope, is because of God's unfailing promises.

When you acquire the habit of hopeful thinking, you will have acquired a powerful tool for improving your life. So if you find yourself falling into the spiritual traps of worry and discouragement, seek the healing touch of Jesus and the encouraging words of fellow Christians. And if you fall into the terrible habit of negative thinking, think again. After all, God's Word teaches us that Christ can overcome every difficulty. And when God makes a promise, He keeps it.

Never yield to gloomy anticipation. Place your hope and confidence in God. He has no record of failure.

Mrs. Charles E. Cowman

— A PRAYER —

Dear Lord, let my hopes begin and end with you. When I am discouraged, let me turn to You. When I am weak, let me find strength in You. You are my Father, and I will place my faith, my trust, and my hopes in You, this day and forever. Amen

KINDNESS NOW

God has chosen you and made you his holy people. He loves you. So always do these things: Show mercy to others, be kind, humble, gentle, and patient.

Colossians 3:12 NCV

Christ showed His love for us by willingly sacrificing His own life so that we might have eternal life: "But God demonstrates his own love for us in this: While we were still sinners, Christ died for us" (Romans 5:8 NIV). We, as Christ's followers, are challenged to share His love with kind words on our lips and praise in our hearts.

Just as Christ has been—and will always be—the ultimate friend to His flock, so should we be Christlike in the kindness and generosity that we show toward others, especially those who are most in need.

When we walk each day with Jesus—and obey the commandments found in God's Holy Word—we become worthy ambassadors for Christ. When we share the love of Christ, we share a priceless gift with the world. As His servants, we must do no less.

Showing kindness to others is one of the nicest things we can do for ourselves.

Janette Oke

— A PRAYER —

Dear Lord, help me see the needs of those around me. Today, let me spread kind words of thanksgiving and celebration in honor of Your Son. Let forgiveness rule my heart, and let my love for Christ be reflected through the acts of kindness that I extend to those who need the healing touch of the Master's hand. Amen

WHO ARE OUR NEIGHBORS?

Do not withhold good from those who deserve it, when it is within your power to act.

Proverbs 3:27 NIV

Who are our neighbors? Jesus answered that question with the story of the Good Samaritan. Our neighbors are any people whom God places in our paths, especially those in need.

We know that we are instructed to love our neighbors, and yet there's so little time . . . and we're so busy. No matter. As Christians, we are commanded by our Lord and Savior to love our neighbors just as we love ourselves. Period.

This very day, you will encounter someone who needs a word of encouragement or a pat on the back or a helping hand or a heartfelt prayer. And, if you don't reach out to that person, who will? If you don't take the time to understand the needs of your neighbors, who will? If you don't love your brothers and sisters, who will? So, today, look for a neighbor in need . . . and then do something to help. Father's orders.

A person who really cares about his or her neighbor, a person who genuinely loves others, is a person who bears witness to the truth.

Anne Graham Lotz

— A PRAYER —

Dear Lord, I want to be a compassionate Christian. Just as I wish to be understood by my family and friends, so, too, will I seek to understand them. Give me empathy for all my neighbors, Father, and let my words and deeds bless them today and every day that I live. Amen

THE DONUT AND THE HOLE

Be careful what you think, because your thoughts run your life.

Proverbs 4:23 NCV

On the wall of a little donut shop, the sign said:

As you travel through life, brother,
Whatever be your goal,
Keep your eye upon the donut,
And not upon the hole.

Are you a Christian who keeps your eye upon the donut, or have you acquired the bad habit of looking only at the hole? Hopefully, you spend most of your waking hours looking at the donut (and thanking God for it).

Christianity and pessimism don't mix. So do yourself a favor: choose to be a hope-filled Christian. Think optimistically about your life and your future. Trust your hopes, not your fears. Take time to celebrate God's glorious creation. And then, when you've filled your heart with hope and gladness, share your optimism with your friends. They'll be better for it, and so will you. But not necessarily in that order.

— A PRAYER —

Lord, let me be an expectant Christian. Let me expect the best from You, and let me look for the best in others. If I become discouraged, Father, turn my thoughts and my prayers to You. Let me trust You, Lord, to direct my life. And, let me be Your faithful, hopeful, optimistic servant every day that I live. Amen

PURPOSE DAY BY DAY

Yet Lord, You are our Father; we are the clay, and You are our potter;
we all are the work of Your hands.

Isaiah 64:8 HCSB

Each morning, as the sun rises in the east, you welcome a new day, one that is filled to the brim with opportunities, with possibilities, and with God. As you contemplate God's blessings in your own life, you should prayerfully seek His guidance for the day ahead.

Discovering God's unfolding purpose for your life is a daily journey, a journey guided by the teachings of God's Holy Word. As you reflect upon God's promises and upon the meaning that those promises hold for you, ask God to lead you throughout the coming day. Let your Heavenly Father direct your steps; concentrate on what God wants you to do now, and leave the distant future in hands that are far more capable than your own: His hands.

There is wonderful freedom and joy in coming to recognize that the fun is in the becoming.

Gloria Gaither

— A PRAYER —

Lord, You have a plan for my life that is grander than I can imagine. Let Your purposes be my purposes. Let Your will be my will. When I am confused, give me clarity. When I am frightened, give me courage. Let me be Your faithful servant, always seeking Your guidance for my life. And, let me always be a shining beacon for Your Son today and every day that I live. Amen

SELF-ACCEPTANCE

You're blessed when you're content with just who you are—no more, no less. That's the moment you find yourselves proud owners of everything that can't be bought.

Matthew 5:5 MSG

Being patient with other people can be difficult. But sometimes, we find it even more difficult to be patient with ourselves. We have high expectations and lofty goals. We want to accomplish things now, not later. And, of course, we want our lives to unfold according to our own timetables, not God's.

Throughout the Bible, we are instructed that patience is the companion of wisdom. Proverbs 16:32 teaches us that "Patience is better than strength" (NCV). And, in 1 Peter 5:6, we are told to "humble yourselves under the mighty hand of God, that He may exalt you in due time" (NKJV).

God's message, then, is clear: we must be patient with all people, beginning with that particular person who stares back at us each time we gaze into the mirror.

Once you loosen up, let yourself be who you are: the wonderful, witty woman whom God will use to encourage and uplift other people.

Barbara Johnson

— A PRAYER —

Lord, I have so much to learn and so many ways to improve myself, but You love me just as I am. Thank You for Your love and for Your Son. And, help me to become the person that You want me to become. Amen

WISE WORDS

The heart of the wise teaches his mouth, and adds learning to his lips.

Proverbs 16:23 NKJV

Think . . . pause . . . then speak: How wise is the woman who can communicate in this way. But all too often, in the rush to have ourselves heard, we speak first and think next . . . with unfortunate results.

God's Word reminds us that "Reckless words pierce like a sword, but the tongue of the wise brings healing" (Proverbs 12:18 NIV). If we seek to be a source of encouragement to friends and family, then we must measure our words carefully. Words are important: they can hurt or heal. Words can uplift us or discourage us, and reckless words, spoken in haste, cannot be erased.

Today, seek to encourage all who cross your path. Measure your words carefully. Speak wisely, not impulsively. Use words of kindness and praise, not words of anger or derision. Remember that you have the power to heal others or to injure them, to lift others up or to hold them back. When you lift them up, your wisdom will bring healing and comfort to a world that needs both.

The battle of the tongue is won not in the mouth, but in the heart.

Annie Chapman

— A PRAYER —

Dear Lord, You have commanded me to choose my words carefully so that I might be a source of encouragement and hope to all whom I meet. Keep me mindful, Lord, that I have influence on many people. Let the words that I speak today be worthy of the One who has saved me forever. Amen

OUT OF BALANCE?

Happy is a man who finds wisdom and who acquires understanding.

Proverbs 3:13 HCSB

Sometimes, amid the concerns of everyday life, we lose perspective. Life seems out of balance as we confront an array of demands that sap our strength and cloud our thoughts. What's needed is a renewed faith, a fresh perspective, and God's wisdom.

Here in the 21st century, commentary is commonplace and information is everywhere. But the ultimate source of wisdom, the kind of timeless wisdom that God willingly shares with His children, is still available from a single unique source: the Holy Bible.

The wisdom of the world changes with the ever-shifting sands of public opinion. God's wisdom does not. His wisdom is eternal. It never changes. And it most certainly is the wisdom that you must use to plan your day, your life, and your eternal destiny.

He teaches us, not just to let us see ourselves correctly, but to help us see him correctly.

Kathy Troccoli

— A PRAYER —

Lord, make me a woman of wisdom and discernment. I seek wisdom, Lord, not as the world gives, but as You give. Lead me in Your ways and teach me from Your Word so that, in time, my wisdom might glorify Your kingdom and Your Son. Amen

GOD'S ABUNDANCE

You did not choose me, but I chose you and appointed you to go and bear fruit—fruit that will last. Then the Father will give you whatever you ask in my name.

John 15:16 NIV

Do you seek God's abundance for yourself and your family? Of course you do. And it's worth remembering that God's rewards are most certainly available to you and yours. The 10th chapter of John tells us that Christ came to earth so that our lives might be filled with abundance. But what, exactly, did Jesus mean when He promised "life . . . more abundantly"? Was He referring to material possessions or financial wealth? Hardly. Jesus offers a different kind of abundance: a spiritual richness that extends beyond the temporal boundaries of this world. This everlasting abundance is available to all who seek it and claim it. May you and your family claim those riches, and may you share Christ's blessings with all who cross your path.

If we were given all we wanted here, our hearts would settle for this world rather than the next.

Elisabeth Elliot

— A PRAYER —

Father, thank You for the joyful, abundant life that is mine through Christ Jesus. Guide me according to Your will, and help me to be a worthy servant through all that I say and do. Give me courage, Lord, to claim the spiritual riches that You have promised, and lead me according to Your plan for my life, today and always. Amen

EMBRACING EVERY STAGE OF LIFE

Youth may be admired for vigor, but gray hair gives prestige to old age.

Proverbs 20:29 MSG

We live in a society that glorifies youth. The messages that we receive from the media are unrelenting: We are told that we must do everything within our power to retain youthful values and a youthful appearance. The goal, we are told, is to remain "forever young"—yet this goal is not only unrealistic, it is also unworthy of women who understand what genuine beauty is, and what it isn't. When it comes to "health and beauty" . . . you should focus more on health than on beauty. In fact, when you take care of your physical, spiritual, and mental health, your appearance will tend to take care of itself. And remember: God loves you during every stage of life—so embrace the aging process for what it is: an opportunity to grow closer to your loved ones and to your Creator.

Youth is not a time of life but a state of mind. It boldly takes risks, seeks adventure, hopes for the best, and displays courage. You are as young as your faith is strong.

Barbara Johnson

— A PRAYER —

Dear Lord, through every stage of life, I will praise You for Your blessings, for Your love, and for Your Son. Let me be a joyful believer every day of my life. Amen

YOUR BELIEFS AND YOUR LIFE

Because the kingdom of God is present not in talk but in power.

1 Corinthians 4:20 NCV

Do you weave your beliefs into the very fabric of your day? If you do, God will honor your good works, and your good works will honor God.

If you seek to be a responsible believer, you must realize that it is never enough to hear the instructions of God; you must also live by them. And it is never enough to wait idly by while others do God's work here on earth. You, too, must act.

Doing God's work is a responsibility that every Christian (including you) should bear. And when you do, your loving Heavenly Father will reward your efforts with a bountiful harvest.

The reason many of us do not ardently believe in the gospel is that we have never given it a rigorous testing, thrown our hard questions at it, or faced it with our most prickly doubts.

Eugene Peterson

— A PRAYER —

Lord, it is so much easier to speak of the righteous life than it is to live it. Let me live righteously, and let my actions be consistent with my beliefs. Let every step that I take reflect Your truth, and let me live a life that is worthy of Your Son. Amen

HE DOES NOT CHANGE

One Lord, one faith, one baptism, one God and Father of all, who is above all and through all and in all.

Ephesians 4:5-6 HCSB

We live in a world that is always changing, but we worship a God who never changes—thank goodness! As believers, we can be comforted in the knowledge that our Heavenly Father is the rock that simply cannot be moved: "I am the Lord, I do not change" (Malachi 3:6 NKJV).

Are you facing difficult circumstances or unwelcome changes? If so, please remember that God is far bigger than any problem you may face. So, instead of worrying about life's inevitable challenges, put your faith in the Father and His only begotten Son: "Jesus Christ is the same yesterday, today, and forever" (Hebrews 13:8 HCSB). And rest assured: It is precisely because your Savior does not change that you can face your challenges with courage for this day and hope for the future.

Live for today, but hold your hands open to tomorrow. Anticipate the future and its changes with joy. There is a seed of God's love in every event, every circumstance, every unpleasant situation in which you may find yourself.

Barbara Johnson

— A PRAYER —

Dear Lord, our world changes, but You are unchanging. When I face challenges that leave me discouraged or fearful, I will turn to You for strength and assurance. Let my trust in You—like Your love for me—be unchanging and everlasting. Amen

FINDING CONTENTMENT

I am not telling you this because I need anything. I have learned to be satisfied with the things I have and with everything that happens. I know how to live when I am poor, and I know how to live when I have plenty. I have learned the secret of being happy at any time in everything that happens.

Philippians 4:11-12 NCV

The preoccupation with happiness and contentment is an ever-present theme in the modern world. We are bombarded with messages that tell us where to find peace and pleasure in a world that worships materialism and wealth. But, lasting contentment is not found in material possessions; genuine contentment is a spiritual gift from God to those who trust in Him and follow His commandments.

Where do we find contentment? If we don't find it in God, we will never find it anywhere else. But, if we put our faith and our trust in Him, we will be blessed with an inner peace that is beyond human understanding. When God dwells at the center of our lives, peace and contentment will belong to us just as surely as we belong to God.

— A PRAYER —

Father, let me be a woman who strives to do Your will here on earth, and as I do, let me find contentment and balance. Let me live in the light of Your will and Your priorities for my life, and when I have done my best, Lord, give me the wisdom to place my faith and my trust in You. Amen

HE DOESN'T FAIL

The LORD is my strength and song, and He has become my salvation.

Exodus 15:2 NASB

When we fail to meet the expectations of others (or, for that matter, the expectations that we have set for ourselves), we may be tempted to abandon hope. Thankfully, on those cloudy days when our strength is sapped and our faith is shaken, there exists God from whom we can draw courage and wisdom.

The words of Isaiah 40:31 teach us that, "Those who wait on the Lord shall renew their strength; they shall mount up with wings like eagles, they shall run and not be weary, they shall walk and not faint" (NKJV).

So if you're feeling defeated or discouraged, think again. And while you're thinking, consider the following advice from Mrs. Charles E. Cowman: "Never yield to gloomy anticipation. Place your hope and confidence in God. He has no record of failure."

The most profane word we use is "hopeless." When you say a situation or person is hopeless, you are slamming the door in the face of God.

Kathy Troccoli

— A PRAYER —

Dear Lord, when I am discouraged, give me perspective and faith. When I am weak, give me strength. When I am fearful, give me courage for the day ahead. I will trust in Your promises, Father, and I will live with the assurance that You are with me not only for this day, but also throughout all eternity. Amen

BEYOND ENVY

Let us not be desirous of vainglory, provoking one another, envying one another.

Galatians 5:26 KJV

Because we are frail, imperfect human beings, we are sometimes envious of others. But God's Word warns us that envy is sin. Thus, we must guard ourselves against the natural tendency to feel resentment and jealousy when other people experience good fortune.

As believers, we have absolutely no reason to be envious of any people on earth. After all, as Christians we are already recipients of the greatest gift in all creation: God's grace. We have been promised the gift of eternal life through God's only begotten Son, and we must count that gift as our most precious possession.

Rather than succumbing to the sin of envy, we should focus on the marvelous things that God has done for us. So here's a surefire formula for a happier, healthier life: Count your own blessings and let your neighbors count theirs. It's the godly way to live.

Discontent dries up the soul.

Elisabeth Elliot

— A PRAYER —

Dear Lord, when I am envious of others, redirect my thoughts to the blessings I have received from You. Make me a thankful Christian, Father, and deliver me from envy. Amen

CHOOSING WISE ROLE MODELS

Spend time with the wise and you will become wise, but the friends of fools will suffer.

Proverbs 13:20 NCV

Here's a simple yet effective way to strengthen your faith: Choose role models whose faith in God is strong.

When you emulate godly people, you become a more godly person yourself. That's why you should seek out mentors who, by their words and their presence, make you a better person and a better Christian.

Today, as a gift to yourself, select, from your friends and family members, a mentor whose judgement you trust. Then listen carefully to your mentor's advice and be willing to accept that advice, even if accepting it requires effort or pain, or both. Consider your mentor to be God's gift to you. Thank God for that gift, and use it for the glory of His kingdom.

It takes a wise person to give good advice, but an even wiser person to take it.

Marie T. Freeman

— A PRAYER —

Dear Lord, thank You for the mentors whom you have placed along my path. When I am troubled, let me turn to them for help, for guidance, for comfort, and for perspective. And Father, let me be a friend and mentor to others, so that my love for You may be demonstrated by my genuine concern for them. Amen

FOLLOWING HIS PLAN

The counsel of the Lord stands forever, the plans of His heart to all generations.

Psalm 33:11 NKJV

You can expect a satisfying and fulfilling life when you follow God's plan for your life. But how can you discern God's will? You should begin by studying God's Word and obeying His commandments. You should watch carefully for His signs, and you should associate with fellow Christians who encourage your spiritual growth. And you should listen to that inner voice that speaks to you in the quiet moments of your daily devotionals.

God intends to use you in wonderful, unexpected ways if you let Him. The decision to seek God's plan and to follow it is yours and yours alone. The consequences of that decision have implications that are both profound and eternal, so choose carefully.

Loving Him means the thankful acceptance of all things that His love has appointed.

Elisabeth Elliot

— A PRAYER —

Lord, let Your will be my will. When I am confused, give me maturity and wisdom. When I am worried, give me courage and strength. Let me be Your faithful servant, Father, always seeking Your guidance and Your will for my life. Amen

TRUST HIM

Trust in Him at all times, you people; pour out your heart before Him;
God is a refuge for us.

Psalm 62:8 NKJV

Sometimes the future seems bright, and sometimes it does not. Yet even when we cannot see the possibilities of tomorrow, God can. As believers, our challenge is to trust an uncertain future to an all-powerful God.

When we trust God, we should trust Him without reservation. We should steel ourselves against the inevitable disappointments of the day, secure in the knowledge that our Heavenly Father has a plan for the future that only He can see.

Can you place your future into the hands of a loving and all-knowing God? Can you live amid the uncertainties of today, knowing that God has dominion over all your tomorrows? If you can, you are wise and you are blessed. When you trust God with everything you are and everything you have, He will bless you now and forever.

Since we can't understand what God does, we must trust everything that God is.

Marie T. Freeman

— A PRAYER —

Lord, when I trust in the things of this earth, I will be disappointed. But, when I put my faith in You, I am secure. In every aspect of my life, Father, let me place my hope and my trust in Your infinite wisdom and Your boundless grace. Amen

DON'T BE WORRIED . . . YOU ARE PROTECTED

But seek first the kingdom of God and His righteousness, and all these things shall be added to you. Therefore do not worry about tomorrow, for tomorrow will worry about its own things. Sufficient for the day is its own trouble.

Matthew 6:33-34 NKJV

Because we are fallible human beings, we worry. Even though we, as Christians, have the assurance of salvation—even though we, as Christians, have the promise of God's love and protection—we find ourselves fretting over the countless details of everyday life.

If you are like most women, you may, on occasion, find yourself worrying about health, about finances, about safety, about relationships, about family, and about countless other challenges of life, some great and some small. Where is the best place to take your worries? Take them to God. Take your troubles to Him, and your fears, and your sorrows. And remember: God is trustworthy . . . and you are protected.

Worry is a cycle of inefficient thoughts whirling around a center of fear.

Corrie ten Boom

— A PRAYER —

Dear Lord, wherever I find myself, let me celebrate more and worry less. When my faith begins to waver, help me to trust You more. Then, with praise on my lips and the love of Your Son in my heart, let me live courageously, faithfully, prayerfully, and thankfully this day and every day. Amen

WHEN WE FACE ADVERSITY

I will be with you when you pass through the waters . . . when you walk through the fire . . . the flame will not burn you. For I the Lord your God, the Holy One of Israel, and your Savior.

Isaiah 43:2-3 HCSB

From time to time, all of us face adversity, discouragement, or disappointment. And, throughout life, we must all endure life-changing personal losses that leave us breathless. When we do, God stands ready to protect us. Psalm 147 promises, "He heals the brokenhearted, and binds their wounds" (v. 3, NIV).

When we are troubled, we must call upon God, and, in His own time and according to His own plan, He will heal us.

Are you anxious? Take those anxieties to God. Are you troubled? Take your troubles to Him. Does your world seem to be trembling beneath your feet? Seek protection from the One who cannot be moved. The same God who created the universe will protect you if you ask Him . . . so ask Him.

You and I need to learn to interpret our circumstances by His love, not interpret His love by our circumstances!

Anne Graham Lotz

— A PRAYER —

Heavenly Father, You are my strength and my refuge. As I journey through this day, I know that I may encounter disappointments and losses. When I am troubled, let me turn to You. Keep me steady, Lord, and renew a right spirit inside of me this day and forever. Amen

LIVING RIGHTEOUSLY

But now you must be holy in everything you do, just as God—who chose you to be his children—is holy. For he himself has said, "You must be holy because I am holy."

1 Peter 1:15-16 NLT

When we seek righteousness in our own lives—and when we seek the companionship of those who do likewise—we reap the spiritual rewards that God intends for us to enjoy. When we behave ourselves as godly women, we honor God. When we live righteously and according to God's commandments, He blesses us in ways that we cannot fully understand.

Today, as you fulfill your responsibilities, hold fast to that which is good, and associate yourself with believers who behave themselves in like fashion. When you do, your good works will serve as a powerful example for others and as a worthy offering to your Creator.

You can't compromise and conquer sin at the same time.

Anonymous

— A PRAYER —

Lord, I pray that my actions will always be consistent with my beliefs. I know that my deeds speak more loudly than my words. May every step that I take reflect Your truth and love, and may others be drawn to You because of my words and my deeds. Amen

TIME TO CELEBRATE

Celebrate God all day, every day. I mean, revel in him!

Philippians 4:4 MSG

Are you living a life of agitation, consternation, or celebration? If you're a believer, it should most certainly be the latter. With Christ as your Savior, every day should be a time of celebration.

Today, celebrate the life that God has given you. Today, put a smile on your face, kind words on your lips, and a song in your heart. Be generous with your praise and free with your encouragement. And then, when you have celebrated life to the fullest, invite your friends to do likewise. After all, this is God's day, and He has given us clear instructions for its use. We are commanded to rejoice and be glad.

How much of our lives are, well, so daily. How often our hours are filled with the mundane, seemingly unimportant things that have to be done, whether at home or work. These very "daily" tasks could become a celebration of praise. "It is through consecration," someone has said, "that drudgery is made divine."

Gigi Graham Tchividjian

— A PRAYER —

Dear Lord, let me celebrate this moment and every moment of life. Today is Your gift to me, Lord. Let me use it to Your glory while giving all the praise to You. Amen

CHOICES, CHOICES, CHOICES

Don't consider yourself to be wise; fear the Lord and turn away from evil.

Proverbs 3:7 HCSB

Life is a series of choices. Each day, we make countless decisions that can bring us closer to God . . . or not. When we live according to God's commandments, we earn for ourselves the abundance and peace that He intends for our lives. But, when we turn our backs upon God by disobeying Him, we bring needless suffering upon ourselves and our families.

Do you seek spiritual abundance that can be yours through the person of God's only begotten Son? Then invite Christ into your heart and live according to His teachings. And, when you confront a difficult decision or a powerful temptation, seek God's wisdom and trust it. When you do, you will receive untold blessings—not only for this day, but also for all eternity.

My story. Your story. How it is told in the end and what the story says depends on what each of us does with Jesus.

Gloria Gaither

— A PRAYER —

Heavenly Father, I have many choices to make. Help me choose wisely as I follow in the footsteps of Your only begotten Son. Amen

BEYOND THE CRISES

But the wisdom that is from above is first pure, then peaceable, gentle, willing to yield, full of mercy and good fruits, without partiality and without hypocrisy.

James 3:17 NKJV

Your decision to seek a deeper relationship with God will not remove all problems from your life; to the contrary, it will bring about a series of personal crises as you constantly seek to say "yes" to God although the world encourages you to do otherwise. You live in a world that seeks to snare your attention and lead you away from God. And it's up to you to resist these forces.

Today, you will face many opportunities to say "yes" to your Creator—and you will also encounter many opportunities to say "no" to Him. Your answers will determine the quality of your day and the direction of your life, so answer carefully.

Knowing God involves an intimate, personal relationship that is developed over time through prayer and getting answers to prayer, through Bible study and applying its teaching to our lives, through obedience and experiencing the power of God, through moment-by-moment submission to Him that results in a moment-by-moment filling of the Holy Spirit.

Anne Graham Lotz

— A PRAYER —

Dear Lord, every day of my life is a journey with You. Today is another day on that journey. Guide my steps today, Father, and keep me mindful that today offers yet another opportunity to celebrate Your blessings, Your love, and Your Son. Amen

SPEAKING WORDS OF ENCOURAGEMENT AND HOPE

The godly give good advice, but fools are destroyed by their lack of common sense.

Proverbs 10:21 NLT

The words that we speak have the power to do great good or great harm. If we speak words of encouragement and hope, we can lift others up. And that's exactly what God commands us to do!

Sometimes, when we feel uplifted and secure, it is easy to speak kind words. Other times, when we are discouraged or tired, we can scarcely summon the energy to uplift ourselves, much less anyone else. God intends that we speak words of kindness, wisdom, and truth, no matter our circumstances, no matter our emotions. When we do, we share a priceless gift with the world, and we give glory to the One who gave His life for us. As believers, we must do no less.

We do have the ability to encourage or discourage each other with the words we say. In order to maintain a positive mood, our hearts must be in good condition.

Annie Chapman

— A PRAYER —

Lord, make me mindful of my words. Make me a powerful source of encouragement to those in need, and let my words and deeds be worthy of Your Son, the One who gives me courage and strength, this day and for all eternity. Amen

MOUNTAIN-MOVING FAITH

I assure you: If anyone says to this mountain, "Be lifted up and thrown into the sea," and does not doubt in his heart, but believes that what he says will happen, it will be done for him.

Mark 11:23 HCSB

Have you ever felt your faith in God slipping away? If so, you are not alone. Every life—including yours—is a series of successes and failures, celebrations and disappointments, joys and sorrows. But even when we feel very distant from God, God is never distant from us.

Jesus taught His disciples that if they had faith, they could move mountains. You can too. When you place your faith, your trust, indeed your life in the hands of Christ Jesus, you'll be amazed at the marvelous things He can do with you and through you. So strengthen your faith through praise, through worship, through Bible study, and through prayer. And trust God's plans. With Him, all things are possible, and He stands ready to open a world of possibilities to you if you have faith.

Faith is an activity. It is something that has to be applied.

Corrie ten Boom

— A PRAYER —

Dear Lord, I want faith that moves mountains. You have big plans for this world and big plans for me. Help me fulfill those plans, Father, as I follow in the footsteps of Your Son. Amen

THE WISDOM TO RESPECT HIM

The fear of the Lord is the beginning of wisdom, and the knowledge of the Holy One is understanding.

Proverbs 9:10 NKJV

Do you have a healthy, fearful respect for God's power? If so, you are both wise and obedient. And, because you are a thoughtful believer, you also understand that genuine wisdom begins with a profound appreciation for God's limitless power.

God praises humility and punishes pride. That's why God's greatest servants will always be those humble men and women who care less for their own glory and more for God's glory. In God's kingdom, the only way to achieve greatness is to shun it. And the only way to be wise is to understand these facts: God is great; He is all-knowing; and He is all-powerful. We must respect Him, and we must humbly obey His commandments, or we must accept the consequences of our misplaced pride.

God is God. Because He is God, He is worthy of my trust and obedience. I will find rest nowhere but in His holy will, a will that is unspeakably beyond my largest notions of what He is up to.

Elisabeth Elliot

— A PRAYER —

Lord, You love me and protect me. I praise You, Father, for your grace, and I respect You for Your infinite power. Let my greatest fear in life be the fear of displeasing You. Amen

GOD'S FORGIVENESS

But God, who is abundant in mercy, because of His great love that He had for us, made us alive with the Messiah even though we were dead in trespasses. By grace you are saved!

Ephesians 2:4-5 HCSB

God's power to forgive, like His love, is infinite. Despite your shortcomings, despite your sins, God offers you immediate forgiveness and eternal life when you accept Christ as your Savior.

As a believer who is the recipient of God's forgiveness, how should you behave towards others? Should you forgive them (just as God has forgiven you), or should you remain embittered and resentful? The answer, of course, is found in God's Word: you are instructed to forgive others. When you do, you not only obey God's command, you also free yourself from a prison of your own making.

When it comes to forgiveness, God doesn't play favorites and neither should you. You should forgive all those who have harmed you (not just the people who have asked for forgiveness or those who have made restitution). Complete forgiveness is God's way, and it should be your way, too. Anything less is an affront to Him and a burden to you.

— A PRAYER —

Dear Lord, I have fallen short of Your commandments, and You have forgiven me. You have blessed me with Your love and Your mercy. Enable me to be merciful toward others, Father, just as You have been merciful to me, and let me share Your love with all whom I meet. Amen

GOD'S CORRECTION

My son, do not despise the chastening of the Lord, nor detest His correction.

Proverbs 3:11 NKJV

The hand of God corrects us when we disobey His commandments. The hand of God guides us when we stray from His chosen path. When our behavior is inconsistent with God's will, our Heavenly Father inevitably disciplines us in the same fashion that a loving parent disciplines a wayward child.

Hebrews 12:5 reminds us that when God chastises us, we should accept His discipline without bitterness or despair. We should, instead, look upon God's instruction as an occasion to repent from our sins, to reorder our priorities, and to realign our lives.

God's correction is purposeful: He intends to guide us back to Him. When we trust God completely and without reservation, He gives us the strength to meet any challenge, the courage to face any trial, and the wisdom to live in His righteousness and in His peace.

Discipline is the refining fire by which talent becomes ability.

Roy L. Smith

— A PRAYER —

Heavenly Father, I am Your child, and I understand that, at times, I need Your discipline. I also understand, Father, that Your discipline and Your love go hand in hand. Help me to accept Your correction—and learn from it—so that I might walk each day in the footsteps of Your Son. Amen

GOD'S ARMOR

Finally, my brethren, be strong in the Lord and in the power of His might. Put on the whole armor of God, that you may be able to stand against the wiles of the devil.

Ephesians 6:10-11 NKJV

In a world filled with dangers and temptations, God is the ultimate armor. In a world filled with misleading messages, God's Word is the ultimate truth. In a world filled with more frustrations than we can count, God's Son offers the ultimate peace. Will you accept God's peace and wear God's armor against the dangers of our world?

Sometimes, in the crush of everyday life, God may seem far away, but He is not. God is everywhere you have ever been and everywhere you will ever go. He is with you night and day; He knows your thoughts and your prayers. His is your ultimate Protector. And, when you earnestly seek His protection, you will find it because He is here—always—waiting patiently for you to reach out to Him.

God will never let you sink under your circumstances. He always provides a safety net and His love always encircles.

Barbara Johnson

— A PRAYER —

Lord, sometimes life is difficult. Sometimes, I am worried, weary, or heartbroken. And sometimes, I encounter powerful temptations to disobey Your commandments. But, when I lift my eyes to You, Father, You strengthen me. When I am weak, You lift me up. Today, I will turn to You for strength, for hope, for direction, and for deliverance. Amen

THE BEST POLICY

He who walks with integrity walks securely, but he who perverts his ways will become known.

Proverbs 10:9 NKJV

As the familiar saying goes, "Honesty is the best policy." For believers, it is far more important to note that honesty is God's policy. And if we are to be servants worthy of our Savior, Jesus Christ, we must be honest and forthright in our communications with others.

Sometimes, honesty is difficult; sometimes, honesty is painful; but always honesty is God's commandment. In the Book of Exodus, God did not command, "Thou shalt not bear false witness when it is convenient." God said, "Thou shalt not bear false witness against thy neighbor." Period.

Sometime soon, perhaps even today, you will be tempted to bend the truth or perhaps even to break it. Resist that temptation. Truth is God's way, and it must also be yours. Period.

Those who are given to white lies soon become color blind.

Anonymous

— A PRAYER —

Dear Lord, You command Your children to walk in truth. Let me follow Your commandment. Give me the courage to speak honestly, and let me walk righteously with You so that others might see Your eternal truth reflected in my words and my deeds. Amen

THE CRUCIAL QUESTION

We know very well that we are not set right with God by rule-keeping but only through personal faith in Jesus Christ.

Galatians 2:16 MSG

The 19th-century writer Hannah Whitall Smith observed, "The crucial question for each of us is this: What do you think of Jesus, and do you yet have a personal acquaintance with Him?" Indeed, the answer to that question determines the quality, the course, and the direction of our lives today and for all eternity.

The old familiar hymn begins, "What a friend we have in Jesus . . . ." No truer words were ever penned. Jesus is the sovereign Friend and ultimate Savior of mankind. Christ showed enduring love for His believers by willingly sacrificing His own life so that we might have eternal life. Now, it is our turn to become His friend.

Let us love our Savior, praise Him, and share His message of salvation with our neighbors and with the world. When we do, we demonstrate that our acquaintance with the Master is not a passing fancy; it is, instead, the cornerstone and the touchstone of our lives.

— A PRAYER —

Dear Heavenly Father, I praise You and thank You for Your priceless gift: Jesus Christ. Let me share the Good News of the One who became a man so that I might become His, not only for today, but also for all eternity. Jesus is my Savior and my strength. I will welcome Him into my heart with love and thanksgiving, today and forever. Amen

LIFE TRIUMPHANT

Shout triumphantly to the Lord, all the earth. Serve the Lord with gladness; come before Him with joyful songs.

Psalm 100:1-2 HCSB

Are you living the triumphant life that God has promised? Or are you, instead, a spiritual shrinking violet? As you ponder that question, consider this: God does not intend that you live a life that is commonplace or mediocre. And He doesn't want you to hide your light "under a basket." Instead, He wants you to "Let your light so shine before men, that they may see your good works and glorify your Father in heaven" (Matthew 5:16 NKJV). In short, God wants you to live a triumphant life so that others might know precisely what it means to be a believer.

The Christian life should be a triumphal celebration, a daily exercise in thanksgiving and praise. Join that celebration today. And while you're at it, make sure that you let others know that you've joined.

The world has never been stable. Jesus Himself was born into the cruelest and most unstable of worlds. No, we have babies and keep trusting and living because the Resurrection is true! The Resurrection was not just a one-time event in history; it is a principle built into the very fabric of our beings, a fact reverberating from every cell of creation: Life wins! Life wins!

Gloria Gaither

— A PRAYER —

Dear Lord, You have given me the gift of love; let me share that gift with others. And, keep me mindful that the essence of love is not to receive it, but to give it, today and forever. Amen

TAKING UP HIS CROSS

Then He said to them all, "If anyone desires to come after Me, let him deny himself, and take up his cross daily, and follow Me. For whoever desires to save his life will lose it, but whoever loses his life for My sake will save it."

Luke 9:23-24 NKJV

When Jesus addressed His disciples, He warned that each one must, "take up his cross and follow me." The disciples must have known exactly what the Master meant. In Jesus' day, prisoners were forced to carry their own crosses to the location where they would be put to death. Thus, Christ's message was clear: in order to follow Him, Christ's disciples must deny themselves and, instead, trust Him completely. Nothing has changed since then.

If we are to be dutiful disciples of the One from Galilee, we must trust Him and we must follow Him. Jesus never comes "next." He is always first. He shows us the path of life.

Do you seek to be a worthy disciple of Jesus? Then pick up His cross today and follow in His footsteps. When you do, you can walk with confidence: He will never lead you astray.

There is not Christianity without a cross, for you cannot be a disciple of Jesus without taking up your cross.

Henry Blackaby

— A PRAYER —

Lord, sometimes life is difficult. But even when I can't see any hope for the future, You are always with me. And, I can live courageously because I know that You are leading me to a place where I can accomplish Your kingdom's work . . . and where You lead, I will follow. Amen

PERSPECTIVE NOW

Teach me Your way, O Lord; I will walk in Your truth.

Psalm 86:11 NKJV

Do you carve out quiet moments each day to offer thanksgiving and praise to your Creator? You should. During these moments of stillness, you will often sense the love and wisdom of our Lord.

The familiar words of Psalm 46:10 remind us to "Be still, and know that I am God" (NKJV). When we do so, we encounter the awesome presence of our loving Heavenly Father, and we are blessed beyond words. But, when we ignore the presence of our Creator, we rob ourselves of His perspective, His peace, and His joy.

Today and every day, make time to be still before God. When you do, you can face the day's complications with the wisdom and power that only He can provide.

When we look at the individual parts of our lives, some things appear unfair and unpleasant. When we take them out of the context of the big picture, we easily drift into the attitude that we deserve better, and the tumble down into the pit of pride begins.

Susan Hunt

— A PRAYER —

Dear Lord, give me wisdom and perspective. Guide me according to Your plans for my life and according to Your commandments. And keep me mindful, Dear Lord, that Your truth is—and will forever be—the ultimate truth. Amen

IT PAYS TO PRAISE

Therefore, through Him let us continually offer up to God a sacrifice of praise, that is, the fruit of our lips that confess His name.

Hebrews 13:15 HCSB

The Bible makes it clear: it pays to praise God. But sometimes, we allow ourselves to become so preoccupied with the demands of everyday life that we forget to say "Thank You" to the Giver of all good gifts.

Worship and praise should be a part of everything we do. Otherwise, we quickly lose perspective as we fall prey to the demands of the moment.

Do you sincerely desire to be a worthy servant of the One who has given you eternal love and eternal life? Then praise Him for who He is and for what He has done for you. And don't just praise Him on Sunday morning. Praise Him all day long, every day, for as long as you live . . . and then for all eternity.

Praise is the sparkplug of faith. Praise gets faith airborne where it can soar above the gravitational forces of this world's cares.

Kay Arthur

— A PRAYER —

Dear Lord, I will praise You today and every day that I live. And, I will praise Your Son, the Savior of my life. Christ's love is boundless and eternal. Let my thoughts, my prayers, my words, and my deeds praise Him now and forever. Amen

COUNTLESS OPPORTUNITIES

*I will instruct you and show you the way to go; with My eye on you,
I will give counsel.*

Psalm 32:8 HCSB

Each waking moment holds the potential to think a creative thought or offer a heartfelt prayer. So even if you're a person with too many demands and too few hours in which to meet them, don't panic. Instead, be comforted in the knowledge that when you sincerely seek to discover God's priorities for your life, He will provide answers in marvelous and surprising ways.

Remember: this is the day that God has made and that He has filled it with countless opportunities to love, to serve, and to seek His guidance. Seize those opportunities. And as a gift to yourself, to your family, and to the world, slow down and establish clear priorities that are pleasing to God. When you do, you will earn the inner peace that is your spiritual birthright: the peace of Jesus Christ. It is yours for the asking. So ask . . . and be thankful.

When we put people before possessions in our hearts, we are sowing seeds of enduring satisfaction.

Beverly LaHaye

— A PRAYER —

Lord, let Your will be my will, let Your priorities be my priorities, and let me grow in faith and in wisdom this day and every day. Amen

REAL REPENTANCE

Come back to the LORD and live!

Amos 5:6 NLT

Genuine repentance requires more than simply offering God apologies for our misdeeds. Real repentance may start with feelings of sorrow and remorse, but it ends only when we turn away from the sin that has heretofore distanced us from our Creator. In truth, we offer our most meaningful apologies to God, not with our words, but with our actions. As long as we are still engaged in sin, we may be "repenting," but we have not fully "repented."

Is there an aspect of your life that is distancing you from your God? If so, ask for His forgiveness, and—just as importantly—stop sinning. Then, wrap yourself in the protection of God's Word. When you do, you will be secure.

Real repentance is always accompanied by godly sorrow. Asking God to forgive us for a sin we are not yet sorry we committed is a waste of time.

Beth Moore

— A PRAYER —

When I stray from Your commandments, Lord, I must not only confess my sins, I must also turn from them. When I fall short, help me to change. When I reject Your Word and Your will for my life, guide me back to Your side. Forgive my sins, Dear Lord, and help me live according to Your plan for my life. Your plan is perfect, Father; I am not. Let me trust in You. Amen

SERVICE AND LOVE

By this we know that we love the children of God, when we love God and keep His commandments.

1 John 5:2 NKJV

Jesus came to earth as a servant of man and the Savior of mankind. One way that we can demonstrate our love for our wonderful Savior is by obeying His commandment to serve one another.

Whom will you choose to serve today? Will you be a woman who cheerfully meets the needs of her family and her friends? And, will you meet those needs with love in your heart and encouragement on your lips? As you plan for the day ahead, remember that the needs are great and the workers are few. And remember that God is doing His very best to enlist able-bodied believers—like you.

We'll know how to lovingly serve others as we trust him to give us the guidance we need.

Sheila Cragg

— A PRAYER —

Lord, You have promised me a life of abundance and joy through Your Son Jesus. Thank You, Lord, for Your blessings, and guide me according to Your will, so that I might be a worthy servant in all that I say and do, this day and every day. Amen

SPIRITUAL GROWTH

But grow in the grace and knowledge of our Lord and Savior Jesus Christ. To Him be the glory both now and forever. Amen.

2 Peter 3:18 NKJV

If we are to grow as Christians and as women, we need both knowledge and wisdom. Knowledge is found in textbooks. Wisdom, on the other hand, is found in God's Holy Word and in the carefully-chosen words of loving parents, family members, and friends. Knowledge is an important building block in a well-lived life, and it pays rich dividends both personally and professionally. But, wisdom is even more important because it refashions not only the mind, but also the heart.

When it comes to your faith, God doesn't intend for you to stand still. As a Christian, you should continue to grow in the love and the knowledge of your Savior as long as you live. How? By studying God's Word every day, by obeying His commandments, and by allowing His Son to reign over your heart.

Be filled with the Holy Spirit; join a church where the members believe the Bible and know the Lord; seek the fellowship of other Christians; learn and be nourished by God's Word and His many promises. Conversion is not the end of your journey—it is only the beginning.

Corrie ten Boom

— A PRAYER —

Dear Lord, thank You for the opportunity to walk with Your Son. And, thank You for the opportunity to grow closer to You each day. I thank You for the person I am . . . and for the person I can become. Amen

REBELS BEWARE

Whoever is stubborn after being corrected many times will suddenly be hurt beyond cure.

Proverbs 29:1 NCV

Since the days of Adam and Eve, human beings have been strong-willed and rebellious. Our rebellion stems, in large part, from an intense desire to do things "our way" instead of "God's way." But when we pridefully choose to forsake God's path for our lives, we do ourselves a sincere injustice . . . and we are penalized because of our stubbornness.

God's Word warns us to be humble, not prideful. God instructs us to be obedient, not rebellious. God wants us to do things His way. When we do, we reap a bountiful harvest of blessings—more blessings than we can count. But when we pridefully rebel against our Creator, we sow the seeds of our own destruction, and we reap a sad, sparse, bitter harvest. May we sow—and reap—accordingly.

God loves us enough to make us ultimately miserable in our rebellion.

Beth Moore

— A PRAYER —

Dear Lord, when I stubbornly rebel against You, give me the wisdom to see my mistakes and the courage to correct them. Amen

FOCUSING ON YOUR HOPES

This hope we have as an anchor of the soul, both sure and steadfast, and which enters the Presence behind the veil.

Hebrews 6:19 NKJV

Paul Valéry observed, "We hope vaguely but dread precisely." How true. All too often, we allow the worries of everyday life to overwhelm our thoughts and cloud our vision. What's needed is clearer perspective, renewed faith, and a different focus.

When we focus on the frustrations of today or the uncertainties of tomorrow, we rob ourselves of peace in the present moment. But, when we focus on God's grace, and when we trust in the ultimate wisdom of God's plan for our lives, our worries no longer tyrannize us.

Today, remember that God is infinitely greater than the challenges that you face. Remember also that your thoughts are profoundly powerful, so guard them accordingly.

No more imperfect thoughts. No more sad memories. No more ignorance. My redeemed body will have a redeemed mind. Grant me a foretaste of that perfect mind as you mirror your thoughts in me today.

Joni Eareckson Tada

— A PRAYER —

Dear Lord, keep my thoughts focused on Your love, Your power, Your promises, and Your Son. When I am worried, I will turn to You for comfort; when I am weak, I will turn to You for strength; when I am troubled, I will turn to You for patience and perspective. Help me guard my thoughts, Father, so that I may honor You today and every day that I live. Amen

FORGIVE EVERYBODY!

And be kind to one another, tenderhearted, forgiving one another, just as God in Christ forgave you.

Ephesians 4:32 NKJV

From time to time, all of us fall prey to a powerful yet subtle temptation: the temptation to judge others. But the Bible teaches us to refrain from such behavior. The warning is unmistakably clear: "Judge not, and ye shall not be judged." In other words, we must refrain from being judgmental . . . or else.

Thankfully, the Bible promises that God has forgiven us (whew!). Now it's our turn to forgive others. So, let us refrain from the temptation to judge our family members, our friends, and our loved ones. And let us refrain from judging people we don't know very well (or people we don't know at all). Instead, let us forgive everybody (including ourselves!) in the same way that God forgives: completely.

If Jesus forgave those who nailed Him to the Cross, and if God forgives you and me, how can you withhold your forgiveness from someone else?

Anne Graham Lotz

— A PRAYER —

Lord, make me a woman who is slow to anger and quick to forgive. When I am bitter, You can change my unforgiving heart. And, when I am angry, Your Word reminds me that forgiveness is Your commandment. Let me be Your obedient servant, Lord, and let me forgive others just as You have forgiven me. Amen

CULTIVATING GOD'S GIFTS

I remind you to keep ablaze the gift of God that is in you.

2 Timothy 1:6 HCSB

All women possess special gifts and talents; you are no exception. But, your gift is no guarantee of success; it must be cultivated and nurtured; otherwise, it will go unused . . . and God's gift to you will be squandered. Today, accept this challenge: value the talent that God has given you, nourish it, make it grow, and share it with the world. After all, the best way to say "Thank You" for God's gift is to use it.

When you hoard the treasures that God has given you, you live in rebellion against His commandments. But, when you obey God by sharing His gifts freely and without fanfare, you invite Him to bless you more and more. Today, be a faithful steward of your talents and treasures. And then prepare yourself for even greater blessings that are sure to come.

The Lord has abundantly blessed me all of my life. I'm not trying to pay Him back for all of His wonderful gifts; I just realize that He gave them to me to give away.

Lisa Whelchel

— A PRAYER —

Lord, I praise You for Your priceless gifts. I give thanks for Your creation, for Your Son, and for the unique talents and opportunities that You have given me. Let me use my gifts for the glory of Your kingdom, this day and every day. Amen

YOUR RELATIONSHIP WITH GOD

Unfailing love surrounds those who trust the LORD.

Psalm 32:10 NLT

St. Augustine observed, "God loves each of us as if there were only one of us." Do you believe those words? Do you seek to have an intimate, one-on-one relationship with your Heavenly Father, or are you satisfied to keep Him at a "safe" distance?

Sometimes, in the crush of our daily duties, God may seem far away, but He is not. God is everywhere we have ever been and everywhere we will ever go. He is with us night and day; He knows our thoughts and our prayers. And, when we earnestly seek Him, we will find Him because He is here, waiting patiently for us to reach out to Him.

Let us reach out to Him today and always. And let us praise Him for the glorious gifts that have transformed us today and forever. Amen.

God loves you whether you like it or not.

Anonymous

— A PRAYER —

Dear Lord, for the love You have shown me and the blessings You have given me, I thank You and I praise You. Your Son died so that I might receive the blessings of eternal love and eternal life. I will praise You today, tomorrow, and forever, Lord, for Your love, for Your mercy, and for Your Son. Amen

A GRAND PLAN

I will instruct you and teach you in the way you should go; I will guide you with My eye.

Psalm 32:8 NKJV

God has plans for your life that are far grander than you can imagine. But He won't force you to follow His will; to the contrary, He has given you free will, the ability to make choices and decisions on your own. The most important decision of your life is, of course, your commitment to accept Jesus Christ as your personal Lord and Savior. And once your eternal destiny is secured, you will undoubtedly ask yourself "What now, Lord?" If you earnestly seek God's will for your life, you will find it . . . in time.

Sometimes, God's plans are crystal clear, but other times, He may lead you through the wilderness before He delivers you to the Promised Land. So be patient, keep praying, and keep seeking His will for your life. When you do, you'll be amazed at the marvelous things that an all-powerful, all-knowing God can do.

God has no problems, only plans. There is never panic in heaven.

Corrie ten Boom

— A PRAYER —

Dear Lord, let me choose Your plans. You created me, and You have called me to do Your work here on earth. Today, I choose to seek Your will and to live it, knowing that when I trust in You, I am eternally blessed. Amen

GUARD YOUR HEART

Guard your heart above all else, for it is the source of life.

Proverbs 4:23 HCSB

You are near and dear to God. He loves you more than you can imagine, and He wants the very best for you. And one more thing: God wants you to guard your heart.

Every day, you are faced with choices . . . more choices than you can count. You can do the right thing, or not. You can be prudent, or not. You can be kind, and generous, and obedient to God. Or not.

Today, the world will offer you countless opportunities to let down your guard and, by doing so, make needless mistakes that may injure you or your loved ones. So be watchful and obedient. Guard your heart by giving it to your Heavenly Father; it is safe with Him.

God has a present will for your life. It is neither chaotic nor utterly exhausting. In the midst of many good choices vying for your time, He will give you the discernment to recognize what is best.

Beth Moore

— A PRAYER —

Dear Lord, in every aspect of my life, let me labor for You. Let my words and deeds honor You, and let my relationships with others be a reflection of the love that You have for me and the love that I have in my heart for You. Amen

WHEN WE LOSE HOPE

Be of good courage, and He shall strengthen your heart, all you who hope in the Lord.

Psalm 31:24 NKJV

As every woman knows, hope is a perishable commodity. Despite God's promises, despite Christ's love, and despite our countless blessings, we frail human beings can still lose hope from time to time. When we do, we need the encouragement of Christian friends, the life-changing power of prayer, and the healing truth of God's Holy Word. If we find ourselves falling into the spiritual traps of worry and discouragement, we should seek the healing touch of Jesus and the encouraging words of fellow Christians. Even though this world can be a place of trials and struggles, God has promised us peace, joy, and eternal life if we give ourselves to Him.

When we think we can't go one more step, when the race becomes painful beyond endurance, when our hearts feel heavy, when our minds become dull, when our spirits are burned out, we have the Parakletos [Holy Spirit], Who comes alongside us, puts His everlasting arms around us, and gently walks with us to the finish.

Anne Graham Lotz

— A PRAYER —

Dear Lord, make me a hope-filled Christian. If I become discouraged, let me turn to You. If I grow weary, let me seek strength in You. In every aspect of my life, I will trust You, Father, today and forever. Amen

KINDNESS IN ACTION

Yes indeed, it is good when you truly obey our Lord's royal command found in the Scriptures: "Love your neighbor as yourself."

James 2:8 NLT

As believers in Christ, we are commanded to treat others as we wish to be treated. This commandment is, indeed, the Golden Rule for Christians of every generation.

Kindness is a choice. Sometimes, when we feel happy or prosperous, we find it easy to be kind. Other times, when we are discouraged or tired, we can scarcely summon the energy to utter a single kind word. But, God's commandment is clear: we must observe the Golden Rule "in everything." God intends that we make the conscious choice to treat others with kindness and respect, no matter our circumstances, no matter our emotions. Kindness, therefore, is a choice that we, as Christians must make many times each day.

When we weave the thread of kindness into the very fabric of our lives, we give a priceless gift to others, and we give glory to the One who gave His life for us. As believers, we must do no less.

— A PRAYER —

Heavenly Father, sometimes this world can become a demanding place, a place where I rush through the day with my eyes focused only on my next step. Slow me down, Lord, and give me wisdom and peace so that I might look beyond my own needs and see the needs of those around me. Today, help me to be generous, compassionate, and understanding. Today, let me spread kind words and deeds to all who cross my path. Today, let the love for Christ shine through me. And let me show kindness to all who need the healing touch of our Master's hand. Amen

OBEDIENCE IN ACTION

Obey God and be at peace with him; this is the way to happiness.

Job 22:21 NCV

Obedience to God is determined, not by words, but by deeds. Talking about righteousness is easy; living righteously is far more difficult, especially in today's temptation-filled world.

Since God created Adam and Eve, we human beings have been rebelling against our Creator. Why? Because we are unwilling to trust God's Word, and we are unwilling to follow His commandments. God has given us a guidebook for righteous living called the Holy Bible. It contains thorough instructions which, if followed, lead to fulfillment, righteousness and salvation. But, if we choose to ignore God's commandments, the results are as predictable as they are tragic.

Unless we are willing to abide by God's laws, all of our righteous proclamations ring hollow. How can we best proclaim our love for the Lord? By obeying Him. And, for further instructions, read the manual.

You may not always see immediate results, but all God wants is your obedience and faithfulness.

Vonette Bright

— A PRAYER —

Dear Lord, make me a woman who is obedient to Your Word. Let me live according to Your commandments. Direct my path far from the temptations and distractions of this world. And, let me discover Your will and follow it, Lord, this day and always. Amen

OPTIMISTIC CHRISTIANITY

Make me hear joy and gladness.

Psalm 51:8 NKJV

Are you an optimistic, hopeful, enthusiastic Christian? You should be. After all, as a believer, you have every reason to be optimistic about life here on earth and life eternal. As C. H. Spurgeon observed, "Our hope in Christ for the future is the mainstream of our joy." But sometimes, you may find yourself pulled down by the inevitable demands and worries of life. If you find yourself discouraged, exhausted, or both, then it's time to take your concerns to God. When you do, He will lift your spirits and renew your strength.

Today, make this promise to yourself and keep it: vow to be a hope-filled Christian. Think optimistically about your life, your profession, your family, and your future. Trust your hopes, not your fears. Take time to celebrate God's glorious creation. And then, when you've filled your heart with hope and gladness, share your optimism with others. They'll be better for it, and so will you.

If you can't tell whether your glass is half-empty or half-full, you don't need another glass; what you need is better eyesight . . . and a more thankful heart.

Marie T. Freeman

— A PRAYER —

Lord, give me faith, optimism, and hope. Let me expect the best from You, and let me look for the best in others. Let me trust You, Lord, to direct my life. And, let me be Your faithful, hopeful, optimistic servant every day that I live. Amen

OUR HOPES AND HIS PEACE

And as they were saying these things, He Himself stood among them. He said to them, "Peace to you!"

Luke 24:36 HCSB

When we accept Jesus as our personal Savior, we are transformed by His grace. We are then free to accept the spiritual abundance and peace that can be ours through the power of the risen Christ.

The familiar and reassuring words of John 14:27 serve as a reminder that Jesus offers peace, not as the world gives, but as He alone gives.

As a gift to yourself, to your family, and to the world, be still, trust God's Word, and claim the inner peace that is your spiritual birthright through Christ. It is a life-altering inner peace that is offered freely by your loving Savior. Accept it and share it today.

Trade God your pieces for His peace.

Anonymous

— A PRAYER —

Dear Lord, we can never know the exact hour when our Savior will return. So let me live each moment as if He might return before my next breath. Let my life be a testimony to the changes He has made in me. And let my thoughts and prayers honor the One who has given me peace, abundance, and eternal life. Amen

LIVING IN
OUR MATERIAL WORLD

There is one who makes himself rich, yet has nothing; And one who makes himself poor, yet has great riches.

Proverbs 13:7 NKJV

On the grand stage of a well-lived life, material possessions should play a rather small role. Of course, we all need the basic necessities of life, but once we meet those needs for ourselves and for our families, the piling up of possessions creates more problems than it solves. Our real riches, of course, are not of this world. We are never really rich until we are rich in spirit.

Do you find yourself constantly wrapped up in the concerns of the material world? If so, it's time to reorder your priorities by turning your thoughts and your prayers to more important matters. And, it's time to begin storing up riches that will endure throughout eternity: the spiritual kind.

I've learned to hold everything loosely because it hurts when God pries my fingers from it.

Corrie ten Boom

— A PRAYER —

Dear Lord, Your Word teaches me to seek first Your kingdom and Your righteousness. Today, I will trust You completely for my needs, both spiritual and material. Thank You, Father, for Your protection, for Your love, and for Your Son. Amen

GOD RESPONDS

Therefore I say to you, whatever things you ask when you pray, believe that you receive them, and you will have them.

Mark 11:24 NKJV

When we petition God, He responds. God's hand is not absent, and it is not distant. It is responsive.

On his second missionary journey, Paul started a small church in Thessalonica. A short time later, he penned a letter that was intended to encourage the new believers at that church. Today, almost 2,000 years later, 1 Thessalonians remains a powerful, practical guide for Christian living.

In his letter, Paul advises members of the new church to "pray without ceasing." His advice applies to Christians of every generation. When we weave the habit of prayer into the very fabric of our days, we invite God to become a partner in every aspect of our lives. When we consult God on an hourly basis, we avail ourselves of His wisdom, His strength, and His love.

Today, allow the responsive hand of God to guide you and help you. Pray without ceasing, and then rest assured: God is listening . . . and responding!

— A PRAYER —

Dear Lord, Your Holy Word commands me to pray without ceasing. Let me take everything to You in prayer. When I am discouraged, You can give me hope. When I am bitter, You can heal my heart. When I am angry, You can help me forgive. In all things great and small, at all times, whether happy or sad, let me seek Your wisdom and Your grace . . . in prayer. Amen

AT PEACE WITH YOUR PURPOSE

The Lord will perfect that which concerns me; Your mercy, O Lord, endures forever.

Psalm 138:8 NKJV

Are you at peace with the direction of your life? If you're a Christian, you should be. Even if God's plans for you are uncertain, His love for you is not.

The words of John 14:27 give us hope: "Peace I leave with you, My peace I give unto you . . . ." Jesus offers us peace, not as the world gives, but as He alone gives. We, as believers, can accept His peace or ignore it.

When we accept the peace of Jesus Christ into our hearts, our lives are transformed. And then, because we possess the gift of peace, we can share that gift with fellow believers, family members, friends, and associates.

Today, as a gift to yourself, to your family, and to your friends, claim the inner peace that is your spiritual birthright: the peace of Jesus Christ. It is offered freely; it has been paid for in full; it is yours for the asking. So ask. And then share.

— A PRAYER —

Dear Lord, You've got something You want me to do—help me to figure out exactly what it is. Give me Your blessings and lead me along a path that is pleasing to You . . . today, tomorrow, and forever. Amen

RESPECTING YOUR TALENTS

Every generous act and every perfect gift is from above, coming down from the Father of lights.

James 1:17 HCSB

Do you place a high value on your talents, your time, your capabilities, and your opportunities? If so, congratulations. But if you've acquired the insidious habit of devaluing your time, your work, or yourself, it's now time for a change.

Pearl Bailey correctly observed, "The first and worst of all frauds is to cheat one's self. All sin is easy after that."

If you've been squandering opportunities or selling yourself short, it's time to rethink the way you think about yourself and your opportunities. No one can seize those opportunities for you, and no one can build up your self-confidence if you're unwilling to believe in yourself. So if you've been talking yourself down, stop. You deserve better. And if you don't give yourself healthy respect, who will?

Christ never resisted the heinous, habitual sinner who was desperate to repent, but He could not abide a religious hypocrite.

Beth Moore

— A PRAYER —

Father, You have given me abilities to be used for the glory of Your kingdom. Give me the courage and the perseverance to use those talents. Keep me mindful that all my gifts come from You, Lord. Let me be Your faithful, humble servant, and let me give You all the glory and all the praise. Amen

HELPFUL WORDS

Careful words make for a careful life; careless talk may ruin everything.
Proverbs 13:3 MSG

This world can be a difficult place, a place where many of our friends and family members are troubled by the inevitable challenges of everyday life. And since we can never be certain who needs our help, we should be careful to speak helpful words to everybody who crosses our paths.

In the book of Ephesians, Paul writes, "Do not let any unwholesome talk come out of your mouths, but only what is helpful for building others up according to their needs, that it may benefit those who listen" (4:29 NIV). Paul reminds us that when we choose our words carefully, we can have a powerful impact on those around us.

Today, let's share kind words, smiles, encouragement, and hugs with family, with friends, and with the world.

Words. Do you fully understand their power? Can any of us really grasp the mighty force behind the things we say? Do we stop and think before we speak, considering the potency of the words we utter?

Joni Eareckson Tada

— A PRAYER —

Dear Lord, make my words pleasing to You. Let me be a source of encouragement to others as I share a message of faith and assurance with the world. Today, I will honor You, Father, by choosing my words carefully, thoughtfully, and lovingly. Amen

WORKING FOR WISDOM

Wisdom is a tree of life to those who embrace her; happy are those who hold her tightly.

Proverbs 3:18 NLT

All of us would like to be wise, but not all of us are willing to do the work that is required to become wise. Wisdom is not like a mushroom; it does not spring up overnight. It is, instead, like an oak tree that starts as a tiny acorn, grows into a sapling, and eventually reaches up to the sky, tall and strong.

To become wise, we must seek God's wisdom and live according to His Word. To become wise, we must seek wisdom with consistency and purpose. To become wise, we must not only learn the lessons of life, we must live by them.

Do you seek wisdom for yourself and for your family? Then keep learning and keep motivating your family members to do likewise. The ultimate source of wisdom, of course, is the Word of God. When you study God's Word and live according to His commandments, you will become wise . . . and you will be a blessing to your family and to the world.

Wisdom is knowledge applied. Head knowledge is useless on the battlefield. Knowledge stamped on the heart makes one wise.

Beth Moore

— A PRAYER —

Dear Lord, I will seek wisdom not as the world gives, but as You give. I will trust Your commandments and I will follow Your Son, this day and forever. Amen

ACCEPTANCE NOW

A man's heart plans his way, but the Lord determines his steps.

Proverbs 16:9 HCSB

Sometimes, we must accept life on its terms, not our own. Life has a way of unfolding, not as we will, but as it will. And sometimes, there is precious little we can do to change things.

When events transpire that are beyond our control, we have a choice: we can either learn the art of acceptance, or we can make ourselves miserable as we struggle to change the unchangeable.

We must entrust the things we cannot change to God. Once we have done so, we can prayerfully and faithfully tackle the important work that He has placed before us: doing something about the things we can change . . . and doing it sooner rather than later.

How changed our lives would be if we could only fly through the days on wings of surrender and trust!

Hannah Whitall Smith

— A PRAYER —

Lord, when I am discouraged, give me hope. When I am impatient, give me peace. When I face circumstances that I cannot change, give me a spirit of acceptance. In all things great and small, let me trust in You, Dear Lord, knowing that You are the Giver of life and the Giver of all things good, today and forever. Amen

ABOUT ANGER

When you are angry, do not sin, and be sure to stop being angry before the end of the day. Do not give the devil a way to defeat you.

Ephesians 4:26-27 NCV

Sometimes, anger is appropriate. Even Jesus became angry when confronted with the moneychangers in the temple. On occasion, you, like Jesus, will confront evil, and when you do, you may respond as He did: vigorously and without reservation. But, more often than not, your frustrations will be of the more mundane variety. As long as you live here on earth, you will face countless opportunities to lose your temper over small, relatively insignificant events: a traffic jam, a spilled cup of coffee, an inconsiderate comment, a broken promise. When you are tempted to lose your temper over the minor inconveniences of life, don't. Turn away from anger, hatred, bitterness, and regret. Turn instead to God.

You will accomplish more by kind words and a courteous manner than by anger and sharp rebuke, which should never be used, except in necessity.

St. Angela Merici

— A PRAYER —

Lord, as a frail human being, I can be quick to anger and slow to forgive. But I know, Lord, that You seek that I live in peace. When I am slow to forgive, Lord, keep me mindful of Your commandment that I love my neighbor as myself. Let me follow in the footsteps of Your Son Jesus who forgave His persecutors, and as I turn away from anger, let me claim for myself the peace that You intend for my life. Amen

GOD'S GUIDEBOOK

All Scripture is given by inspiration of God, and is profitable for doctrine, for reproof, for correction, for instruction in righteousness, that the man of God may be complete, thoroughly equipped for every good work.

2 Timothy 3:16-17 NKJV

God has given us a guidebook for living called the Holy Bible. It contains thorough instructions which, if followed, lead to fulfillment, righteousness, and salvation. But, if we choose to ignore God's commandments, the results are as predictable as they are tragic.

God has given us the Bible for the purpose of knowing His promises, His power, His commandments, His wisdom, His love, and His Son. As we study God's teachings and apply them to our lives, we live by the Word that shall never pass away.

Today, let us follow God's commandments, and let us conduct our lives in such a way that we might be shining examples to our students, to our families, and, most importantly, to those who have not yet found Christ.

If we neglect the Bible, we cannot expect to benefit from the wisdom and direction that result from knowing God's Word.

Vonette Bright

— A PRAYER —

Dear Lord, Your scripture is a light unto the world; let me study it, trust it, and share it with all who cross my path. In all that I do, help me be a woman who is a worthy witness for You as I share the Good News of Your perfect Son and Your perfect Word. Amen

WORSHIP HIM

But an hour is coming, and is now here, when the true worshipers will worship the Father in spirit and truth. Yes, the Father wants such people to worship Him. God is Spirit, and those who worship Him must worship in spirit and truth.

John 4:23-24 HCSB

Where do we worship? In our hearts or in our church? The answer is both. As Christians who have been saved by a loving, compassionate Creator, we are compelled not only to worship the Creator in our hearts but also to worship Him in the presence of fellow believers.

We live in a world that is teeming with temptations and distractions—a world where good and evil struggle in a constant battle to win our hearts and souls. Our challenge, of course, is to ensure that we cast our lot on the side of God. One way to ensure that we do so is by the practice of regular, purposeful worship with our families. When we worship God faithfully and fervently, we are blessed.

— A PRAYER —

Heavenly Father, this world can be a place of distractions and temptations. But when I worship You, Lord, You direct my path and You cleanse my heart. Let today and every day be a time of worship and praise. Let me worship You in everything that I think and do. Thank You, Lord, for the priceless gift of Your Son Jesus. Let me be worthy of that gift, and let me give You the praise and the glory forever. Amen

A GOD OF INFINITE POSSIBILITIES

We are hard pressed on every side, yet not crushed; we are perplexed, but not in despair.

2 Corinthians 4:8 NKJV

As we travel the roads of life, all of us are confronted with streets that seem to be dead ends. When we do, we may become discouraged. After all, we live in a society where expectations can be high and demands even higher.

If you find yourself enduring difficult circumstances, remember that God remains in His heaven. If you become discouraged with the direction of your day or your life, turn your thoughts and prayers to Him. He is a God of possibility, not negativity. He will guide you through your difficulties and beyond them. And then, with a renewed spirit of optimism and hope, you can thank the Giver of all things good for gifts that are simply too profound to fully understand and for treasures that are too numerous to count.

Every misfortune, every failure, every loss may be transformed. God has the power to transform all misfortunes into "God-sends."

Mrs. Charles E. Cowman

— A PRAYER —

Heavenly Father, You are my strength and refuge. I can face the difficulties of this day because You are with me. You are my light and pathway. As I follow You, Father, I can overcome adversity just as Jesus overcame this world. Amen

ASK HIM

Until now you have asked for nothing in My name. Ask and you will receive, that your joy may be complete.

John 16:24 HCSB

God gives the gifts; we, as believers, should accept them—but oftentimes, we don't. Why? Because we fail to trust our Heavenly Father completely, and because we are, at times, surprisingly stubborn. Luke 11 teaches us that God does not withhold spiritual gifts from those who ask. Our obligation, quite simply, is to ask for them.

Are you a woman who asks God to move mountains in your life, or are you expecting Him to stumble over molehills? Whatever the size of your challenges, God is big enough to handle them. Ask for His help today, with faith and with fervor, and then watch in amazement as your mountains begin to move.

God makes prayer as easy as possible for us. He's completely approachable and available, and He'll never mock or upbraid us for bringing our needs before Him.

Shirley Dobson

— A PRAYER —

Dear Lord, I will be a woman of prayer. I will pray about matters great and small. I will bring my concerns to You, Father. I will listen for Your voice, and I will follow in the footsteps of Your Son. Amen

BEYOND THE STATUS QUO

You were taught to leave your old self—to stop living the evil way you lived before. That old self becomes worse, because people are fooled by the evil things they want to do. But you were taught to be made new in your hearts, to become a new person. That new person is made to be like God—made to be truly good and holy.

Ephesians 4:22-24 NCV

It has been said that a rut is nothing more than a grave with both ends kicked out. That's a thought worth pondering. Have you made your life an exciting adventure, or have you allowed the distractions of everyday life to rob you of a sense of God's purpose?

As a believing Christian, you have every reason to celebrate. So if you find yourself feeling as if you're stuck in a rut or in an unfortunate circumstance or in a difficult relationship, abandon the status quo by making the changes that your heart tells you are right. After all, in God's glorious kingdom, there should be no place for disciples who are dejected, discouraged, or disheartened. God has a far better plan than that, and so should you.

No matter how little we can change about our circumstances, we always have a choice about our attitude toward the situation.

Vonette Bright

— A PRAYER —

Dear Lord, let my words and actions show the world the changes that You have made in my life. You sent Your Son so that I might have abundant life and eternal life. Thank You, Father, for my Savior, Christ Jesus. I will follow Him, honor Him, and share His Good News, this day and every day. Amen

THE BEST DAY TO CELEBRATE

Rejoice in the Lord always. I will say it again: Rejoice!

Philippians 4:4 HCSB

What is the best day to celebrate life? This one! Today and every day should be a day of prayer and celebration as we consider the Good News of God's free gift: salvation through Jesus Christ.

What do you expect from the day ahead? Are you expecting God to do wonderful things, or are you living beneath a cloud of apprehension and doubt? The familiar words of Psalm 118:24 remind us of a profound yet simple truth: "This is the day which the LORD hath made" (KJV). Our duty, as believers, is to rejoice in God's marvelous creation.

For Christians, every day begins and ends with God and His Son. Christ came to this earth to give us abundant life and eternal salvation. We give thanks to our Maker when we treasure each day. May we use our time here on earth to serve God, to celebrate His marvelous gifts, and to share His Good News with the world.

This is my story, this is my song, praising my Savior all the day long; this is my story, this is my song, praising my Savior all the day long.

Fanny Crosby

— A PRAYER —

Lord God, You have created a grand and glorious universe that is far beyond human understanding. The heavens proclaim Your handiwork, and every star in the sky tells of Your power. Let me celebrate You and Your marvelous creation, Father, and let me give thanks for this day. Today is Your gift to me, Lord. Let me use it to Your glory while giving all the praise to You. Amen

REAL CHRISTIANITY

But now in Christ Jesus you who formerly were far off have been brought near by the blood of Christ. For He Himself is our peace.

Ephesians 2:13-14 NASB

What is "real" Christianity? Think of it as an ongoing relationship—an all-encompassing relationship with God and with His Son Jesus. It is inevitable that your life must be lived in relationship to God. The question is not if you will have a relationship with Him; the burning question is whether or not that relationship will be one that seeks to honor Him or one that seeks to ignore Him.

We live in a world that discourages heartfelt devotion and obedience to God. Everywhere we turn, or so it seems, we are confronted by a mind-numbing assortment of distractions, temptations, obligations, and frustrations. Yet even on our busiest days, God beckons us to slow down and consult Him. When we do, we avail ourselves of the peace and abundance that only He can give.

The Christian lifestyle is not one of legalistic do's and don'ts, but one that is positive, attractive, and joyful.

Vonette Bright

— A PRAYER —

Dear Lord, thank You for the gift of Your Son Jesus, my personal Savior. Let me be a worthy servant of Christ, and let me be ever grateful for His love. Amen

YOUR DAILY JOURNEY

He said to them all, "If anyone desires to come after Me, let him deny himself, and take up his cross daily, and follow Me. For whoever desires to save his life will lose it, but whoever loses his life for My sake will save it."

Luke 9:23-24 NKJV

Even the most inspired women can, from time to time, find themselves running on empty. Why? Because the inevitable demands of daily life can drain us of our strength and rob us of the joy that is rightfully ours in Christ. Thankfully, God stands ready to renew our spirits, even on the darkest of days. God's Word is clear: When we genuinely lift our hearts and prayers to Him, He renews our strength.

Are you almost too weary to lift your head? Then bow it—in prayer. Offer your concerns and your needs to your Father in heaven. He is always at your side, offering His love and His strength.

Your search to discover God's purpose for your life is not a destination; it is a journey that unfolds day by day. And, that's exactly how often you should seek direction from your Creator: one day at a time, each day followed by the next, without exception.

God calls us to seek him daily in order to serve him daily.

Sheila Cragg

— A PRAYER —

Dear Lord, every day of my life is a journey with You. Today is another day on that journey. Let me celebrate this day, and let me use it in ways that will serve You and give honor to Your Son. Amen

THE POWER OF ENCOURAGEMENT

He comforts us in all our affliction, so that we may be able to comfort those who are in any kind of affliction, through the comfort we ourselves receive from God.

2 Corinthians 1:4 HCSB

The 118th Psalm reminds us, "This is the day which the Lord hath made; we will rejoice and be glad in it" (v. 24 KJV). As we rejoice in this day that the Lord has given us, let us remember that an important part of today's celebration is the time we spend comforting those in need.

Each day provides countless opportunities to encourage others and to assist those who need our help. When we do, we spread seeds of hope and happiness.

Today, when you encounter someone who needs a helping hand or a comforting word, be generous with both. You possess the power to make the world a better place one person—and one hug—at a time. When you use that power wisely, you make your own corner of the world a kinder, gentler, happier place.

Encouragement is the oxygen of the soul.

John Maxwell

— A PRAYER —

Dear Lord, make me a source of genuine, lasting encouragement to my family and friends. Today, I will celebrate Your blessings, and I will share Your Good News with those who cross my path. Let my words and deeds be worthy of Your Son, the One who gives me strength and salvation. Amen

FAITH THAT WORKS

For in it the righteousness of God is revealed from faith to faith; as it is written, "The just shall live by faith."

Romans 1:17 NKJV

Through every stage of your life, God stands by your side, ready to strengthen you and protect you, if you have faith in Him. When you place your faith, your trust, indeed your life in the hands of Christ Jesus, you'll be amazed at the marvelous things He can do with you and through you.

So make this promise to yourself and keep it: make certain that your faith is a faith that works. How? You can strengthen your faith through praise, through worship, through Bible study, and through prayer. When you do so, you'll learn to trust God's plans. With Him, all things are possible, and He stands ready to open a world of possibilities to you, if you have faith.

It is not my ability, but my response to God's ability, that counts.

Corrie ten Boom

— A PRAYER —

Lord, as I take the next steps on my life's journey, I will take them with You. Because of my faith in You, I can be courageous and strong. I will lean upon You, Father—and trust You—this day and forever. Amen

FORGIVENESS NOW

He who says he is in the light, and hates his brother, is in darkness until now.

1 John 2:9 NKJV

Forgiveness is seldom easy, but it is always right. When we forgive those who have hurt us, we honor God by obeying His commandments. But when we harbor bitterness against others, we disobey God—with predictably unhappy results.

Are you easily frustrated by the inevitable shortcomings of others? Are you a prisoner of bitterness or regret? If so, perhaps you need a refresher course in the art of forgiveness.

If there exists even one person, alive or dead, whom you have not forgiven (and that includes yourself), follow God's commandment and His will for your life: forgive that person today. And remember that bitterness, anger, and regret are not part of God's plan for your life. Forgiveness is.

Doing an injury puts you below your enemy; revenging an injury makes you even with him; forgiving an injury sets you above him!

Anonymous

— A PRAYER —

Dear Lord, let forgiveness rule my heart, even when forgiveness is difficult. Let me be Your obedient servant, Lord, and let me be a woman who forgives others just as You have forgiven me. Amen

GOD CAN HANDLE IT

God—His way is perfect; the word of the Lord is pure. He is a shield to all who take refuge in Him.

Psalm 18:30 HCSB

In 1967, a diving accident left Joni Eareckson Tada a quadriplegic. But she didn't give up. Unable to use her hands, she taught herself to paint fine art by holding a brush between her teeth. Then, the determined Mrs. Tada began writing. To date, she's completed over thirty books, and her ministry, Joni and Friends, touches the lives of millions.

Jesus said, "In this world you will have trouble. But take heart! I have overcome the world." So the next time you face a difficult day or an unexpected challenge, remember Joni's journey. If she could meet her challenges, so can you. So take heart, trust, and remember that no problem is too big for God.

As God's children, we are the recipients of lavish love—a love that motivates us to keep trusting even when we have no idea what God is doing.

Beth Moore

— A PRAYER —

Dear Lord, whatever "it" is, You can handle it! Let me turn to You when I am fearful or worried. You are my loving Heavenly Father, sufficient in all things and I will always trust You. Amen

HIS LOVE

You are my God, and I will give you thanks; you are my God, and I will exalt you. Give thanks to the LORD, for he is good; his love endures forever.

Psalm 118:28-29 NIV

God loves you—His love for you is deeper and more profound than you can imagine. God's love for you is so great that He sent His only Son to this earth to die for your sins and to offer you the priceless gift of eternal life.

You must decide whether or not to accept God's gift. Will you ignore it or embrace it? Will you return it or neglect it? Will you invite Christ to dwell in the center of your heart, or will you relegate Him to a position of lesser importance? The decision is yours, and so are the consequences. So choose wisely . . . and choose today.

I think God knew that the message we sometimes need to hear today is not what a great and mighty God we serve, but rather what a tender, loving Father we have, even when He says no.

Lisa Whelchel

— A PRAYER —

Thank You, Lord, for Your love. Your love is boundless, infinite, and eternal. Today, let me pause and reflect upon Your love for me, and let me share that love with all those who cross my path. Amen

GOD IS AT WORK

The Lord will perfect that which concerns me; Your mercy, O Lord, endures forever.

Psalm 138:8 NKJV

Whether you realize it or not, God is busily working in you and through you. He has things He wants you to do and people He wants you to help. Your assignment, should you choose to accept it, is to seek the will of God and to follow it.

Elisabeth Elliot said, "I believe that in every time and place it is within our power to acquiesce in the will of God—and what peace it brings to do so!" And Corrie ten Boom observed, "Surrendering to the Lord is not a tremendous sacrifice, not an agonizing performance. It is the most sensible thing you can do."

So, as you make plans for the future, make sure that your plans conform to God's plans—that's the safest and best way to live.

When things happen which dismay, we ought to look to God for His meaning and remember that He is not taken by surprise nor can His purposes be thwarted in the end.

Elisabeth Elliot

— A PRAYER —

Lord, today, I will seek Your will for my life. You have a plan for me, Father. Let me discover it and live it, knowing that when I trust in You, I am eternally blessed. Amen

HOLINESS BEFORE HAPPINESS

If they serve Him obediently, they will end their days in prosperity and their years in happiness.

Job 36:11 HCSB

Because you are an imperfect human being, you are not "perfectly" happy—and that's perfectly okay with God. He is far less concerned with your happiness than He is with your holiness.

God continuously reveals Himself in everyday life, but He does not do so in order to make you contented; He does so in order to lead you to His Son. So don't be overly concerned with your current level of happiness: it will change. Be more concerned with the current state of your relationship with Christ: He does not change. And because your Savior transcends time and space, you can be comforted in the knowledge that in the end, His joy will become your joy . . . for all eternity.

Perfect obedience would be perfect happiness, if only we had perfect confidence in the power we were obeying.

Corrie ten Boom

— A PRAYER —

Lord, let me be a woman who celebrates life. Let me rejoice in the gift of this day, and let me praise You for the gift of Your Son. Let me be a joyful Christian, Lord, as I share Your Good News with friends, with family, and with the world. Amen

WHO DESERVES THE CREDIT?

Nevertheless God, who comforts the downcast, comforted us . . . .

2 Corinthians 7:6 NKJV

When we experience success, it's easy to proclaim, "I did that!" But it's wrong. Dietrich Bonhoeffer was correct when he observed, "It is very easy to overestimate the importance of our own achievements in comparison with what we owe others." In other words, reality breeds humility.

Who are the greatest among us? Are they the proud and the powerful? Hardly. The greatest among us are the humble servants who care less for their own glory and more for God's glory. If we seek greatness in God's eyes, we must forever praise God's good works, not our own.

If you're tempted to overestimate your own accomplishments, resist that temptation. Instead of puffing out your chest and saying, "Look at me!" give credit where credit is due, starting with God. And, rest assured: There is no such thing as a self-made man. All of us are made by God . . . and He deserves the glory, not us.

— A PRAYER —

Lord, let me be a woman with a humble spirit. Keep me mindful, Dear God, that all my gifts come from You. When I feel prideful, remind me that You sent Your Son to be a humble carpenter and that Jesus was ridiculed and crucified on a cross. Let me grow beyond my need for earthly praise, Lord, and when I seek approval, let me look only to You. Amen

THE GIFT OF LAUGHTER

Oh, clap your hands, all you peoples! Shout to God with the voice of triumph!

Psalm 47:1 NKJV

Laughter is a gift from God, a gift that He intends for us to use. Yet sometimes, because of the inevitable stresses of everyday living, we fail to find the fun in life. When we allow life's inevitable disappointments to cast a pall over our lives and our souls, we do a profound disservice to ourselves and to our loved ones.

As Christians we have every reason to be cheerful and to be thankful. Our blessings from God are beyond measure, starting, of course, with a gift that is ours for the asking, God's gift of salvation through Christ Jesus.

Few things in life are more absurd than the sight of a grumpy, sour-faced Christian. So today, as you go about your daily activities, approach life with a smile and a chuckle. After all, God created laughter for a reason . . . and Father indeed knows best. So laugh!

Laughter may not necessarily get you out of the tunnel, but it will definitely light your way.

Barbara Johnson

— A PRAYER —

Dear Lord, laughter is Your gift. Today and every day, put a smile on my face, and let me share that smile with all who cross my path . . . and let me laugh. Amen

DEMONSTRATING OUR LOVE

For this is the love of God, that we keep His commandments. And His commandments are not burdensome.

1 John 5:3 NKJV

How can we demonstrate our love for God? By accepting His Son as our personal Savior and by placing Christ squarely at the center of our lives and our hearts. Jesus said that if we are to love Him, we must obey His commandments (John 14:15). Thus, our obedience to the Master is an expression of our love for Him.

In Ephesians 2:10 we read, "For we are His workmanship, created in Christ Jesus for good works" (NKJV). These words are instructive: We are not saved by good works, but for good works. Good works are not the root, but rather the fruit of our salvation.

Today, let the fruits of your stewardship be a clear demonstration of your love for Christ. When you do, your good heart will bring forth many good things for yourself and for God. Christ has given you spiritual abundance and eternal life. You, in turn, owe Him good treasure from a single obedient heart: yours.

Peter said, "No, Lord!" But he had to learn that one cannot say "No" while saying "Lord" and that one cannot say "Lord" while saying "No."

Corrie ten Boom

— A PRAYER —

Dear Heavenly Father, You have blessed me with a love that is infinite and eternal. Let me demonstrate my love for You by obeying Your commandments. Make me a faithful servant, Father, today and throughout eternity. And, let me show my love for You by sharing Your message and Your love with others. Amen

PASSION AND PURPOSE

May He grant you according to your heart's desire, and fulfill all your purpose.

Psalm 20:4 NKJV

We all need to discover a purpose for our lives, a purpose that excites us and causes us to live each day with passion.

Anna Quindlen had this advice: "Consider the lilies of the field. Look at the fuzz on a baby's ear. Read in the backyard with the sun on your face. Learn to be happy. And think of life as a terminal illness, because, if you do, you will live it with joy and passion, as it ought to be lived."

If you have not yet discovered a passionate pursuit that blesses you and your world, don't allow yourself to become discouraged. Instead, keep searching and keep trusting that with God's help, you can—and will—find a meaningful way to serve your neighbors, your Creator, and yourself.

I don't know about you, but I want to do more than survive life—I want to mount up like the eagle and glide over rocky crags, nest in the tallest of trees, dive for nourishment in the deepest of mountain lakes, and soar on the wings of the wind.

Barbara Johnson

— A PRAYER —

Lord, let me find my strength in You. When I am weary, give me rest. When I feel overwhelmed, let me look to You for my priorities. Let Your passion be my passion, Lord, and let Your way be my way, today and forever. Amen

WHOM SHOULD WE PLEASE?

Therefore, whether we are at home or away, we make it our aim to be pleasing to Him. For we must all appear before the judgment seat of Christ, so that each may be repaid for what he has done in the body, whether good or bad.

2 Corinthians 5:9-10 HCSB

As a member-in-good-standing in this highly competitive, 21st-century world, you know that the demands and expectations of everyday living can seem burdensome, even overwhelming at times. Keeping up with the Joneses can become a fulltime job if you let it. A better strategy, of course, is to stop trying to please the neighbors and to concentrate, instead, upon pleasing God.

Perhaps you have set your goals high; if so, congratulations! You're willing to dream big dreams, and that's a very good thing. But as you consider your life's purpose, don't allow your quest for excellence to interfere with the spiritual journey that God has planned for you.

As a believer, your instructions are clear: you must strive to please God. How do you please Him? By accepting His Son and obeying His commandments. All other concerns—including, but not limited to, keeping up with the Joneses—are of little or no importance.

— A PRAYER —

Dear Lord, other people may encourage me to stray from Your path, but I wish to follow in the footsteps of Your Son. Give me the vision to see the right path—and the wisdom to follow it— today and every day of my life. Amen

REAL PROSPERITY

Now godliness with contentment is great gain. For we brought nothing into this world, and it is certain we can carry nothing out. And having food and clothing, with these we shall be content.

1 Timothy 6:6-8 NKJV

We live in an era of prosperity, a time when many of us have been richly blessed with an assortment of material possessions that our forebears could have scarcely imagined. As believers living in these prosperous times, we must be cautious: we must keep prosperity in perspective.

The world stresses the importance of material possessions; God does not. The world offers the promise of happiness through wealth and public acclaim; God offers the promise of peace through His Son. When in doubt, we must distrust the world and trust God. The world often makes promises that it cannot keep, but when God makes a promise, He keeps it, not just for a day or a year or a lifetime, for all eternity.

— A PRAYER —

Lord, sometimes, the world's perspective can lead me astray. Sometimes I become confused; sometimes, in the busyness of my daily life, I lose perspective. Help me, Lord, to see the world through Your eyes. Give me guidance and wisdom and perspective. Lead me according to Your plan for my life and according to Your commandments. And keep me ever mindful, Father, that Your reality is the ultimate reality, and that Your truth is the ultimate truth, now and forever. Amen

PRAY ABOUT YOUR PLANS

Your Father knows the things you have need of before you ask Him.

Matthew 6:8 NKJV

Your search to discover God's plan unfolding for your life is not a destination to be reached; it is a path to be traveled, a journey that unfolds every day of your life. And, that's exactly how often you should seek direction from your Creator: one day at a time, each day followed by the next, without exception.

Daily prayer and meditation is a matter of will and habit. You must willingly organize your time by carving out quiet moments with God, and you must form the habit of daily worship. When you do, you'll discover that no time is more precious than the silent moments you spend with your Heavenly Father.

The quality of your spiritual life will be in direct proportion to the quality of your prayer life. Prayer changes things, and it changes you. Today, weave the power of prayer into the very fabric of your life. Don't limit your prayers to meals or to bedtime; pray constantly. God is listening; He wants to hear from you; and you most certainly need to hear from Him.

— A PRAYER —

Dear Lord, let my plans and hopes be pleasing to You. When I turn my thoughts away from You and Your Word, I suffer. But when I place my faith in You, I am secure. Let me live according to Your commandments. Direct my path far from the temptations and distractions of this world. And, let me discover Your will and follow it, Father, this day and always. Amen

OBEDIENCE AND CONTENTMENT

Happy is the man who fears the Lord, taking great delight in His commandments.

Psalm 112:1 HCSB

When we conduct ourselves in ways that are opposed to God's commandments, we rob ourselves of God's peace. When we fall prey to the temptations and distractions of our irreverent age, we rob ourselves of God's blessings. When we become preoccupied with material possessions or personal status, we forfeit the contentment that is rightfully ours in Christ.

Where can we find the kind of contentment that Paul describes in Philippians 4:11? Is it a result of wealth or power or fame? Hardly. Genuine contentment is a gift from God to those who follow His commandments and accept His Son. It is a gift that must be discovered and rediscovered throughout life. It is a gift that we claim when we allow Christ to dwell at the center of our lives.

Those who are God's without reserve are, in every sense, content.

Hannah Whitall Smith

— A PRAYER —

Father, show me how to be ambitious in Your work. Let me strive to do Your will here on earth, and as I do, let me find contentment and balance. Let me live in the light of Your will and Your priorities for my life, and when I have done my best, Lord, give me the wisdom to place my faith and my trust in You. Amen

WHEN THE PATH IS DARK

When my anxious thoughts multiply within me, Your consolations delight my soul.

Psalm 94:19 NASB

Even the most faithful Christians are overcome by occasional bouts of fear and doubt. You are no different. When you feel that your faith is being tested to its limits, seek the comfort and assurance of the One who sent His Son as a sacrifice for you.

Have you ever felt your faith in God slipping away? If so, you are not alone. Every life—including yours—is a series of successes and failures, celebrations and disappointments, joys and sorrows, hopes and doubts.

But even when you feel very distant from God, remember that God is never distant from you. When you sincerely seek His presence, He will touch your heart, calm your fears, and restore your soul.

We are most vulnerable to the piercing winds of doubt when we distance ourselves from the mission and fellowship to which Christ has called us.

Joni Eareckson Tada

— A PRAYER —

Dear Lord, when I am filled with uncertainty and doubt, give me faith. In the dark moments of life, keep me mindful of Your healing power and Your infinite love, so that I may live courageously and faithfully today and every day. Amen

ETERNAL LIFE:
GOD'S PRICELESS GIFT

Jesus said, "Everyone who drinks from this water will get thirsty again. But whoever drinks from the water that I will give him will never get thirsty again—ever! In fact, the water I will give him will become a well of water springing up within him for eternal life."

John 4:13-14 HCSB

Your ability to envision the future, like your life here on earth, is limited. God's vision, however, is not burdened by any such limitations. He sees all things, He knows all things, and His plans for you endure for all time.

God's plans are not limited to the events of life-here-on-earth. Your Heavenly Father has bigger things in mind for you . . . much bigger things. So praise the Creator for the gift of eternal life and share the Good News with all who cross your path. You have given your heart to the Son, so you belong to the Father—today, tomorrow, and for all eternity.

If you are a believer, your judgment will not determine your eternal destiny. Christ's finished work on Calvary was applied to you the moment you accepted Christ as Savior.

Beth Moore

— A PRAYER —

Lord, You have given me the priceless gift of eternal life through Your Son Jesus. Keep the hope of heaven fresh in my heart. While I am in this world, help me to pass through it with faith in my heart and praise on my lips for You. Amen

HE LOVES YOU

Therefore humble yourselves under the mighty hand of God, that He may exalt you in due time, casting all your care upon Him, for He cares for you.

1 Peter 5:6-7 NKJV

When we worship God with faith and assurance, when we place Him at the absolute center of our lives, we invite His love into our hearts. In turn, we grow to love Him more deeply as we sense His love for us. St. Augustine wrote, "I love you, Lord, not doubtingly, but with absolute certainty. Your Word beat upon my heart until I fell in love with you, and now the universe and everything in it tells me to love you." Let us pray that we, too, will turn our hearts to our Heavenly Father, knowing with certainty that He loves us and that we love Him.

God is love, and God's love is perfect. When we open ourselves to His perfect love, we are touched by the Creator's hand, and we are transformed, not just for a day, but for all eternity.

Today, as you carve out quiet moments of thanksgiving and praise for your Heavenly Father, open yourself to His presence and to His love. He is here, waiting. His love is here, always. Accept it—now—and be blessed.

— A PRAYER —

Dear Lord, Your love for me is infinite and eternal. Let me acknowledge Your love, accept Your love, and share Your love. Make me a woman of compassion, understanding, and forgiveness. And let the love that I feel in my heart be expressed through kind words, good deeds and heartfelt prayers. Amen

FORGIVENESS AND THE GOLDEN RULE

Therefore, whatever you want others to do for you, do also the same for them—this is the Law and the Prophets.

Matthew 7:12 HCSB

How should we treat other people? God's Word is clear: we should treat others in the same way that we wish to be treated. This Golden Rule is easy to understand but, at times, difficult to live by.

Because we are imperfect human beings, we are, on occasion, selfish, thoughtless, unforgiving, or even cruel. God commands us to behave otherwise. He teaches us to rise above our own imperfections and to treat others with mercy and compassion. When we observe God's Golden Rule, we help build His kingdom here on earth.

The words of Matthew 7:12 remind us that, as believers in Christ, we are commanded to forgive others just as we wish to be forgive by them. This commandment is, indeed, the Golden Rule for Christians of every generation. When we weave the thread of forgiveness into the very fabric of our lives, we give glory to the One who first forgave us.

— A PRAYER —

Dear Lord, today, I will make forgiveness a priority in my life. I will honor Your Word by obeying it. I will turn my thoughts, my faith, and my prayers to You. I will seek Your will and follow it, Father, this day and always. Amen

HIS WONDROUS HANDIWORK

Then God saw everything that He had made, and indeed it was very good.

Genesis 1:31 NKJV

As we pause to examine God's wondrous handiwork, one thing is clear: God is, indeed, a miracle worker. Throughout history, He has intervened in the course of human events in ways which can't be explained by science or human rationale.

God's miracles are not limited to special occasions, nor are they witnessed by a select few. God is crafting His wonders all around us: the miracle of the birth of a new baby; the miracle of a world renewing itself with every sunrise; the miracle of lives transformed by God's love and by His grace. Each day God's miraculous handiwork is evident for all to see and to experience.

The Psalmist reminds us that the heavens are a declaration of God's glory. May we never cease to praise the Father for a universe that stands as an awesome testimony to His presence, to His power, and to His love.

Knowing God's sovereignty and unconditional love imparts a beauty to life . . . and to you.

Kay Arthur

— A PRAYER —

Dear Lord, You have created a world that is glorious to behold yet impossible to comprehend. I praise You for Your creation, Father, and for the sense of awe and wonder that You have placed in my heart. Today, as I pause to admire Your handiwork, I praise You for Your miraculous creation. This is the day that You have made, and I will rejoice in it. Amen

OUR GREATEST REFUGE

For you need endurance, so that after you have done God's will, you may receive what was promised.

Hebrews 10:36 HCSB

God is our greatest refuge. When every earthly support system fails, God remains steadfast, and His love remains unchanged. When we encounter life's inevitable disappointments and setbacks, God remains faithful. When we suffer losses that leave us breathless, God is always with for us, always ready to respond to our prayers, always working in us and through us to turn tragedy into triumph.

Author and speaker Patsy Clairmont observed, "If you are walking toward Jesus to the best of your ability, he will see you through life's unpredictable waters—but you must risk launching the boat." And that's sound advice because even during life's most difficult days, God stands by us. Our job, of course, is to return the favor and stand by Him.

Worries carry responsibilities that belong to God, not to you. Worry does not enable us to escape evil; it makes us unfit to cope with it when it comes.

Corrie ten Boom

— A PRAYER —

Lord, You are my Shepherd. You care for me; You comfort me; You watch over me; and You have saved me. I will praise You, Father, for Your glorious works, for Your protection, for Your love, and for Your Son. Amen

HONORING GOD

Honor the Lord with your possessions, and with the firstfruits of all your increase; so your barns will be filled with plenty.

Proverbs 3:9-10 NKJV

Whom will you choose to honor today? If you honor God and place Him at the center of your life, every day is a cause for celebration. But if you fail to honor your Heavenly Father, you're asking for trouble, and lots of it.

At times, your life is probably hectic, demanding, and complicated. When the demands of life leave you rushing from place to place with scarcely a moment to spare, you may fail to pause and thank your Creator for the blessings He has bestowed upon you. But that's a big mistake.

Do you sincerely seek to be a worthy servant of the One who has given you eternal love and eternal life? Then honor Him for who He is and for what He has done for you. And don't just honor Him on Sunday morning. Praise Him all day long, every day, for as long as you live . . . and then for all eternity.

If you are willing to honor a person out of respect for God, you can be assured that God will honor you.

Beth Moore

— A PRAYER —

Dear Lord, You have commanded that I have no gods before You. Let me place You first in my heart, Father, and let me accept the salvation of Your Son Jesus. Then, let me encourage others to accept Your love and Your grace. Amen

OUR BEST FRIEND

Greater love has no one than this, that he lay down his life for his friends.

John 15:13 NIV

Who's the best friend this world has ever had? Jesus, of course. And when you form a life-changing relationship with Him, He will be your best friend, too . . . your friend forever.

Jesus has offered to share the gifts of everlasting life and everlasting love with the world and with you. If you make mistakes, He'll stand by you. If you fall short of His commandments, He'll still love you. If you feel lonely or worried, He can touch your heart and lift your spirits.

Jesus wants you to enjoy a happy, healthy, abundant life. He wants you to walk with Him and to share His Good News. You can do it. And with a friend like Jesus, you will.

Jesus was the Savior Who would deliver them not only from the bondage of sin but also from meaningless wandering through life.

Anne Graham Lotz

— A PRAYER —

Dear Lord, You sent Your Son to die on a cross so that I might have eternal life. And because Jesus was a man who walked this earth, You possess a perfect understanding of all humanity, including my own frailties and shortcomings. I praise You, Lord, for Your love, for Your forgiveness, for Your grace, and for Your Son. Let me share the Good News of Jesus Christ, the One who became a man so that I might become His, not only for today, but also for all eternity. Amen

WALKING IN THE LIGHT

I have come as a light into the world, that whoever believes in Me should not abide in darkness.

John 12:46 NKJV

God's Holy Word instructs us that Jesus is, "the way, the truth, and the life" (John 14:6-7). Without Christ, we are as far removed from salvation as the east is removed from the west. And without Christ, we can never know the ultimate truth: God's truth.

Truth is God's way: He commands His believers to live in truth, and He rewards those who do so. Jesus is the personification of God's liberating truth, a truth that offers salvation to mankind.

Do you seek to walk with God? Do you seek to feel His presence and His peace? Then you must walk in truth; you must walk in the light; you must walk with the Savior. There is simply no other way.

Light is stronger than darkness—darkness cannot "comprehend" or "overcome" it.

Anne Graham Lotz

— A PRAYER —

Heavenly Father, You are the way and the truth and the light. Today—as I follow Your way and share Your Good News—let me be a worthy example to others and a worthy servant to You. Amen

HIS PEACE

But now in Christ Jesus you who once were far off have been brought near by the blood of Christ. For He Himself is our peace.

Ephesians 2:13-14 NKJV

On many occasions, our outer struggles are simply manifestations of the inner conflicts that we feel when we stray from God's path. What's needed is a refresher course in God's promise of peace. The beautiful words of John 14:27 remind us that Jesus offers peace, not as the world gives, but as He alone gives: "Peace I leave with you. My peace I give to you. I do not give to you as the world gives. Your heart must not be troubled or fearful" (HCSB).

As believers, our challenge is straightforward: we should welcome Christ's peace into our hearts and then, as best we can, share His peace with our neighbors.

Today, as a gift to yourself, to your family, and to your friends, invite Christ to preside over every aspect of your life. It's the best way to live and the surest path to peace . . . today and forever.

Where the soul is full of peace and joy, outward surroundings and circumstances are of comparatively little account.

Hannah Whitall Smiith

— A PRAYER —

Dear Lord, let me accept the peace and abundance that You offer through Your Son Jesus. You are the Giver of all things good, Father, and You give me peace when I draw close to You. Help me to trust Your will, to follow Your commands, and to accept Your peace, today and forever. Amen

MAKING GOD'S PRIORITIES YOUR PRIORITIES

Teach me, O Lord, the way of Your statutes, and I shall keep it to the end.

Psalm 119:33 NKJV

Sometimes, amid the demands of daily life, we lose perspective. Life seems out of balance, and the pressures of everyday living seem overwhelming. What's needed is a fresh perspective, a restored sense of balance . . . and God.

Negative thoughts are habit-forming; thankfully, so are positive ones. With practice, you can form the habit of focusing on God's priorities and your possibilities. When you do, you'll soon discover that you will spend less time fretting about your challenges and more time praising God for His gifts.

When you call upon the Lord and prayerfully seek His will, He will give you wisdom and perspective. When you make God's priorities your priorities, He will direct your steps and calm your fears. So today and every day hereafter, pray for a sense of balance and perspective. And remember: your thoughts are intensely powerful things, so handle them with care.

— A PRAYER —

Dear Lord, when the pace of my life becomes frantic, slow me down and give me perspective. Give me the wisdom to realize that the problems of today are only temporary but that Your love is eternal. When I become discouraged, keep me steady and sure, so that I might do Your will here on earth and then live with You forever in heaven. Amen

PAUSE AND PRAISE

Is anyone among you suffering? He should pray. Is anyone cheerful? He should sing praises.

James 5:13 HCSB

Because we have been saved by God's only Son, we must never lose hope in the priceless gifts of eternal love and eternal life. And, because we are so richly blessed, we must approach our Heavenly Father with reverence and thanksgiving.

Sometimes, in our rush "to get things done," we simply don't stop long enough to pause and thank our Creator for the countless blessings He has bestowed upon us. But when we slow down and express our gratitude to the One who made us, we enrich our own lives and the lives of those around us.

Thanksgiving should become a habit, a regular part of our daily routines. God has blessed us beyond measure, and we owe Him everything, including our eternal praise. Let us praise Him today, tomorrow, and throughout eternity.

The best moment to praise God is always the present one.

Marie T. Freeman

— A PRAYER —

Lord, Your hand created the smallest grain of sand and the grandest stars in the heavens. You watch over Your entire creation, and You watch over me. Thank You, Lord, for loving this world so much that You sent Your Son to die for our sins. Let me always be grateful for the priceless gift of Your Son, and let me praise Your holy name forever. Amen

FIRST THINGS FIRST

First pay attention to me, and then relax. Now you can take it easy—you're in good hands.

Proverbs 1:33 MSG

"First things first." These words are easy to speak but hard to put into practice. For busy women living in a demanding world, placing first things first can be difficult indeed. Why? Because so many people are expecting so many things from us!

If you're having trouble prioritizing your day, perhaps you've been trying to organize your life according to your own plans, not God's. A better strategy, of course, is to take your daily obligations and place them in the hands of the One who created you. To do so, you must prioritize your day according to God's commandments, and you must seek His will and His wisdom in all matters. Then, you can face the day with the assurance that the same God who created our universe out of nothingness will help you place first things first in your own life.

The manifold rewards of a serious, consistent prayer life demonstrate clearly that time with our Lord should be our first priority.

Shirley Dobson

— A PRAYER —

Dear Lord, let Your purposes be my purposes. Let Your priorities be my priorities. Let Your will be my will. Let Your Word be my guide. And, let me grow in faith and in wisdom today and every day. Amen

HE RENEWS

A final word: Be strong with the Lord's mighty power.

Ephesians 6:10 NLT

God's Word is clear: When we genuinely lift our hearts and prayers to Him, He renews our strength. Are you almost too weary to lift your head? Then bow it. Offer your concerns and your fears to your Father in heaven. He is always at your side, offering His love and His strength.

Are you troubled or anxious? Take your anxieties to God in prayer. Are you weak or worried? Delve deeply into God's Holy Word and sense His presence in the quiet moments of the early morning. Are you spiritually exhausted? Call upon fellow believers to support you, and call upon Christ to renew your spirit and your life. Your Savior will not let you down. To the contrary, He will lift you up when you ask Him to do so. So what, dear friend, are you waiting for?

It is important that we take time out for ourselves—for relaxation, for refreshment.

Ruth Bell Graham

— A PRAYER —

Dear Lord, sometimes the demands of the day leave me discouraged and frustrated. Renew my strength, Father, and give me patience and perspective. Today and every day, let me draw comfort and courage from Your promises, from Your love, and from Your Son. Amen

OPPORTUNITIES FOR SERVICE

So then, we must pursue what promotes peace and what builds up one another.

Romans 14:19 HCSB

You're a special person, created by God, and He has unique work for you to do. Do you acknowledge your own uniqueness, and do you celebrate the one-of-kind opportunities that God has placed before you? Hopefully so. But if you're like too many women, you may have fallen into a trap—the trap of taking yourself and your opportunities for granted.

God created you with a surprising array of talents, and He placed you precisely where you are—at a time and place of His choosing. God has done His part by giving you life, love, blessings, and more opportunities than you can count. Your particular situation is unique and so are your opportunities for service.

In the very place where God has put us, whatever its limitations, whatever kind of work it may be, we may indeed serve the Lord Christ.

Elisabeth Elliot

— A PRAYER —

Father in heaven, when Jesus humbled Himself and became a servant, He also became an example for His followers. Today, as I serve my family and friends, I do so in the name of Jesus, my Lord and Master. Guide my steps, Father, and let my service be pleasing to You. Amen

STILLNESS

Be still, and know that I am God.

Psalm 46:10 NKJV

Are you so busy that you rush through the day with scarcely a single moment for quiet contemplation and prayer? If so, it's time to reorder your priorities.

If we are to maintain righteous minds and compassionate hearts, we must take time each day for prayer and for meditation. We must make ourselves still in the presence of our Creator. We must quiet our minds and our hearts so that we might sense God's will, God's love, and God's Son.

Has the busy pace of life robbed you of the peace that might otherwise be yours through Jesus Christ? Nothing is more important than the time you spend with your Savior. So be still and claim the inner peace that is your spiritual birthright: the peace of Jesus Christ.

Be quiet enough to hear God's whisper.

Anonymous

— A PRAYER —

Dear Lord, let me be still before You. When I am hurried or distracted, slow me down and redirect my thoughts. When I am confused, give me perspective. Keep me mindful, Father, that You are always with me. And let me sense Your presence today, tomorrow, and forever. Amen

USING YOUR TALENTS

As each one has received a gift, minister it to one another, as good stewards of the manifold grace of God.

1 Peter 4:10 NKJV

Your talents, resources, and opportunities are all gifts from the Giver of all things good. And the best way to say "Thank You" for these gifts is to use them.

Do you have a particular talent? Hone your skill and use it. Do you possess financial resources? Share them. Have you been blessed by a particular opportunity, or have you experienced unusual good fortune? Use your good fortune to help others.

When you share the gifts God has given you—and when you share them freely and without fanfare—you invite God to bless you more and more. So today, do yourself and the world a favor: be a faithful steward of your talents and treasures. And then prepare yourself for even greater blessings that are sure to come.

Employ whatever God has entrusted you with, in doing good, all possible good, in every possible kind and degree.

John Wesley

— A PRAYER —

Lord, You have blessed me with a love that is far beyond my limited understanding. You loved me before I was ever born; You sent Your Son Jesus to redeem me from my sins; You have given me the gift of eternal life. And, You have given me special talents; let me use those talents to the best of my ability and to the glory of Your kingdom so that I might be a good and faithful servant this day and forever. Amen

BEYOND PESSIMISM

But if we hope for what we do not see, we eagerly wait for it with patience.

Romans 8:25 HCSB

When you decided to allow Christ to rule over your heart, you entitled yourself to share in His promise of spiritual abundance and eternal joy. Have you claimed that entitlement? Are you an upbeat believer? Are you a person whose hopes and dreams are alive and well? Hopefully so. But sometimes, when pessimism and doubt invade your thoughts, you won't feel like celebrating. Why? Because thoughts are extremely powerful things.

If you've allowed pessimism to creep into your mind and heart, you should spend more time thinking about your blessings and less time fretting about your hardships. Then, you should take time to thank the Giver of all things good for gifts that are, in truth, far too numerous to count.

I became aware of one very important concept I had missed before: my attitude—not my circumstances—was what was making me unhappy.

Vonette Bright

— A PRAYER —

Dear Lord, let my thoughts and prayers honor You. When I become fearful or discouraged, let me trust You. And when I encounter the evils of this world, let me turn to You for strength and wisdom. Amen

EXPECT A MIRACLE

And Jesus looking upon them saith, With men it is impossible, but not with God: for with God all things are possible.

Mark 10:27 KJV

When you invite Christ to rule over your heart, you avail yourself of His power. And make no mistake about it: You and Christ, working together, can do miraculous things. In fact, miraculous things are exactly what Christ intends for you to do, but He won't force you to do great things on His behalf. The decision to become a full-fledged participant in His power is a decision that you must make for yourself.

Jesus made this promise: "I assure you: The one who believes in Me will also do the works that I do" (John 14:12 HCSB). In other words, when you put absolute faith in Christ, you can share in His power. So today, trust the Savior's promise—and expect a miracle in His name.

Faith means believing in realities that go beyond sense and sight. It is the awareness of unseen divine realities all around you.

Joni Eareckson Tada

— A PRAYER —

Dear Lord, absolutely nothing is impossible for You. Let me trust in Your power and in Your miracles. When I lose hope, give me faith; when others lose hope, let me tell them of Your glorious works. Today, Lord, keep me mindful that You are a God of infinite possibilities and infinite love. Amen

GOD'S WILL FOR YOU

The world and its desires pass away, but the man who does the will of God lives forever.

1 John 2:17 NIV

As human beings with limited understanding, we can never fully comprehend the will of God. But as believers in a benevolent God, we must always trust the will of our Heavenly Father.

Before His crucifixion, Jesus went to the Mount of Olives and poured out His heart to God (Luke 22). Jesus knew of the agony that He was destined to endure, but He also knew that God's will must be done. We, like our Savior, face trials that bring fear and trembling to the very depths of our souls, but like Christ, we, too, must ultimately seek God's will, not our own.

As this day unfolds, seek God's will for your own life and obey His Word. When you entrust your life to Him completely and without reservation, He will give you the strength to meet any challenge, the courage to face any trial, and the wisdom to live in His righteousness and in His peace.

The Will of God will never take you where the Grace of God will not protect you.

Anonymous

— A PRAYER —

Heavenly Father, in these quiet moments before this busy day unfolds, I come to You. I will study Your Word and seek Your guidance. Give me the wisdom to know Your will for my life and the courage to follow wherever You may lead me, today and forever. Amen

WHOM DO YOU TRUST?

The one who understands a matter finds success, and the one who trusts in the Lord will be happy.

Proverbs 16:20 HCSB

Where will you place your trust today? Will you trust in the ways of the world, or will you trust in the Word and the will of your Creator?

If you aspire to do great things for God's kingdom, you will trust Him completely.

Trusting God means trusting Him in every aspect of your life. You must trust Him with your relationships. You must trust Him with your finances. You must follow His commandments and pray for His guidance. Then, you can wait patiently for God's revelations and for His blessings.

When you trust your Heavenly Father without reservation, you can rest assured: in His own fashion and in His own time, God will bless you in ways that you never could have imagined. So trust Him, and then prepare yourself for the abundance and joy that will most certainly be yours through Him.

Sometimes the very essence of faith is trusting God in the midst of things He knows good and well we cannot comprehend.

Beth Moore

— A PRAYER —

Dear Lord, I will turn my concerns over to You. I will trust Your love, Your wisdom, Your plan, Your promises, and Your Son—today and every day that I live. Amen

YOUR NEXT MOVE

It is better to take refuge in the Lord than to trust in man.

Psalm 118:8 NIV

Does God have a plan for your life? Of course He does! Every day of your life, He is trying to lead you along a path of His choosing . . . but He won't force you to follow. God has given you free will, the opportunity to make decisions for yourself. The choices are yours: either you will choose to obey His Word and seek His will, or you will choose to follow a different path.

Today, as you carve out a few quiet moments to commune with your Heavenly Father, ask Him to renew your sense of purpose. God's plans for you may be far bigger than you imagine, but He may be waiting for you to make the next move—so today, make that move prayerfully, faithfully, and expectantly. And after you've made your move, trust God to make His.

How much of our lives are, well, so daily. How often our hours are filled with the mundane, seemingly unimportant things that have to be done, whether at home or work. These very "daily" tasks could become a celebration of praise. "It is through consecration," someone has said, "that drudgery is made divine."

Gigi Graham Tchividjian

— A PRAYER —

Dear Lord, thank You for the gift of Your Son Jesus, my personal Savior. I will be His faithful, obedient servant, and I will make radical changes in my life for Him. I offer my life to You, Lord, so that I might live with passion and with purpose. And I will praise You for Your Son and for Your everlasting love. Amen

DISCIPLINING YOURSELF

So roll up your sleeves, put your mind in gear, be totally ready to receive the gift that's coming when Jesus arrives. Don't lazily slip back into those old grooves of evil, doing just what you feel like doing. You didn't know any better then; you do now. As obedient children, let yourselves be pulled into a way of life shaped by God's life, a life energetic and blazing with holiness.

1 Peter 1:13-15 MSG

God's Word is clear: as believers, we are called to lead lives of discipline, diligence, moderation, and maturity. But the world often tempts us to do otherwise. Everywhere we turn, or so it seems, we are faced with powerful temptations to behave in undisciplined, ungodly ways—but God has far better plans for our days and for our lives.

God's Word instructs us to be disciplined in our thoughts and our actions; God's Word warns us against the dangers of impulsive behavior. God's Word teaches us that diligence is rewarded and laziness is not.

Do you seek to reap the rewards that God offers those who lead disciplined lives? If so, then you must learn to discipline yourself . . . before God does.

— A PRAYER —

Dear Lord, make me a woman of discipline and righteousness. Let my conduct show others what it means to be a faithful Christian, and let me follow Your will and Your Word, today and every day. Amen

THE IMPORTANCE OF WORDS

No rotten talk should come from your mouth, but only what is good for the building up of someone in need, in order to give grace to those who hear.

Ephesians 4:29 HCSB

How important are the words we speak? More important than we may realize. Our words have echoes that extend beyond place or time. If our words are encouraging, we can lift others up; if our words are hurtful, we can hold others back.

Do you seek to be a source of encouragement to others? And, do you seek to be a worthy ambassador for Christ? If so, you must speak words that are worthy of your Savior. So avoid angry outbursts. Refrain from impulsive outpourings. Terminate tantrums. Instead, speak words of encouragement and hope to your family and friends, who, by the way, most certainly need all the hope and encouragement they can find.

It is time that the followers of Jesus revise their language and learn to speak respectfully of non-Christian peoples.

Lottie Moon

— A PRAYER —

Lord, You have warned me that I will be judged by the words I speak. And, You have commanded me to choose my words carefully so that I might be a source of encouragement and hope to my family and to the world. Let the words that I speak today be worthy of the One who has saved me forever. Amen

SEEKING HIS WISDOM

Wisdom is the principal thing; therefore get wisdom. And in all your getting, get understanding.

Proverbs 4:7 NKJV

Do you seek the wisdom that only God can give? If so, ask Him for it! If you ask God for guidance, He will not withhold it. If you petition Him sincerely, and if you genuinely seek to form a relationship with Him, your Heavenly Father will guide your steps and enlighten your heart. But be forewarned: You will not acquire God's wisdom without obeying His commandments. Why? Because God's wisdom is more than just a collection of thoughts; it is, first and foremost, a way of life.

Wisdom is as wisdom does. So if you sincerely seek God's wisdom, don't be satisfied to learn something; make up your mind to become something. And then, as you allow God to remake you in the image of His Son, you will most surely become wise.

Knowledge can be found in books or in school. Wisdom, on the other hand, starts with God . . . and ends there.

Marie T. Freeman

— A PRAYER —

Dear Lord, when I trust in the wisdom of the world, I am often led astray, but when I trust in Your wisdom, I build my life upon a firm foundation. Today and every day I will trust Your Word and follow it, knowing that the ultimate wisdom is Your wisdom and the ultimate truth is Your truth. Amen

MOVING PAST THE PAST

One thing I do, forgetting those things which are behind and reaching forward to those things which are ahead, I press toward the goal for the prize of the upward call of God in Christ Jesus.

Philippians 3:13-14 NKJV

Manmade plans are fallible; God's plans are not. Yet whenever life takes an unexpected turn, we are tempted to fall into the spiritual traps of worry, self-pity, or bitterness. God intends that we do otherwise.

The old saying is familiar: "Forgive and forget." But when we have been hurt badly, forgiveness is often difficult and forgetting is downright impossible. Since we can't forget yesterday's troubles, we should learn from them. Yesterday has much to teach us about tomorrow. We may learn from the past, but we should never live in the past.

So if you're trying to forget the past, don't waste your time. Instead, try a different approach: learn to accept the past and live in the present. Then, you can focus your thoughts and your energies, not on the struggles of yesterday, but instead on the profound opportunities that God has placed before you today.

— A PRAYER —

Dear Lord, let me live in the present, not the past. Let me focus on my blessings, not my sorrows. Give me the wisdom to be thankful for the gifts that I do have, not bitter about the things that I don't have. Let me accept what was, let me give thanks for what is, and let me have faith in what most surely will be: the promise of eternal life with You. Amen

WHEN CALAMITY STRIKES

Why am I so depressed? Why this turmoil within me? Put your hope in God, for I will still praise Him, my Savior and my God.

Psalm 42:11 HCSB

When calamity strikes anywhere in the world, we may be confronted with real-time images, images that breed anxiety. And as we stare transfixed at our television screens, we may fall prey to fear, discouragement, worry, or all three. But our Father in heaven has other plans. God has promised that we may lead lives of abundance, not anxiety. In fact, His Word instructs us to "be anxious for nothing" (Philippians 4:6). But how can we put our fears to rest? By taking those fears to God and leaving them there.

As you face the challenges of daily life, you may find yourself becoming anxious. If so, turn every one of your concerns over to your Heavenly Father. The same God who created the universe will comfort you if you ask Him . . . so ask Him and trust Him. And then watch in amazement as your anxieties melt into the warmth of His loving hands.

Emotions we have not poured out in the safe hands of God can turn into feelings of hopelessness and depression. God is safe.

Beth Moore

— A PRAYER —

Lord, sometimes this world is a difficult place, and, as a frail human being, I am fearful. When I am worried, restore my faith. When I am anxious, turn my thoughts to You. When I grieve, touch my heart with Your enduring love. And, keep me mindful, Lord, that nothing, absolutely nothing, will happen this day that You and I cannot handle together. Amen

A BOOK UNLIKE ANY OTHER

Your word is a lamp for my feet and a light on my path.

Psalm 119:105 HCSB

God's Word is unlike any other book. The words of Matthew 4:4 remind us that, "Man shall not live by bread alone but by every word that proceedeth out of the mouth of God" (KJV). As believers, we are instructed to study the Bible and meditate upon its meaning for our lives, yet far too many Bibles are laid aside by well-intentioned believers who would like to study the Bible if they could "just find the time."

Warren Wiersbe observed, "When the child of God looks into the Word of God, he sees the Son of God. And, he is transformed by the Spirit of God to share in the glory of God." God's Holy Word is, indeed, a transforming, life-changing, one-of-a-kind treasure. And it's up to you—and only you—to use it that way.

The Bible is like no other book. Treat it that way!

Marie T. Freeman

— A PRAYER —

Lord, You've given me instructions for life here on earth and for life eternal. I will use the Bible as my guide. I will study it and meditate upon it as I trust You, Lord, to speak to me through Your Holy Word. Amen

WHY ME?

I have heard your prayer, I have seen your tears; surely I will heal you.

2 Kings 20:5 NKJV

When life unfolds according to our wishes, or when we experience unexpected good fortune, we find it easy to praise God's plan. That's when we greet change with open arms. But sometimes the changes that we must endure are painful. When we struggle through the difficult days of life, as we must from time to time, we may ask ourselves, "Why me?" The answer, of course, is that God knows, but He isn't telling . . . yet.

Have you endured a difficult transition that has left your head spinning or your heart broken? If so, you have a clear choice to make: either you can cry and complain, or you can trust God and get busy fixing what's broken. The former is a formula for disaster; the latter is a formula for a well-lived life.

Jesus did not promise to change the circumstances around us. He promised great peace and pure joy to those who would learn to believe that God actually controls all things.

Corrie ten Boom

— A PRAYER —

Dear Lord, I will seek Your plan for my life. Even when I don't understand why things happen, I will trust You. Even when I am uncertain of my next step, I will trust You. There are many things that I cannot do, Lord, and there are many things that I cannot understand. But one thing I can do is to trust You always. And I will. Amen

CLAIMING CONTENTMENT IN A DISCONTENTED WORLD

But godliness with contentment is a great gain.

1 Timothy 6:6 HCSB

Everywhere we turn, or so it seems, the world promises us contentment and happiness. We are bombarded by messages offering us the "good life" if only we will purchase products and services that are designed to provide happiness, success, and contentment. But the contentment that the world offers is fleeting and incomplete. Thankfully, the contentment that God offers is all encompassing and everlasting.

Happiness depends less upon our circumstances than upon our thoughts. When we turn our thoughts to God, to His gifts, and to His glorious creation, we experience the joy that God intends for His children. But, when we focus on the negative aspects of life—or when we disobey God's commandments—we cause ourselves needless suffering.

Do you sincerely want to be a contented Christian? Then set your mind and your heart upon God's love and His grace. Seek first the salvation that is available through a personal relationship with Jesus Christ, and then claim the joy, the contentment, and the spiritual abundance that God offers His children.

— A PRAYER —

Dear Lord, You offer me contentment and peace; let me accept Your peace. Help me to trust Your Word, to follow Your commandments, and to welcome the peace of Jesus into my heart, today and forever. Amen

WHEN FAITH SLIPS AWAY

Immediately the father of the child cried out and said with tears, "Lord, I believe; help my unbelief!"

Mark 9:24 NKJV

Sometimes, like Jesus' disciples, we feel threatened by the storms of life. During these moments, when our hearts are flooded with uncertainty, we must remember that God is not simply near, He is here.

Have you ever felt your faith in God slipping away? If so, you are in good company. Even the most faithful Christians are, at times, beset by occasional bouts of discouragement and doubt. But even when you feel far removed from God, God never leaves your side. He is always with you, always willing to calm the storms of life. When you sincerely seek His presence—and when you genuinely seek to establish a deeper, more meaningful relationship with His Son—God will calm your fears, answer your prayers, and restore your soul.

Resisting His will for your life will cause you to doubt.

Anne Graham Lotz

— A PRAYER —

Dear God, sometimes this world can be a puzzling place, filled with uncertainty and doubt. When I am unsure of my next step, keep me mindful that You are always near and that You can overcome any challenge. Give me faith, Father, and let me remember always that with Your love and Your power, I can live courageously and faithfully today and every day. Amen

GUARDING AGAINST EVIL

Turn from your evil ways and keep My commandments and statutes according to all the law I commanded your ancestors and sent to you through My servants the prophets.

2 Kings 17:13 HCSB

This world is God's creation, and it contains the wonderful fruits of His handiwork. But, the world also contains countless opportunities to stray from God's will. Temptations are everywhere, and the devil, it seems, never takes a day off. Our task, as believers, is to turn away from temptation and to place our lives squarely in the center of God's will.

In his letter to Jewish Christians, Peter offered a stern warning: "Your adversary, the devil, prowls around like a roaring lion, seeking someone to devour" (1 Peter 5:8 NASB). What was true in New Testament times is equally true in our own. Evil is indeed abroad in the world, and Satan continues to sow the seeds of destruction far and wide. As Christians, we must guard our hearts by earnestly wrapping ourselves in the protection of God's Holy Word. When we do, we are protected.

Holiness has never been the driving force of the majority. It is, however, mandatory for anyone who wants to enter the kingdom.

Elisabeth Elliot

— A PRAYER —

Dear Lord, give me the wisdom to recognize evil and the courage to fight it, today and every day of my life. Amen

FACING YOUR FEARS

They won't be afraid of bad news; their hearts are steady because they trust the Lord.

Psalm 112:7 NCV

Do you prefer to face your fears rather than run from them? If so, you will be blessed because of your willingness to live courageously.

When Paul wrote Timothy, he reminded his young protégé that the God they served was a bold God, and God's spirit empowered His children with boldness also. Like Timothy, we face times of uncertainty and fear. God's message is the same to us, today, as it was to Timothy: We can live boldly because the spirit of God resides in us.

So today, as you face the challenges of everyday living, remember that God is with you . . . and you are protected.

Whether our fear is absolutely realistic or out of proportion in our minds, our greatest refuge is Jesus Christ.

Luci Swindoll

— A PRAYER —

Your Word reminds me, Lord, that even when I walk through the valley of the shadow of death, I need fear no evil, for You are with me, and You comfort me. Thank You, Lord, for a perfect love that casts out fear. Let me live courageously and faithfully this day and every day. Amen

PRAYING ABOUT FORGIVENESS

The intense prayer of the righteous is very powerful.

James 5:16 HCSB

Jesus made it clear to His disciples: they should pray always. And so should we. Genuine, heartfelt prayer changes things and it changes us. When we lift our hearts to our Father in heaven, we open ourselves to a never-ending source of divine wisdom and infinite love.

Do you have questions that you simply can't answer? Ask for the guidance of your Father in heaven. Have you been unable to forgive yourself for something you did long ago? God has forgiven you; now it's your turn to forgive yourself. Do you sincerely seek the gift of peace and wholeness that only God can give? Then obey His commandments and accept the grace of His only begotten Son.

Whatever your need, no matter how great or small, pray about it. And remember: God is not just near; He is here, and He's ready to talk with you. Now.

If you can't seem to forgive someone, pray for that person and keep praying for him or her until, with God's help, you've removed the poison of bitterness from your heart.

Marie T. Freeman

— A PRAYER —

Dear Lord, when I am bitter or frustrated, give me a forgiving heart. When I am angry, give me patience; when I am worried, give me perspective. Today and every day, renew my soul; let me draw comfort and courage from Your promises, from Your love, and from Your Son. Amen

GOD'S SOVEREIGNTY

Can you solve the mysteries of God? Can you discover everything there is to know about the Almighty? Such knowledge is higher than the heavens—but who are you? It is deeper than the underworld—what can you know in comparison to him? It is broader than the earth and wider than the sea.

Job 11:7-9 NLT

God is sovereign. He reigns over the entire universe, and He reigns over your little corner of that universe. Your challenge is to recognize God's sovereignty and live in accordance with His commandments. Sometimes, of course, this is easier said than done.

Your Heavenly Father may not always reveal Himself as quickly (or as clearly) as you would like. But rest assured: God is in control, God is here, and God intends to use you in wonderful, unexpected ways. He desires to lead you along a path of His choosing. Your challenge is to watch, to listen, to learn . . . and to follow.

Knowing God's sovereignty and unconditional love imparts a beauty to life . . . and to you.

Kay Arthur

— A PRAYER —

Dear Lord, You are the sovereign God of the universe. You rule over our world, and I will allow You to rule over my heart. I will obey Your commandments, Father, and I will study Your Word. I will seek Your will for my life, and I will allow Your Son to reign over my heart . . . today and every day of my life. Amen

HOPE NOW

Let us hold on to the confession of our hope without wavering, for He who promised is faithful.

Hebrews 10:23 HCSB

Despite God's promises, despite Christ's love, and despite our countless blessings, we frail human beings can still lose hope from time to time. When we do, we need the encouragement of Christian friends, the life-changing power of prayer, and the healing truth of God's Holy Word.

If you find yourself falling into the spiritual traps of worry and discouragement, seek the healing touch of Jesus and the encouraging words of fellow Christians. And remember the words of our Savior: "These things I have spoken unto you, that in me ye might have peace. In the world ye shall have tribulation: but be of good cheer; I have overcome the world" (John 16:33 KJV). This world can be a place of trials and tribulations, but as believers, we are secure. God has promised us peace, joy, and eternal life. And, of course, God keeps His promises today, tomorrow, and forever.

— A PRAYER —

Dear Lord, make me a woman of hope. If I become discouraged, let me turn to You. If I grow weary, let me seek strength in You. When I face disappointments, let me seek Your will and trust Your Word. In every aspect of my life, I will trust You, Father, so that my heart will be filled with faith and hope, this day and forever. Amen

SHARING THE JOY

Glory in His holy name; let the hearts of those rejoice who seek the Lord! Seek the Lord and His strength; seek His face evermore!

1 Chronicles 16:10-11 NKJV

God's intends that His joy should become our joy. He intends that we, His children, should share His love, His joy, and His peace. Yet sometimes, amid the inevitable hustle and bustle of life-here-on-earth, we don't feel much like sharing. So we forfeit—albeit temporarily—God's joy as we wrestle with the challenges of everyday life.

If, today, your heart is heavy, open the door of your soul to your Heavenly Father. When you do, He will renew your spirit. And, if you already have the joy of Christ in your heart, share it freely. When you discover ways to share your joy, you will have discovered a wonderful way to say, "I love you" to your family, to your friends, and, most especially, to your God.

God gives to us a heavenly gift called joy, radically different in quality from any natural joy.

Elisabeth Elliot

— A PRAYER —

Dear Lord, You have given me so many blessings; let me celebrate Your gifts. Make me thankful, loving, responsible, and wise. I praise You, Father, for the gift of Your Son and for the priceless gift of salvation. Make me a joyful Christian and a worthy example to my loved ones, today and every day. Amen

LOVING GOD

You shall love the LORD your God with all your heart and with all your soul and with all your might.

Deuteronomy 6:5 NASB

If you want to know God in a more meaningful way, you'll need to open up your heart and let Him in.

C. S. Lewis observed, "A person's spiritual health is exactly proportional to his love for God." If you hope to receive a full measure of God's spiritual blessings, you must invite your Creator to rule over your heart. When you honor God in this way, His love expands to fill your heart and bless your life.

St. Augustine wrote, "I love you, Lord, not doubtingly, but with absolute certainty. Your Word beat upon my heart until I fell in love with you, and now the universe and everything in it tells me to love you."

Today, open your heart to the Father. And let your obedience be a fitting response to His never-ending love.

Telling the Lord how much you love Him and why is what praise and worship are all about.

Lisa Whelchel

— A PRAYER —

Dear Heavenly Father, You have blessed me with a love that is infinite and eternal. Let me love You, Lord, more and more each day. Make me a loving servant, Father, today and throughout eternity. And, let me show my love for You by sharing Your message and Your love with others. Amen

ACKNOWLEDGING GOD'S SOVEREIGNTY

However, I did give them this command: Obey Me, and then I will be your God, and you will be My people. You must walk in every way I command you so that it may go well with you.

Jeremiah 7:23 HCSB

Proverbs 3:6 makes this promise: if you acknowledge God's sovereignty over every aspect of your life, He will guide your path. And, as you prayerfully consider the path that God intends for you to take, here are things you should do: You should study His Word and be ever-watchful for His signs. You should associate with fellow believers who will encourage your spiritual growth. You should listen carefully to that inner voice that speaks to you in the quiet moments of your daily devotionals. And, as you continually seek God's unfolding purpose for your life, you should be patient. Your Heavenly Father may not always reveal Himself as quickly as you would like. But rest assured: God is here, and He intends to use you in wonderful, unexpected ways. He desires to lead you along a path of His choosing. Your challenge is to watch, to listen, to learn . . . and to follow.

God is, must be, our answer to every question and every cry of need.

Hannah Whitall Smith

— A PRAYER —

Dear Lord, each day I will walk with You. As we walk together, I pray that Your presence will be reflected in my life, and that Your love will dwell within my heart this day and every day. Amen

PLANNING (AND WORKING) FOR THE FUTURE

The plans of the diligent lead to profit as surely as haste leads to poverty.

Proverbs 21:5 NIV

Are you willing to plan for the future—and are you willing to work diligently to accomplish the plans that you've made? The Book of Proverbs teaches that the plans of hardworking people (like you) are rewarded.

If you desire to reap a bountiful harvest from life, you must plan for the future while entrusting the final outcome to God. Then, you must do your part to make the future better (by working dutifully), while acknowledging the sovereignty of God's hands over all affairs, including your own.

Are you in a hurry for success to arrive at your doorstep? Don't be. Instead, work carefully, plan thoughtfully, and wait patiently. Remember that you're not the only one working on your behalf: God, too, is at work. And with Him as your partner, your ultimate success is guaranteed.

Plan ahead—it wasn't raining when Noah built the ark.

Anonymous

— A PRAYER —

Dear Lord, give me the wisdom to accept the past and the insight to plan for the future. And help me align my plans with Your plans, Father, this day and every day. Amen

PRAYER NOW

Be joyful because you have hope. Be patient when trouble comes, and pray at all times.

Romans 12:12 NCV

Prayer is a powerful tool for communicating with our Creator; it is an opportunity to commune with the Giver of all things good. Prayer is not a thing to be taken lightly or to be used infrequently. Prayer should never be reserved for mealtimes or for bedtimes; it should be an ever-present focus in our daily lives.

In his first letter to the Thessalonians, Paul wrote, "Rejoice evermore. Pray without ceasing. In every thing give thanks: for this is the will of God in Christ Jesus concerning you" (5:17-18 KJV). Paul's words apply to every Christian of every generation.

Today, instead of turning things over in our minds, let us turn them over to God in prayer. Instead of worrying about our decisions, let's trust God to help us make them. Today, let us pray constantly about things great and small. God is listening, and He wants to hear from us. Now.

— A PRAYER —

Dear Lord, Your Holy Word commands me to pray without ceasing. Let me take everything to You in prayer. When I am discouraged, let me pray. When I am lonely, let me take my sorrows to You. When I grieve, let me take my tears to You, Father, in prayer. And when I am joyful, let me offer up prayers of thanksgiving. In all things great and small, at all times, whether happy or sad, let me seek Your wisdom and Your grace . . . in prayer. Amen

WORKING FOR THE HARVEST

I have seen that there is nothing better than for a person to enjoy his activities, because that is his reward. For who can enable him to see what will happen after he dies?

Ecclesiastes 3:22 HCSB

Once the season for planting is upon us, the time to plant seeds is when we make time to plant seeds. And when it comes to planting God's seeds in the soil of eternity, the only certain time that we have is now. Yet because we are fallible human beings with limited vision and misplaced priorities, we may be tempted to delay.

If we hope to reap a bountiful harvest for God, for our families, and for ourselves, we must plant now by defeating a dreaded human frailty: the habit of procrastination. Procrastination often results from our shortsighted attempts to postpone temporary discomfort.

A far better strategy is this: Whatever "it" is, do it now. When you do, you won't have to worry about "it" later.

Never fail to do something because you don't feel like it. Sometimes you just have to do it now, and you'll feel like it later.

Marie T. Freeman

— A PRAYER —

Dear Lord, when I am confronted with things that need to be done, give me the courage and the wisdom to do them now, not later. Amen

THE MERRY-GO-ROUND

I will give you a new heart and put a new spirit in you....

Ezekiel 36:26 NIV

For busy women living in a fast-paced world, life may seem like a merry-go-round that never stops turning. If that description seems to fit your life, then you may find yourself running short of patience or strength, or both.

When you feel tired or discouraged, there is a source from which you can draw the power needed to recharge your spiritual batteries. That source is God.

Are you exhausted or troubled? Weak or worried? Worn out or burned out? If so, take time to rest, and take time to have a heart-to-heart talk with God. When you do, you'll discover that the Creator of the universe can help you gain a renewed sense of hope and a fresh perspective . . . your job is to let Him do it.

He is the God of wholeness and restoration.

Stormie Omartian

— A PRAYER —

Lord, You are my rock and my strength. When I grow weary, let me turn my thoughts and my prayers to You. When I am discouraged, restore my faith in You. Let me always trust in Your promises, Lord, and let me draw strength from those promises and from Your unending love. Amen

AS THE WORLD GROWS LOUDER

Be silent before the Lord and wait expectantly for Him.

Psalm 37:7 HCSB

The world seems to grow louder day by day, and our senses seem to be invaded at every turn. If we allow the distractions of a clamorous society to separate us from God's peace, we do ourselves a profound disservice. Our task, as dutiful believers, is to carve out moments of silence in a world filled with noise.

If we are to maintain righteous minds and compassionate hearts, we must take time each day for prayer and for meditation. We must make ourselves still in the presence of our Creator. We must quiet our minds and our hearts so that we might sense God's will and His love.

Has the busy pace of life robbed you of the peace that God has promised? If so, it's time to reorder your priorities and your life. Nothing is more important than the time you spend with your Heavenly Father. So be still and claim the inner peace that is found in the silent moments you spend with God.

A quiet morning with a loving God puts the events of the upcoming day into proper perspective.

Janette Oke

— A PRAYER —

Dear Lord, in the quiet moments of this day, I will turn my thoughts and prayers to You. In silence I will sense Your presence, and I will seek Your will for my life, knowing that when I accept Your peace, I will be blessed today and throughout eternity. Amen

DEPENDING UPON GOD

Depend on the Lord and his strength; always go to him for help. Remember the miracles he has done; remember his wonders and his decisions.

Psalm 105:4-5 NCV

God's love and support never changes. From the cradle to the grave, God has promised to give you the strength to meet any challenge. God has promised to lift you up and guide your steps if you let Him. God has promised that when you entrust your life to Him completely and without reservation, He will give you the courage to face any trial and the wisdom to live in His righteousness.

God's hand uplifts those who turn their hearts and prayers to Him. Will you count yourself among that number? Will you accept God's peace and wear God's armor against the temptations and distractions of our dangerous world? If you do, you can live courageously and optimistically, knowing that you have been forever touched by the loving, unfailing, uplifting hand of God.

No matter how heavy the burden, daily strength is given, so I expect we need not give ourselves any concern as to what the outcome will be. We must simply go forward.

Annie Armstrong

— A PRAYER —

Dear Lord, let me turn to You for strength. When I am weak, You lift me up. When my spirit is crushed, You comfort me. When I am victorious, Your Word reminds me to be humble. Today and every day, I will turn to You, Father, for strength, for hope, for wisdom, and for salvation. Amen

A WORLD FILLED WITH TEMPTATIONS

Look straight ahead, and fix your eyes on what lies before you. Mark out a straight path for your feet; then stick to the path and stay safe. Don't get sidetracked; keep your feet from following evil.

Proverbs 4:25-27 NLT

Have you noticed that this world is filled to the brim with temptations? Unless you've been living the life of a hermit, you've observed that temptations, both great and small, are everywhere.

Some temptations are small; eating a second scoop of ice cream, for example, is tempting, but not very dangerous. Other temptations, however, are not nearly so harmless. The devil is working 24/7, and he's causing pain and heartache in more ways than ever before. Thankfully, in the battle against Satan, we are never alone. God is always with us, and He gives us the power to resist temptation whenever we ask Him for the strength to do so.

In a letter to believers, Peter offered a stern warning: "Your adversary the devil walks about like a roaring lion, seeking whom he may devour" (1 Peter 5:8 NKJV). As Christians, we must take that warning seriously, and we must behave accordingly.

— A PRAYER —

Dear Lord, this world is filled with temptations, distractions, and frustrations. When I turn my thoughts away from You and Your Word, Lord, I suffer bitter consequences. But, when I trust in Your commandments, I am safe. Direct my path far from the temptations and distractions of the world. Let me discover Your will and follow it, Dear Lord, this day and always. Amen

THE GIFT OF TIME

Hard work means prosperity; only fools idle away their time.

Proverbs 12:11 NLT

Time is a nonrenewable gift from God. But sometimes, we treat our time here on earth as if it were not a gift at all: We may be tempted to invest our lives in trivial pursuits and petty diversions. But our Father beckons each of us to a higher calling.

An important element of our stewardship to God is the way that we choose to spend the time He has entrusted to us. Each waking moment holds the potential to do a good deed, to say a kind word, or to offer a heartfelt prayer. Our challenge, as believers, is to use our time wisely in the service of God's work and in accordance with His plan for our lives.

Each day is a special treasure to be savored and celebrated. May we—as Christians who have so much to celebrate—never fail to praise our Creator by rejoicing in His glorious creation and by using it wisely.

There were endless demands on Jesus' time. Still he was able to make that amazing claim of "completing the work you gave me to do." (John 17:4 NIV)

Elisabeth Elliot

— A PRAYER —

Dear Lord, You have given me a wonderful gift: time here on earth. Let me use it wisely—for the glory of Your kingdom and the betterment of Your world—today and every day. Amen

HE IS AT WORK

You are the God who works wonders; You revealed Your strength among the peoples.

Psalm 77:14 HCSB

Do you believe that God is at work in the world? And do you also believe that nothing is impossible for Him? If so, then you also believe that God is perfectly capable of doing things that you, as a mere human being with limited vision and limited understanding, would deem to be utterly impossible. And that's precisely what God does.

Since the moment that He created our universe out of nothingness, God has made a habit of doing miraculous things. And He still works miracles today. Expect Him to work miracles in your own life, and then be watchful. With God, absolutely nothing is impossible, including an amazing assortment of miracles that He stands ready, willing, and able to perform for you and yours.

Our helplessness can be a healthy sign. This is always a good place to begin a task that seems completely impossible

Catherine Marshall

— A PRAYER —

Heavenly Father, You are the miracle worker of life; let me trust in Your power and Your love. With You, Father, all things are possible. Keep me mindful that You are a God of power and possibilities, and let me never place limitations upon You, the Designer and Creator of the Universe. Amen

HIS GOLDEN RULE

If you really carry out the royal law prescribed in Scripture, You shall love your neighbor as yourself, you are doing well.

James 2:8 HCSB

As Christians, we are instructed to be courteous and compassionate. As believers, we are called to be gracious, humble, gentle, and kind. But sometimes, we fall short. Sometimes, amid the busyness and confusion of everyday life, we may neglect to share a kind word or a kind deed. This oversight hurts others, and it hurts us as well.

Today, slow yourself down and be alert for those who need your smile, your kind words, or your helping hand. Make kindness a centerpiece of your dealings with others. They will be blessed, and you will be, too. So make this promise to yourself and keep it: honor Christ by obeying His Golden Rule. He deserves no less. And neither, for that matter, do they.

It is one of the most beautiful compensations of life that no one can sincerely try to help another without helping herself.

Barbara Johnson

— A PRAYER —

Dear Lord, I thank You for friends and family members who practice the Golden Rule. Because I expect to be treated with kindness, let me be kind. Because I wish to be loved, let me be loving. Because I need forgiveness, let me be merciful. In all things, Lord, let me live by the Golden Rule, and let me express my gratitude to those who offer kindness and generosity to me. Amen

BEARING WITNESS TO THE TRUTH

A person who does not have the Spirit does not accept the truths that come from the Spirit of God. That person thinks they are foolish and cannot understand them, because they can only be judged to be true by the Spirit. The spiritual person is able to judge all things, but no one can judge him.

1 Corinthians 2:14-15 NCV

When God's spirit touches our hearts, we are confronted by a powerful force: the awesome, irresistible force of God's Truth. In response to that force, we will either follow God's lead by allowing Him to guide our thoughts and deeds, or we will resist God's calling and accept the consequences of our rebellion.

Today, as you fulfill the responsibilities that God has placed before you, ask yourself this question: "Do my thoughts and actions bear witness to the ultimate Truth that God has placed in my heart, or am I allowing the pressures of everyday life to overwhelm me?" It's a profound question that only you can answer. You be the judge.

To worship Him in truth means to worship Him honestly, without hypocrisy, standing open and transparent before Him.

Anne Graham Lotz

— A PRAYER —

Dear Lord, You have shown me the truth and the way through Your Son Jesus. Let me trust the promises of the Savior, and let me share His truth today and every day that I live. Amen

ACCEPTANCE TODAY

I have learned to be content whatever the circumstances.

Philippians 4:11 NIV

Are you embittered by a personal tragedy that you did not deserve and cannot understand? If so, it's time to accept the unchangeable past and to have faith in the promise of tomorrow. It's time to trust God completely—and it's time to reclaim the peace—His peace—that can and should be yours.

On occasion, you will be confronted with situations that you simply don't understand. But God does. And He has a reason for everything that He does.

God doesn't explain Himself in ways that we, as mortals with limited insight and clouded vision, can comprehend. So, instead of understanding every aspect of God's unfolding plan for our lives and our universe, we must be satisfied to trust Him completely. We cannot know God's motivations, nor can we understand His actions. We can, however, trust Him, and we must.

Surrender to the Lord is not a tremendous sacrifice, not an agonizing performance. It is the most sensible thing you can do.

Corrie ten Boom

— A PRAYER —

Father, the events of this world unfold according to a plan that I cannot fully understand. But You understand. Help me to trust You, Lord, even when I am grieving. Help me to trust You even when I am confused. Today, in whatever circumstances I find myself, let me trust Your will and accept Your love . . . completely. Amen

DURING DIFFICULT DAYS

I called to the Lord in my distress; I called to my God. From His temple He heard my voice.

2 Samuel 22:7 HCSB

All of us face difficult days. Sometimes even the most optimistic women can become discouraged, and you are no exception. If you find yourself enduring difficult circumstances, perhaps it's time for an extreme intellectual makeover—perhaps it's time to focus more on your strengths and opportunities, and less on the challenges that confront you. And one more thing: perhaps it's time to put a little more faith in God.

Your Heavenly Father is a God of possibility, not negativity. He will guide you through your difficulties and beyond them. And then, with a renewed spirit of optimism and hope, you can thank the Giver of all things good for gifts that are simply too numerous to count.

Losing everything sure has a way of teaching you how to appreciate the tender gifts that come directly from the Lord's hand.

Lisa Whelchel

— A PRAYER —

Dear Lord, in the dark moments of my life, help me to remember that You, my Savior, are always near and that You can overcome any challenge. Keep me mindful of Your love and Your power, so that I may live courageously and faithfully today and every day. Amen

YOUR REASONS TO REJOICE

Keep your eyes focused on what is right, and look straight ahead to what is good.

Proverbs 4:25 NCV

As a Christian woman, you have every reason to rejoice. God is in His heaven; Christ has risen, and dawn has broken on another day of life. But, when the demands of life seem great, you may find yourself feeling exhausted, discouraged, or both. That's when you need a fresh supply of hope . . . and God is ready, willing, and able to supply it.

The advice contained in Proverbs 4:5 is clear-cut: "Keep your eyes focused on what is right, and look straight ahead to what is good" (NCV). That's why you strive to maintain a positive, can-do attitude—an attitude that pleases God.

As you face the challenges of the coming day, use God's Word as a tool for directing your thoughts. When you do, your attitude will be pleasing to God, pleasing to your friends, and pleasing to yourself.

I could go through this day oblivious to the miracles all around me, or I could tune in and "enjoy."

Gloria Gaither

— A PRAYER —

Lord, I pray for an attitude that is Christlike. Whatever my circumstances, whether good or bad, triumphal or tragic, let my response reflect a God-honoring attitude of optimism, faith, and love for You. Amen

TODAY'S BIBLE READING
Old Testament: Psalms 36-38
New Testament: Acts 28:1-10

GOD'S ETERNAL PRESENCE

And the world with its lust is passing away, but the one who does God's will remains forever.

1 John 2:17 HCSB

God's hand is ever-present and everlasting. He has created the universe—and everything in it—out of nothingness. God's hand is everywhere you have ever been, and it is everywhere you will ever be. Your obligation, as a believer, is to reach out to Him and accept the peace, the love, the abundance, and the grace that He has offered.

Are you tired? Discouraged? Fearful? Be comforted. God's hand is with you. Are you worried or anxious? Be confident in God's power. He will never desert you. Are you grieving? Know that God understands your suffering. And rest assured that He will comfort you and that, in time, He will dry your tears.

Throughout every season of life, in times of celebration or sorrow, in times of victory or defeat, God's hand is not just near; it is always here. So why not reach out to Him right now?

God expresses His love toward us by His uninterrupted presence in our lives.

Charles Stanley

— A PRAYER —

Dear Lord, You are with me always. Help me feel Your presence in every situation and every circumstance. Today, Dear God, let me feel You and acknowledge Your presence, Your love, and Your Son. Amen

PROTECTED
BY THE HAND OF GOD

*For whatever is born of God overcomes the world. And this is the
victory that has overcome the world—our faith.*

1 John 5:4 NKJV

Have you ever faced challenges that seemed too big to handle?
Have you ever faced big problems that, despite your best efforts,
simply could not be solved? If so, you know how uncomfortable
it is to feel helpless in the face of difficult circumstances. Thankfully, even when there's nowhere else to turn, you can turn your
thoughts and prayers to God, and He will respond.

God's hand uplifts those who turn their hearts and prayers
to Him. Count yourself among that number. When you do, you
can live courageously and joyfully, knowing that "this too will
pass"—but that God's love for you will not. And you can draw
strength from the knowledge that you are a marvelous creation,
loved, protected, and uplifted by the ever-present hand of God.

Prayer is our pathway not only to divine protection, but also to a
personal, intimate relationship with God.

Shirley Dobson

— A PRAYER —

Lord, You have promised to protect me, and I will trust You. Today,
I will live courageously as I place my hopes, my faith, and my life
in Your hands. Let my life be a testimony to the transforming
power of Your love, Your grace, and Your Son. Amen

GOD'S POLICY

Lying lips are an abomination to the Lord, but those who deal truthfully are His delight.

Proverbs 12:22 NKJV

From the time we are children, we are taught that honesty is the best policy, but sometimes, it is so hard to be honest and so easy to be less than honest. So, we convince ourselves that it's alright to tell "little white lies." But there's a problem: Little white lies tend to grow up, and when they do, they cause havoc and pain in our lives.

For Christian believers, the issue of honesty is not a topic for debate. Honesty is not just the best policy, it is God's policy, pure and simple. And if we are to be servants worthy of our Savior, Jesus Christ, we avoid all lies, white or otherwise.

Sometime soon, perhaps even today, you will be tempted to sow the seeds of deception, perhaps in the form of a "harmless" white lie. Resist that temptation. Truth is God's way, and a lie—of whatever color—is not.

— A PRAYER —

Heavenly Father, You instruct Your children to seek truth and to live righteously. Help me always to live according to Your commandments. Sometimes, Lord, speaking the truth is difficult, but let me always speak truthfully and forthrightly. And, let me walk righteously and courageously so that others might see Your grace reflected in my words and my deeds. Amen

THE BREAD OF LIFE

And Jesus said to them, "I am the bread of life. He who comes to Me shall never hunger, and he who believes in Me shall never thirst."

John 6:35 NKJV

He was the Son of God, but He wore a crown of thorns. He was the Savior of mankind, yet He was put to death on a rough-hewn cross made of wood. He offered His healing touch to an unsaved world, and yet the same hands that had healed the sick and raised the dead were pierced with nails.

Jesus Christ, the Son of God, was born into humble circumstances. He walked this earth, not as a ruler of men, but as the Savior of mankind. His crucifixion, a torturous punishment that was intended to end His life and His reign, instead became the pivotal event in the history of all humanity.

Jesus is the bread of life. Accept His grace. Share His love. And follow in His footsteps.

In your greatest weakness, turn to your greatest strength, Jesus, and hear Him say, "My grace is sufficient for you, for My strength is made perfect in weakness" (2 Corinthians 12:9, NKJV).

Lisa Whelchel

— A PRAYER —

Dear Lord, today I will abide in Jesus. I will look to Him as my Savior, and I will follow in His footsteps. I will strive to please Him, and I will separate myself from the evils of this world. Thank You, Lord, for Your Son. Today, I will count Him as my dearest friend, and I will share His transforming message with a world in desperate need of His peace. Amen

LISTENING TO GOD

The one who is from God listens to God's words. This is why you don't listen, because you are not from God.

John 8:47 HCSB

Sometimes God speaks loudly and clearly. More often, He speaks in a quiet voice—and if you are wise, you will be listening carefully when He does. To do so, you must carve out quiet moments each day to study His Word and sense His direction.

Can you quiet yourself long enough to listen to your conscience? Are you attuned to the subtle guidance of your intuition? Are you willing to pray sincerely and then to wait quietly for God's response? Hopefully so. Usually God refrains from sending His messages on stone tablets or city billboards. More often, He communicates in subtler ways. If you sincerely desire to hear His voice, you must listen carefully, and you must do so in the silent corners of your quiet, willing heart.

When we come to Jesus stripped of pretensions, with a needy spirit, ready to listen, He meets us at the point of need.

Catherine Marshall

— A PRAYER —

Lord, Your Holy Word is a light unto the world; let me study it, trust it, and share it with all who cross my path. Let me discover You, Father, in the quiet moments of the day. And, in all that I say and do, help me to be a worthy witness as I share the Good News of Your perfect Son and Your perfect Word. Amen

HIS PATH

I will instruct you and teach you in the way you should go; I will guide you with My eye.

Psalm 32:8 NKJV

How will you respond to Christ's sacrifice? Will you take up His cross and follow Him (Luke 9:23), or will you choose another path? When you place your hopes squarely at the foot of the cross, when you place Jesus squarely at the center of your life, you will be blessed.

The 19th-century writer Hannah Whitall Smith observed, "The crucial question for each of us is this: What do you think of Jesus, and do you yet have a personal acquaintance with Him?" Indeed, the answer to that question determines the quality, the course, and the direction of our lives today and for all eternity.

Let us put down our old ways and pick up His cross. Let us walk the path that He walked.

It is God to whom and with whom we travel, while He is the End of our journey, He is also at every stopping place.

Elisabeth Elliot

— A PRAYER —

Dear Lord, this world is filled with so many temptations, distractions, and frustrations. When I turn my thoughts away from You and Your Word, I suffer. But when I turn my thoughts, my faith, and my prayers to You, I am safe. Direct my path, Father, and let me discover Your will for me today and every day that I live. Amen

SPIRITUAL TRAPS

Why are you cast down, O my soul? And why are you disquieted within me? Hope in God; for I shall yet praise Him, the help of my countenance and my God.

Psalm 42:11 NKJV

Pessimism and Christianity don't mix. Why? Because Christians have every reason to be optimistic about life here on earth and life eternal.

Sometimes, despite our trust in God, we may fall into the spiritual traps of worry, frustration, anxiety, or sheer exhaustion, and our hearts become heavy. What's needed is plenty of rest, a large dose of perspective, and God's healing touch, but not necessarily in that order.

Today, make this promise to yourself and keep it: vow to be a hope-filled Christian. Think optimistically about your life, your profession, and your future. Trust your hopes, not your fears. Take time to celebrate God's glorious creation. And then, when you've filled your heart with hope and gladness, share your optimism with others. They'll be better for it, and so will you. But not necessarily in that order.

We never get anywhere—nor do our conditions and circumstances change—when we look at the dark side of life.

Mrs. Charles E. Cowman

— A PRAYER —

Lord, I pray for an attitude that is Christlike. Whatever my situation, whether good or bad, happy or sad, let me respond with an attitude of optimism, faith, and love for You. Amen

PEACE AND PRAYER

Rejoice always! Pray constantly. Give thanks in everything, for this is God's will for you in Christ Jesus.

1 Thessalonians 5:16-18 HCSB

Do you seek a more peaceful life? Then you must lead a prayerful life. Do you have questions that you simply can't answer? Ask for the guidance of your Father in heaven. Do you sincerely seek the gift of everlasting love and eternal life? Accept the grace of God's only begotten Son.

When you weave the habit of prayer into the very fabric of your day, you invite God to become a partner in every aspect of your life. When you consult God on an constant basis, you avail yourself of His wisdom, His strength, and His love. And, because God answers prayers according to His perfect timetable, your petitions to Him will transform your family, your world, and yourself.

Today, turn everything over to your Creator in prayer. Instead of worrying about your next decision, decide to let God lead the way. Don't limit your prayers to meals or to bedtime. Pray constantly about things great and small. God is listening, and He wants to hear from you. Now.

Jesus practiced secret prayer and asked us to follow His example.

Catherine Marshall

— A PRAYER —

Dear Lord, make me a person whose constant prayers are pleasing to You. Let me come to You often with concerns both great and small. And, when You answer my prayers, Father, let me trust Your answers, today and forever. Amen

BEYOND PROCRASTINATION

Now, Lord, what do I wait for? My hope is in You.

Psalm 39:7 HCSB

The habit of procrastination takes a two-fold toll on its victims. First, important work goes unfinished; second (and more importantly), valuable energy is wasted in the process of putting off the things that remain undone. Procrastination results from an individual's short-sighted attempt to postpone temporary discomfort. What results is a senseless cycle of 1. delay, followed by 2. worry, followed by 3. a panicky and often futile attempt to "catch up." Procrastination is, at its core, a struggle against oneself; the only antidote is action.

Once you acquire the habit of doing what needs to be done when it needs to be done, you will avoid untold trouble, worry, and stress. So learn to defeat procrastination by paying less attention to your fears and more attention to your responsibilities. God has created a world that punishes procrastinators and rewards men and women who "do it now." In other words, life doesn't procrastinate. Neither should you.

Do the unpleasant work first and enjoy the rest of the day.

Marie T. Freeman

— A PRAYER —

Dear Lord, today is a new day. Help me tackle the important tasks immediately, even if those tasks are unpleasant. Don't let me put off until tomorrow what I should do today. Amen

A NEW SENSE OF JOY

Take my yoke upon you, and learn of me; for I am meek and lowly in heart: and ye shall find rest unto your souls. For my yoke is easy, and my burden is light.

Matthew 11:29-30 KJV

Even the most inspired Christian women can, from time to time, find themselves running on empty. The demands of daily life can drain us of our strength and rob us of the joy that is rightfully ours in Christ. Are you tired or troubled? Turn your heart toward God in prayer. Are you weak or worried? Take the time—or, more accurately, make the time—to delve deeply into God's Holy Word. Are you spiritually depleted? Call upon fellow believers to support you, and call upon Christ to renew your spirit and your life. When you do, you'll discover that the Creator of the universe stands always ready and always able to create a new sense of wonderment and joy in you.

But while relaxation is one thing, refreshment is another. We need to drink frequently and at length from God's fresh springs, to spend time in the Scripture, time in fellowship with Him, time worshiping Him.

Ruth Bell Graham

— A PRAYER —

Dear Lord, You can make all things new. I am a new creature in Christ Jesus, and when I fall short in my commitment, You can renew my effort and my enthusiasm. When I am weak or worried, restore my strength, Lord, for my own sake and for the sake of Your kingdom. Amen

SERVING OTHERS

Each one of us needs to look after the good of the people around us, asking ourselves, "How can I help?" That's exactly what Jesus did. He didn't make it easy for himself by avoiding people's troubles, but waded right in and helped out. "I took on the troubles of the troubled," is the way Scripture puts it.

Romans 15:2-3 MSG

We live in a world that glorifies power, prestige, fame, and money. But the words of Jesus teach us that the most esteemed men and women in this world are not the self-congratulatory leaders of society but are instead the humblest of servants.

Today, you may feel the temptation to build yourself up in the eyes of your neighbors. Resist that temptation. Instead, serve your neighbors quietly and without fanfare. Find a need and fill it . . . humbly. Lend a helping hand . . . anonymously. Share a word of kindness . . . with quiet sincerity. As you go about your daily activities, remember that the Savior of all humanity made Himself a servant, and we, as His followers, must do no less.

Through our service to others, God wants to influence our world for Him.

Vonette Bright

— A PRAYER —

Dear Lord, give me a servant's heart. When Jesus humbled Himself and became a servant, He also became an example for His followers. Make me a faithful steward of my gifts, and let me share with those in need. Amen

SEARCHING FOR STRENGTH

God is our refuge and strength, a very present help in trouble.

Psalm 46:1 NKJV

Where you go to find strength? The gym? The health food store? The espresso bar? There's a better source of strength, of course, and that source is God. He is a never-ending source of strength and courage if you call upon Him.

Are you an energized Christian? You should be. But if you're not, you must seek strength and renewal from the source that will never fail: that source, of course, is your Heavenly Father. And rest assured—when you sincerely petition Him, He will give you all the strength you need to live victoriously for Him.

Have you "tapped in" to the power of God? Have you turned your life and your heart over to Him, or are you muddling along under your own power? The answer to this question will determine the quality of your life here on earth and the destiny of your life throughout all eternity. So start tapping in—and remember that when it comes to strength, God is the Ultimate Source.

— A PRAYER —

Dear Heavenly Father, You are my strength and my protector. When I am troubled, You comfort me. When I am discouraged, You lift me up. When I am afraid, You deliver me. Let me turn to You, Lord, when I am weak. In times of adversity, let me trust Your plan, Lord, and whatever my circumstances, let me look to You for my strength and my salvation. Amen

BEYOND THE TEMPTATIONS

Then Jesus told him, "Go away, Satan! For it is written: You must worship the Lord your God, and you must serve Him only."

Matthew 4:10 HCSB

After fasting forty days and nights in the desert, Jesus was tempted by Satan. Christ used Scripture to rebuke the devil (Matthew 4:1-11). We must do likewise. The Holy Bible provides us with a perfect blueprint for righteous living. If we consult that blueprint daily and follow it carefully, we build our lives according to God's plan.

We live in a world that is brimming with opportunities to stray from God's will. Ours is a society filled with temptations, a place where it is all too easy to disobey God. We, like our Savior, must guard ourselves against these temptations. We do so, in part, through prayer and through a careful reading of God's Word.

The battle against Satan is ongoing. Be vigilant, and call upon your Heavenly Father to protect you. When you petition Him with a sincere heart, God will be your shield, now and forever.

— A PRAYER —

Lord, life is filled with temptations to stray from Your chosen path. Keep me mindful that the life I live and the words I speak bear testimony to my faith. Make me a faithful servant of Your Son, and lead me far from the temptations of this world. Make me a righteous woman, Lord, and let my actions point others to You. Amen

THE QUALITY OF OUR THOUGHTS

Let the words of my mouth and the meditation of my heart be acceptable in Your sight, O Lord, my strength and my Redeemer.

Psalm 19:14 NKJV

Do you pay careful attention to the quality of your thoughts? And are you careful to direct those thoughts toward topics that are uplifting, enlightening, and pleasing to God? If so, congratulations. But if you find that your thoughts are hijacked from time to time by the negativity that seems to have invaded our troubled world, you are not alone. Ours is a society that focuses on—and often glamorizes—the negative aspects of life, and that's unfortunate.

God intends that you experience joy and abundance. So, today and every day hereafter, celebrate the life that God has given you by focusing your thoughts upon those things that are worthy of praise (Philippians 4:8). And while you're at it, count your blessings instead of your hardships. When you do, you'll undoubtedly offer words of thanks to your Heavenly Father for gifts that are simply too numerous to count.

— A PRAYER —

Dear Lord, let my thoughts and my actions demonstrate the difference that Your Son has made in my life. Let me live righteously, and let my actions be consistent with my beliefs. Let every step that I take reflect Your truth, and let me live a life that is worthy of Your Son. Amen

THE MIRACLE WORKER

Is anything impossible for the Lord?

Genesis 18:14 HCSB

God is a miracle worker. Throughout history He has intervened in the course of human events in ways that cannot be explained by science or human rationale. And He's still doing so today.

God's miracles are not limited to special occasions, nor are they witnessed by a select few. God is crafting His wonders all around us: the miracle of the birth of a new baby; the miracle of a world renewing itself with every sunrise; the miracle of lives transformed by God's love and grace. Each day, God's handiwork is evident for all to see and experience.

Today, seize the opportunity to inspect God's hand at work. His miracles come in a variety of shapes and sizes, so keep your eyes and your heart open. Be watchful, and you'll soon be amazed.

Are you looking for a miracle? If you keep your eyes wide open and trust in God, you won't have to look very far.

Marie T. Freeman

— A PRAYER —

Heavenly Father, Your infinite power is beyond human understanding. With You, Lord, nothing is impossible. Keep me always mindful of Your power, and let me share the glorious message of Your miracles. When I lose hope, give me faith; when others lose hope, let me tell them of Your glory and Your works. Today, Lord, let me expect the miraculous, let me praise You, and let me give thanks for Your miracles. Amen

HIS PLAN

The steps of the Godly are directed by the Lord. He delights in every detail of their lives. Though they stumble, they will not fall, for the Lord holds them by the hand.

Psalm 37:23-24 NLT

God has a plan for our world and for our lives—He does not do things by accident. God is willful and intentional, but we cannot always understand His purposes. Why? Because we are mortal beings with limited understanding. And although we cannot fully comprehend the will of God, we should always trust His will.

As this day unfolds, seek God's will and obey His Word. When you entrust your life to Him without reservation, He will give you the courage to meet any challenge, the strength to endure any trial, and the wisdom to live in His righteousness and in His peace.

The only safe place is in the center of God's will. It is not only the safest place. It is also the most rewarding and the most satisfying place to be.

Gigi Graham Tchividjian

— A PRAYER —

Dear Lord, You are the Creator of the universe, and I know that Your plan for my life is grander than I can imagine. Let Your purposes be my purposes. Let Your will be my will. When I am confused, give me clarity. When I am worried, give me strength. Let me be Your faithful servant, Lord, always seeking Your guidance and Your will for my life. Let me live this day and every day according to Your commandments and with the assurance of Your promises, in Jesus' name I pray. Amen

SEEKING HIS BLESSINGS

Commit everything you do to the Lord. Trust him, and he will help you.

Psalm 37:5 NLT

When our dreams come true and our plans prove successful, we find it easy to thank our Creator and easy to trust His divine providence. But in times of sorrow or hardship, we may find ourselves questioning God's plans for our lives.

On occasion, you will confront circumstances that trouble you to the very core of your soul. It is during these difficult days that you must find the wisdom and the courage to trust your Heavenly Father despite your circumstances.

Are you a woman who seeks God's blessings for yourself and your family? Then trust Him. Trust Him with your relationships. Trust Him with your priorities. Follow His commandments and pray for His guidance. Trust the Father day by day, moment by moment—in good times and in trying times. Then, wait patiently for God's revelations, and prepare yourself for the abundance and peace that will most certainly be yours when you do.

To know God as He really is—in His essential nature and character—is to arrive at a citadel of peace that circumstances may storm, but can never capture.

Catherine Marshall

— A PRAYER —

Today, Lord, I will trust You and seek Your will for my life. You have a plan for me, Father. Let me discover it and live it, knowing that when I trust in You, I am eternally blessed. Amen

SPIRITUAL ABUNDANCE

These things I have spoken to you, that My joy may remain in you, and that your joy may be full.

John 15:11 NKJV

God does not promise us abundance. He promises that we "might have life" and that we "might have it more abundantly" if we accept His grace, His blessings, and His Son (John 10:10). When we commit our hearts and our days to the One who created us, we experience spiritual abundance through the grace and sacrifice of His Son, Jesus. But, when we focus our thoughts and energies, not upon God's perfect will for our lives, but instead upon our own unending assortments of earthly needs and desires, we inevitably forfeit the spiritual abundance that might otherwise be ours.

Today and every day, seek God's will for your life and follow it. Today, turn your worries and your concerns over to your Heavenly Father. Today, seek God's wisdom, follow His commandments, trust His judgment, and honor His Son. When you do, spiritual abundance will be yours, not just for this day, but for all eternity.

— A PRAYER —

Dear Lord, thank You for the joyful, abundant life that is mine through Christ Jesus. Guide me according to Your will, and help me become a woman whose life is a worthy example to others. Give me courage, Lord, to claim the spiritual riches that You have promised, and show me Your plan for my life, today and forever. Amen

WHEN YOUR FAITH IS TESTED

Blessed be the God and Father of our Lord Jesus Christ, the Father of mercies and the God of all comfort. He comforts us in all our affliction, so that we may be able to comfort those who are in any kind of affliction, through the comfort we ourselves receive from God.

2 Corinthians 1:3-4 HCSB

When the sun is shining and all is well, it is easy to have faith. But, when life takes an unexpected turn for the worse, as it will from time to time, your faith will be tested. In times of trouble and doubt, God remains faithful to you—and you must retain faith in God.

Social activist Jane Addams observed, "You do not know what life means when all the difficulties are removed. It's like eating a sweet dessert the first thing in the morning." And so it is with your own life.

So the next time you spot storm clouds on the horizon, remind yourself that every difficult day must come to an end . . . and when tough times are tough, tough women (like you) are tougher.

While chastening is always difficult, if we look to God for the lesson we should learn, we will see spiritual fruit.

Vonette Bright

— A PRAYER —

Dear Lord, when I face the inevitable disappointments of life, give me perspective and faith. When I am discouraged, give me the strength to trust Your promises and follow Your will. Then, when I have done my best, Father, let me live with the assurance that You are firmly in control, and that Your love endures forever. Amen

WHAT'S YOUR ATTITUDE?

Set your mind on the things above, not on the things that are on earth.

Colossians 3:2 NASB

What's your attitude today? Are you fearful, angry, bored, or worried? Are you worried more about pleasing your friends than about pleasing your God? Are you confused, bitter, or pessimistic? If so, God wants to have a little talk with you.

God created you in His own image, and He wants you to experience joy and abundance. But, God will not force His joy upon you; you must claim it for yourself. So today, and every day thereafter, celebrate this life that God has given you. Think optimistically about yourself and your future. Give thanks to the One who has given you everything, and trust in your heart that He wants to give you so much more.

The difference between winning and losing is how we choose to react to disappointment.

Barbara Johnson

— A PRAYER —

Lord, I have so many reasons to be thankful; let my attitude be a reflection of the many blessings I have received. Make me a woman whose thoughts are Christlike and whose hopes are worthy of the One who has given me so much. Amen

CELEBRATING HIS GIFTS

Be glad and rejoice, because your reward is great in heaven.

Matthew 5:12 HCSB

Do you celebrate the gifts God has given you? Do you pray without ceasing? Do you rejoice in the beauty of God's glorious creation? You should. But perhaps, as a busy woman living in a demanding world, you have been slow to count your gifts and even slower to give thanks to the Giver.

As God's children, we are all blessed beyond measure, and we should celebrate His blessings every day that we live. The gifts we receive from God are multiplied when we share them with others. Today is a non-renewable resource—once it's gone, it's gone forever. Our responsibility—as believers—is to give thanks for God's gifts and then to use them in the service of God's will and in the service of His people.

God has blessed us beyond measure, and we owe Him everything, including our praise. And let us remember that for those of us who have been saved by God's only begotten Son, every day is a cause for celebration.

— A PRAYER —

Lord, Your desire is that I be complete in Your joy. Joy begets celebration. Today, I celebrate the life and the work You have given me, and I celebrate the lives of my friends and family. Thank You, Father, for Your love, for Your blessings, and for Your joy. Let me treasure Your gifts and share them this day and forever. Amen

CHOOSING TO WALK IN HIS FOOTSTEPS

But seek first the kingdom of God and His righteousness, and all these things shall be added to you.

Matthew 6:33 NKJV

Because we are creatures of free will, we make choices—lots of them. When we make choices that are pleasing to our Heavenly Father, we are blessed. When we make choices that cause us to walk in the footsteps of God's Son, we enjoy the abundance that Christ has promised to those who follow Him. But when we make choices that are displeasing to God, we sow seeds that have the potential to bring forth a bitter harvest.

Today, as you encounter the challenges of everyday living, you will make hundreds of choices. Choose wisely. Make your thoughts and your actions pleasing to God. And remember: every choice that is displeasing to Him is the wrong choice—no exceptions.

If you are going to be a person who is committed to the Word of God, you will have to learn to be led by the Spirit and not by your emotions.

Joyce Meyer

— A PRAYER —

Lord, help me to make choices that are pleasing to You. Help me to be honest, patient, and kind. And above all, help me to follow the teachings of Jesus, not just today, but every day. Amen

WHEN SOLUTIONS AREN'T EASY

For God has not given us a spirit of fearfulness, but one of power, love, and sound judgment.

2 Timothy 1:7 HCSB

Sometimes, we all face problems that defy easy solutions. If you find yourself facing a difficult decision, here's a simple formula for making the right choice: let God decide. Instead of fretting about your future, pray about it.

When you consult your Heavenly Father early and often, you'll soon discover that the quiet moments you spend with God can be very helpful. Many times, God will quietly lead you along a path of His choosing, a path that is right for you.

So the next time you arrive at one of life's inevitable crossroads, take a moment or two to bow your head and have a chat with the Ultimate Advisor. When you do, you'll never stay lost for long.

There may be no trumpet sound or loud applause when we make a right decision, just a calm sense of resolution and peace.

Gloria Gaither

— A PRAYER —

Lord, help me to make decisions that are pleasing to You. Help me to be honest, patient, thoughtful, and obedient. And above all, help me to follow the teachings of Jesus, not just today, but every day. Amen

A BEACON OF ENCOURAGEMENT

Be of good comfort, be of one mind, live in peace; and the God of love and peace will be with you.

2 Corinthians 13:11 NKJV

One of the reasons that God placed you here on earth is so that you might become a beacon of encouragement to the world. As a faithful follower of the One from Galilee, you have every reason to be hopeful, and you have every reason to share your hopes with others. When you do, you will discover that hope, like other human emotions, is contagious.

As a follower of Christ, you are instructed to choose your words carefully so as to build others up through wholesome, honest encouragement (Ephesians 4:29). So look for the good in others and celebrate the good that you find. As the old saying goes, "When someone does something good, applaud—you'll make two people happy."

A hug is the ideal gift . . . one size fits all.

Anonymous

— A PRAYER —

Dear Lord, You have loved me eternally, and cared for me faithfully. Just as You have lifted me up, Lord, let me also lift up others in a spirit of encouragement, optimism, and hope. Today and every day, let me share Your healing message so that I might encourage others. And, Lord, may the glory be Yours. Amen

FAITH AND WHOLENESS

Now the just shall live by faith.

Hebrews 10:38 NKJV

A suffering woman sought healing in an unusual way: she simply touched the hem of Jesus' garment. When she did, Jesus turned and said, "Daughter, be of good comfort; thy faith hath made thee whole" (Matthew 9:22 KJV). We, too, can be made whole when we place our faith completely and unwaveringly in the person of Jesus Christ.

Concentration camp survivor Corrie ten Boom wrote, "There is no pit so deep that God's love is not deeper still." Christians take note: Genuine faith in God means faith in all circumstances, happy or sad, joyful or tragic.

Your Heavenly Father is standing at the door of your heart. If you reach out to Him in faith, He will give you peace and heal your broken spirit. Be content to touch even the smallest fragment of the Master's garment, and He will make you whole.

Some people think that I have great faith, but that is not true. I do not have great faith—I have faith in a great God!

Corrie ten Boom

— A PRAYER —

Father, in the dark moments of my life, help me to remember that You are always near and that You can overcome any challenge. Keep me mindful of Your love and Your power, so that I may live courageously and faithfully today and every day. Amen

HOW OFTEN MUST WE FORGIVE?

Then Peter came to Him and said, "Lord, how often shall my brother sin against me, and I forgive him? Up to seven times?" Jesus said to him, "I do not say to you, up to seven times, but up to seventy times seven."

Matthew 18:21-22 NKJV

How often must we forgive family members and friends? More times than we can count. Our children are precious but imperfect; so are our spouses and our friends. We must, on occasion, forgive those who have injured us; to do otherwise is to disobey God.

Are you easily frustrated by the inevitable imperfections of others? Are you a prisoner of bitterness and regret? If so, perhaps you need a refresher course in the art of forgiveness.

If there exists even one person, alive or dead, whom you have not forgiven (and that includes yourself), follow God's commandment and His will for your life: forgive. Bitterness, anger, and regret are not part of God's plan for your life. Forgiveness is.

As you forgive others, winter will soon make way for springtime as fresh joy pushes up through the soil of your heart.

Barbara Johnson

— A PRAYER —

Dear Lord, Your ability to forgive is limitless; mine is not. Keep me mindful of Your commandment to forgive others—and to keep forgiving them—just as I have been forgiven by You. Amen

WHO RULES?

You shall have no other gods before Me.

Exodus 20:3 NKJV

Who rules your heart? Is it God, or is it something else? Do you give God your firstfruits or your last? Have you given Christ your heart, your soul, your talents, your time, and your testimony, or have you given Him little more than a few hours each Sunday morning?

In the book of Exodus, God warns that we should place no gods before Him. Yet all too often, we place our Lord in second, third, or fourth place as we worship the gods of pride, greed, power, or lust. When we unwittingly place possessions or relationships above our love for the Creator, we must seek His forgiveness and repent from our sins.

Does God rule your heart? Make certain that the honest answer to this question is a resounding yes. In the life of every righteous believer, God comes first. And that's precisely the place that He deserves in your heart.

— A PRAYER —

Dear Lord, I will have no other gods before You. You sent Your Son Jesus to die on a cross for my sins. Jesus endured indignity, suffering, and death so that I might live. Because He lives, I, too, have Your promise of eternal life. Let me share this Good News, Lord, with a world that so desperately needs Your healing hand and the salvation of Your Son. Amen

HOW MUCH DOES GOD LOVE YOU?

For God loved the world in this way: He gave His only Son, so that everyone who believes in Him will not perish but have eternal life.

John 3:16 HCSB

How much does God love you? To answer that question, you need only to look at the cross. God's love for you is so great that He sent His only Son to this earth to die for your sins and to offer you the priceless gift of eternal life.

You must decide whether or not to accept God's gift. Will you ignore it or embrace it? Will you return it or neglect it? Will you invite Christ to dwell in the center of your heart, or will you relegate Him to a position of lesser importance? The decision is yours, and so are the consequences. So choose wisely . . . and choose today.

Love is not something God does; love is something God is.

Beth Moore

— A PRAYER —

Dear Lord, You have given me so much more than I deserve. You have blessed me with Your love and Your mercy. Help me be merciful toward others, Father, just as You have been merciful toward me, and let me share Your love with a world that desperately needs Your mercy and Your Son. Amen

HIS SURPRISING PLANS

But as it is written: What no eye has seen and no ear has heard, and what has never come into a man's heart, is what God has prepared for those who love Him.

1 Corinthians 2:9 HCSB

God has big plans for your life, wonderful, surprising plans . . . but He won't force those plans upon you. To the contrary, He has given you free will, the ability to make decisions on your own. Now, it's up to you to make those decisions wisely.

If you seek to live in accordance with God's plan for your life, you will study His Word, you will be attentive to His instructions, and you will be watchful for His signs. You will associate with fellow believers who, by their words and actions, will encourage your spiritual growth. You will assiduously avoid those two terrible temptations: the temptation to sin and the temptation to squander time. And finally, you will listen carefully, even reverently, to the conscience that God has placed in your heart.

God intends to use you in wonderful, unexpected ways if you let Him. Let Him. When you do, you'll be thoroughly surprised by the creativity and the beauty of His plans.

With God, it's never "Plan B" or "second best." It's always "Plan A." And, if we let Him, He'll make something beautiful of our lives.

Gloria Gaither

— A PRAYER —

Lord, You have a plan for my life. Let me discover it and live it. Today, I will seek Your will, knowing that when I trust in You, dear Father, I am eternally blessed. Amen

HOPE AND HAPPINESS

Blessed is he whose help is the God of Jacob, whose hope is in the LORD his God, the Maker of heaven and earth, the sea, and everything in them—the LORD, who remains faithful forever.

Psalm 146:5-6 NIV

Hope and happiness are traveling companions. And if you're a Christian, you have every reason to be hopeful. After all, God is good; His love endures; and He has offered you the priceless gift of eternal life. But sometimes, in life's darker moments, you may lose sight of these blessings, and when you do, it's easy to lose hope.

Are you a hope-filled woman? You should be. God has promised you peace, joy, and eternal life. And, of course, God keeps His promises today, tomorrow, and forever, amen!

Make God's will the focus of your life day by day. If you seek to please Him and Him alone, you'll find yourself satisfied with life.

Kay Arthur

— A PRAYER —

Dear Lord, You are my strength and my joy. I will rejoice in the day that You have made, and I will give thanks for the countless blessings that You have given me. Let me be a joyful Christian, Father, as I share the Good News of Your Son, and let me praise You for all the marvelous things You have done. Amen

THE WISDOM TO BE HUMBLE

Who is wise and understanding among you? Let him show by good conduct that his works are done in the meekness of wisdom.

James 3:13 NKJV

Humility is not, in most cases, a naturally occurring human trait. Most of us, it seems, are more than willing to overestimate our own accomplishments. We are tempted to say, "Look how wonderful I am!" hoping all the while that the world will agree with our own self-appraisals. But those of us who fall prey to the sin of pride should beware—God is definitely not impressed by our prideful proclamations.

God honors humility . . . and He rewards those who humbly serve Him. So if you've acquired the wisdom to be humble, then you are to be congratulated. But if you've not yet overcome the tendency to overestimate your own accomplishments, then God still has some important (and perhaps painful) lessons to teach you—lessons about humility that you still need to learn.

If you know who you are in Christ, your personal ego is not an issue.

Beth Moore

— A PRAYER —

Lord, make me a woman with a humble heart. Keep me mindful, Dear God, that all my gifts come from You. Let me grow beyond my need for earthly praise, Lord, and when I seek approval, let me look only to You. Amen

THE MEDICINE OF LAUGHTER

A joyful heart is good medicine, but a broken spirit dries up the bones.

Proverbs 17:22 HCSB

Laughter is medicine for the soul, but sometimes, amid the stresses of the day, we forget to take our medicine. Instead of viewing our world with a mixture of optimism and humor, we allow worries and distractions to rob us of the joy that God intends for our lives.

So the next time you find yourself dwelling upon the negatives of life, refocus your attention to things positive. The next time you find yourself falling prey to the blight of pessimism, stop yourself and turn your thoughts around. And, if you see your glass as "half-empty," rest assured that your spiritual vision is impaired.

Today, as you go about your daily activities, approach life with a smile on your lips and hope in your heart. And laugh every chance you get. After all, God created laughter for a reason . . . and Father indeed knows best. So laugh!

Laughter dulls the sharpest pain and flattens out the greatest stress. To share it is to give a gift of health.

Barbara Johnson

— A PRAYER —

Lord, when I begin to take myself or my life too seriously, let me laugh. When I rush from place to place, slow me down, Lord, and let me laugh. Put a smile on my face, Dear Lord, and let me share that smile with all who cross my path . . . and let me laugh. Amen

OBEDIENCE MATTERS

Follow the whole instruction the Lord your God has commanded you, so that you may live, prosper, and have a long life in the land you will possess.

Deuteronomy 5:33 HCSB

Are you living outside the commandments of God? If so, you are inviting untold suffering into your own life and into the lives of your loved ones. God's commandments are not "suggestions," and they are not "helpful hints." They are, instead, immutable laws which, if followed, lead to repentance, salvation, and abundance. But if you disobey the commandments of our Heavenly Father or His Son, you will most surely reap a harvest of bitterness and regret.

Would you like a time-tested formula for successful living? Here is a formula that is proven and true: Study God's Word and obey it. Does this sound too simple? Perhaps it is simple, but it is also the only way to reap the marvelous riches that God has in store for you.

There is sharp necessity for giving Christ absolute obedience. The devil bids for our complete self-will. To whatever extent we give this self-will the right to be master over our lives, we are, to an extent, giving Satan a toehold.

Catherine Marshall

— A PRAYER —

Dear Lord, today, I will choose to please You and only You. I will obey Your commandments, and I will praise You for Your gifts, for Your love, and for Your Son. Amen

EXPECTING GOD'S BLESSINGS

My cup runs over. Surely goodness and mercy shall follow me all the days of my life; and I will dwell in the house of the Lord forever.

Psalm 23:5-6 NKJV

As you look at the landscape of your life, do you see opportunities, possibilities, and blessings, or do you focus, instead, upon the more negative scenery? Do you spend more time counting your blessings or your misfortunes? If you've acquired the unfortunate habit of focusing too intently upon the negative aspects of life, then your spiritual vision is in need of correction.

Today is yet another gift from God, and it presents yet another opportunity to thank Him for His gifts . . . or not. And if you're wise, you'll give thanks early and often.

The way that you choose to view the scenery around you will have a profound impact on the quality, the tone, and the direction of your life. The more you focus on the beauty that surrounds you, the more beautiful your own life becomes.

Don't miss the beautiful colors of the rainbow while you're looking for the pot of gold at the end of it!

Barbara Johnson

— A PRAYER —

Heavenly Father, You love me, You care for me, and You protect me. You have given me the priceless gift of eternal life through the sacrifice that Christ made on the cross at Calvary. Because of You, Father, and because of Your Son, I can live each day with celebration in my heart and praise on my lips. Let me always be thankful, and let me share the Good News of Jesus as I turn my thoughts to You this day and always. Amen

GOD SEES

For am I now trying to win the favor of people, or God? Or am I striving to please people? If I were still trying to please people, I would not be a slave of Christ.

Galatians 1:10 HCSB

The world sees you as you appear to be; God sees you as you really are . . . He sees your heart, and He understands your intentions. The opinions of others should be relatively unimportant to you; however, God's view of you—His understanding of your actions, your thoughts, and your motivations—should be vitally important.

Few things in life are more futile than "keeping up appearances" for the sake of neighbors. What is important, of course, is pleasing your Father in heaven. You please Him when your intentions are pure and your actions are just.

Are you trying to keep up with the Joneses? Don't even try . . . you've got better things to do—far better things—like pleasing your Father in heaven.

It is comfortable to know that we are responsible to God and not to man. It is a small matter to be judged of man's judgement.

Lottie Moon

— A PRAYER —

Dear Lord, today I will worry less about pleasing other people and more about pleasing You. I will honor You with my thoughts, my actions, and my prayers. And I will worship You, Father, with thanksgiving in my heart, this day and forever. Amen

YOUR POTENTIAL

Have faith in the Lord your God, and you will stand strong. Have faith in his prophets, and you will succeed.

2 Chronicles 20:20 NCV

Do you expect your future to be bright? Are you willing to dream king-sized dreams . . . and are you willing to work diligently to make those dreams happen? Hopefully so—after all, God promises that we can do "all things" through Him. Yet most of us live far below our potential. We take half measures; we dream small dreams; we waste precious time and energy on the distractions of the world. But God has other plans for us.

Warren Wiersbe observed, "You were born with tremendous potential. When you were born again through faith in Jesus Christ, God added spiritual gifts to your natural talents." These words apply to you. You possess great potential, potential that you must use or forfeit. And the time to fulfill that potential is now.

If all things are possible with God, then all things are possible to him who believes in him.

Corrie ten Boom

— A PRAYER —

Dear Lord, today and every day I will praise You. I will come to You with hope in my heart and words of gratitude on my lips. Let me follow in the footsteps of Your Son, and let my thoughts, my prayers, my words, and my deeds praise You now and forever. Amen

TRUSTING HIS ANSWERS

Trust in the Lord with all your heart, and do not rely on your own understanding; think about Him in all your ways, and He will guide you on the right paths.

Proverbs 3:5-6 HCSB

God answers our prayers. What God does not do is this: He does not always answer our prayers as soon as we might like, and He does not always answer our prayers by saying "Yes." God isn't an order-taker, and He's not some sort of cosmic vending machine. Sometimes—even when we want something very badly—our loving Heavenly Father responds to our requests by saying "No," and we must accept His answer, even if we don't understand it.

God answers prayers not only according to our wishes but also according to His master plan. We cannot know that plan, but we can know the Planner . . . and we must trust His wisdom, His righteousness, and His love. Always.

Often I have made a request of God with earnest pleadings even backed up with Scripture, only to have Him say "No" because He had something better in store.

Ruth Bell Graham

— A PRAYER —

Dear Lord, I will be a woman of prayer. I will take everything to You in prayer, and when I do, I will trust Your answers. Amen

QUIET TIME

In quietness and confidence shall be your strength.

Isaiah 30:15 NKJV

We live in a noisy world, a world filled with distractions, frustrations, and complications. But if we allow the distractions of a clamorous world to separate us from God's peace, we do ourselves a profound disservice.

If we seek to maintain righteous minds and compassionate hearts, we must take time each day for prayer and for meditation.

Are you one of those busy women who rush through the day with scarcely a single moment for quiet contemplation and prayer? If so, it's time to reorder your priorities. Nothing is more important than the time you spend with your Savior. So be still and claim the inner peace that is your spiritual birthright: the peace of Jesus Christ. It is offered freely; it has been paid for in full; it is yours for the asking. So ask. And then share.

Commitment to His lordship on Easter, at revivals, or even every Sunday is not enough. We must choose this day—and every day—whom we will serve. This deliberate act of the will is the inevitable choice between habitual fellowship and habitual failure.

Beth Moore

— A PRAYER —

Lord, Your Holy Word is a light unto the world; let me study it, trust it, and share it with all who cross my path. Let me discover You, Father, in the quiet moments of the day. And, in all that I say and do, help me to be a worthy witness as I share the Good News of Your perfect Son and Your perfect Word. Amen

YOUR OWN WORST CRITIC?

But godliness with contentment is a great gain.

1 Timothy 6:6 HCSB

Are you your own worst critic? If so, it's time to become a little more understanding of the woman you see whenever you look into the mirror.

Millions of words have been written about various ways to improve self-image and increase self-esteem. Yet, maintaining a healthy self-image is, to a surprising extent, a matter of doing three things: 1. behaving ourselves 2. thinking healthy thoughts 3. finding a purpose for your life that pleases your Creator and yourself.

The Bible affirms the importance of self-acceptance by teaching Christians to love others as they love themselves (Matthew 22:37-40). God accepts us just as we are. And, if He accepts us—faults and all—then who are we to believe otherwise?

Being loved by Him whose opinion matters most gives us the security to risk loving, too—even loving ourselves.

Gloria Gaither

— A PRAYER —

Dear Lord, keep me mindful that I am a special person, created by You, loved by You, and saved by Your Son. Amen

SPIRITUAL GIFTS

Go after a life of love as if your life depended on it—because it does. Give yourselves to the gifts God gives you. Most of all, try to proclaim his truth.

1 Corinthians 14:1 MSG

All of us have spiritual gifts, and if we're wise, we continue to refine those gifts every day. The journey toward spiritual maturity lasts a lifetime. As Christians, we can and should continue to grow in the love and the knowledge of our Savior as long as we live. When we cease to grow, either emotionally or spiritually, we do ourselves a profound disservice. But, if we study God's Word, if we obey His commandments, and if we live in the center of His will, we will not be "stagnant" believers; we will, instead, be growing Christians . . . and that's exactly what God intends for us to be.

Life is a series of decisions. Each day, we make decisions that can, and should, bring us closer to God. When we live according to the principles contained in God's Holy Word, we embark upon a journey of spiritual maturity that results in life abundant and life eternal.

— A PRAYER —

Dear Lord, Your richest gifts are spiritual, not material. The Holy Scripture tells me that You are at work in my life, continuing to help me grow and to mature in the faith. Show me Your wisdom, Father, and let me live according to Your Word and Your will. Amen

NO SHORTCUTS

Do not lack diligence; be fervent in spirit; serve the Lord.

Romans 12:11 HCSB

The world often tempts us with instant gratification: get rich—today; lose weight—today; have everything you want—today. Yet life's experiences and God's Word tell us that the best things in life require heaping helpings of both time and work.

It has been said, quite correctly, that there are no shortcuts to any place worth going. For believers, it's important to remember that hard work is not simply a proven way to get ahead, it's also part of God's plan for His children.

So do yourself this favor: don't look for shortcuts . . . because there aren't any.

Ultimately things work out best for those who make the best of the way things work out.

Barbara Johnson

— A PRAYER —

Lord, I know that You desire a bountiful harvest for all Your children. But, You have instructed us that we must sow before we reap, not after. Help me, Lord, to sow the seeds of Your abundance everywhere I go. Let me be diligent in all my undertakings and give me patience to wait for Your harvest. In time, Lord, let me reap the harvest that is found in Your will for my life. Amen

ACCEPTING HIS WILL

Should we take only good things from God and not trouble?

Job 2:10 NCV

All of us must, from time to time, endure days filled with suffering and pain. And as human beings with limited understanding, we can never fully understand the plans of our Father in heaven. But as believers in a benevolent God, we must always trust Him.

When Jesus went to the Mount of Olives, He poured out His heart to God (Luke 22). Jesus knew of the agony that He was destined to endure, but He also knew that God's will must be done.

We, like our Savior, face trials that bring fear and trembling to the very depths of our souls, but like Christ, we, too, must seek God's will, not our own. When we learn to accept God's will without reservation, we experience the peace that He offers to wise believers who trust Him completely.

Part of waiting upon the Lord is telling God that you want only what He wants—whatever it is.

Kay Arthur

— A PRAYER —

Lord, give me the wisdom to accept Your will. When I am confused, give me maturity. When I am worried, give me perspective. Let me be Your faithful servant, Father, always seeking Your guidance and Your will for my life. Amen

THE APPROPRIATE RESPONSE TO EVIL

So rid yourselves of all wickedness, all deceit, hypocrisy, envy, and all slander.

1 Peter 2:1 HCSB

Sometimes, anger can be a good thing. In the 21st chapter of Matthew, we are told how Christ responded when He confronted the evildoings of those who had invaded His Father's house of worship: "Then Jesus went into the temple of God and drove out all those who bought and sold in the temple, and overturned the tables of the money changers and the seats of those who sold doves. And He said to them, 'It is written, "My house shall be called a house of prayer," but you have made it a "den of thieves"'" (12-13 NKJV). Thus Jesus demonstrated that righteous indignation is an appropriate response to evil.

When you come face-to-face with the devil's handiwork, don't be satisfied to remain safely on the sidelines. Instead, follow in the footsteps of your Savior. Jesus never compromised with evil, and neither should you.

Of two evils, choose neither.

C. H. Spurgeon

— A PRAYER —

Lord, give me the wisdom to know when anger is appropriate. Give me the courage to fight injustice, the wisdom to avoid temptation, and the perseverance to follow in the footsteps of Your Son every day of my life. Amen

TO STUDY OR NOT TO STUDY?

Man shall not live by bread alone, but by every word that proceeds from the mouth of God.

Matthew 4:4 NKJV

If you really want to know God, you should read the book He wrote. It's called the Bible, and it is one of the most important tools that God uses to direct your steps and transform your life.

As you seek to build a deeper relationship with your Creator, you must decide whether God's Word will be a bright spotlight that guides your path every day or a tiny nightlight that occasionally flickers in the dark. The decision to study the Bible—or not—is yours and yours alone. But make no mistake: the way that you choose to use your Bible will have a profound impact on you and your loved ones.

Your Bible is waiting patiently on your bookshelf . . . now, what are you going to do about it?

Sin will keep you from the Bible but the Bible can keep you from sin.

Anonymous

— A PRAYER —

Heavenly Father, You have given me the gift of Your Holy Word. Let me study it, and let me live according to its principles. Let me read Your Word, meditate upon it, and share its joyous message with the world, today and every day. Amen

HE REWARDS INTEGRITY

The integrity of the upright will guide them, but the perversity of the unfaithful will destroy them.

Proverbs 11:3 NKJV

The Bible makes it clear that God rewards integrity just as surely as He punishes duplicity. So, if we seek to earn the kind of lasting rewards that God bestows upon those who obey His commandments, we must make honesty the hallmark of our dealings with others.

Character is built slowly over a lifetime. Character is the sum of every right decision, every honest word, every noble thought, and every heartfelt prayer. It is built upon a foundation of industry, generosity, and humility. Character is a precious thing—difficult to build but easy to tear down. As believers in Christ, we must seek to live each day with discipline, honesty, and faith. When we do, integrity becomes a habit. And God smiles.

Often, our character is at greater risk in prosperity than in adversity.

Beth Moore

— A PRAYER —

Lord, You are my Father in heaven. You search my heart and know me far better than I know myself. May I be Your worthy servant, and may I live according to Your commandments. Let me be a person of integrity, Lord, and let my words and deeds be a testimony to You, today and always. Amen

THE NEW YOU

Therefore if anyone is in Christ, he is a new creature; the old things passed away; behold, new things have come.

2 Corinthians 5:17 HCSB

Think, for a moment, about the "old" you, the person you were before you invited Christ to reign over your heart. Now, think about the "new" you, the person you have become since then. Is there a difference between the "old" you and the "new and improved" version? There should be! And that difference should be noticeable not only to you but also to others.

The Bible clearly teaches that when we welcome Christ into our hearts, we become new creations through Him. Our challenge, of course, is to behave ourselves like new creations. When we do, God fills our hearts, He blesses our endeavors, and transforms our lives . . . forever.

If you are God's child, you are no longer bound to your past or to what you were. You are a brand new creature in Christ Jesus.

Kay Arthur

— A PRAYER —

Lord, when I accepted Jesus as my personal Savior, You changed me forever and made me whole. Let me share Your Son's message with my friends, with my family, and with the world. You are a God of love, redemption, conversion, and salvation. I will praise You today and forever. Amen

BIG DREAMS

With God's power working in us, God can do much, much more than anything we can ask or imagine.

Ephesians 3:20 NCV

She was born in rural Mississippi and lived with her grandmother in a house that had no indoor plumbing. She made it to college in Nashville, where she got her start in television. Over time, she moved to the top of her profession, and today, her show, *Oprah*, is an unparalleled hit.

When questioned about her journey to the top, Oprah said, "God can dream a bigger dream than we can dream for ourselves." She was right. So try Oprah's formula: increase the size of your dreams. Because the Good Lord's plan for each of us is big, very big. But it's up to us to accept the part, to step up on stage, and to perform.

Allow your dreams a place in your prayers and plans. God-given dreams can help you move into the future He is preparing for you.

Barbara Johnson

— A PRAYER —

Dear Lord, give me the courage to dream and the faithfulness to trust in Your perfect plan. When I am worried or weary, give me strength for today and hope for tomorrow. Keep me mindful of Your healing power, Your infinite love, and Your eternal salvation. Amen

FELLOWSHIP AND HOPE

I want their hearts to be encouraged and joined together in love, so that they may have all the riches of assured understanding, and have the knowledge of God's mystery—Christ.

Colossians 2:2 HCSB

Every believer—including you—needs to be part of a community of faith. Your association with fellow Christians should be uplifting, enlightening, encouraging, and consistent.

Are you an active member of your fellowship? Are you a builder of bridges inside the four walls of your church and outside it? Do you contribute to God's glory by contributing your time and your talents to a close-knit band of hope-filled believers? Hopefully so. The fellowship of believers is intended to be a powerful tool for spreading God's Good News and uplifting His children. And God intends for you to be a fully contributing member of that fellowship. Your intentions should be the same.

In God's economy you will be hard-pressed to find many examples of successful "Lone Rangers."

Luci Swindoll

— A PRAYER —

Heavenly Father, You have given me a community of supporters called the church. Let our fellowship be a reflection of the love we feel for each other and the love we feel for You. Amen

FORGIVENESS AND SPIRITUAL GROWTH

He who says he is in the light, and hates his brother, is in darkness until now.

1 John 2:9 NKJV

Forgiveness is an exercise in spiritual growth: the more we forgive, the more we grow. Conversely, bitterness makes spiritual growth impossible: when our hearts are filled with resentment and anger, there is no room left for love.

As Christians, we can and should continue to grow in the love and the knowledge of our Savior as long as we live. When we cease to grow, either emotionally or spiritually, we do ourselves and our loved ones a profound disservice. But, if we study God's Word, if we obey His commandments, and if we live in the center of His will, we will not be "stagnant" believers; we will, instead, be growing Christians . . . and that's exactly what God wants for our lives.

In those quiet moments when we open our hearts to God, the Creator who made us keeps remaking us. He gives us direction, perspective, wisdom, and courage. And the appropriate moment to accept His spiritual gifts is always this one.

— A PRAYER —

Lord, when it is difficult to forgive those who have hurt me, I will draw strength from You. When forgiveness is hard work, I will persevere. You have given me the gift of forgiveness, Father; I will share that gift today, tomorrow, and forever. Amen

ACTIONS SPEAK LOUDER

For the kingdom of God is not in talk but in power.

1 Corinthians 4:20 HCSB

Our words speak, but our actions speak much more loudly. And whether we like it or not, all of us are role models. Since our friends and family members observe our actions, we are obliged to act in ways that demonstrate what it means to be a follower of Christ. As the old saying goes, "It's good to be saved and know it! But it's even better to be saved and show it!"

Today, make this promise to your God and to yourself: promise to be the kind of role model that honors your Heavenly Father and His only begotten Son. When you do so, you will be an ambassador for Christ and a positive role model to a world that needs both.

In your desire to share the gospel, you may be the only Jesus someone else will ever meet. Be real and be involved with people.

Barbara Johnson

— A PRAYER —

Lord, make me a worthy example to my family and friends. And, let my words and my deeds serve as a testimony to the changes You have made in my life. Let me praise You, Father, by following in the footsteps of Your Son, and let others see Him through me. Amen

GOD'S FAITHFULNESS

God is faithful, by whom you were called into the fellowship of His Son, Jesus Christ our Lord.

1 Corinthians 1:9 NKJV

God is faithful to us even when we are not faithful to Him. God keeps His promises to us even when we stray far from His path. God offers us countless blessings, but He does not force His blessings upon us. If we are to experience His love and His grace, we must claim them for ourselves.

God is with you. Listen prayerfully to the quiet voice of your Heavenly Father. Talk with God often; seek His guidance; watch for His signs; listen to the wisdom that He shares through the reliable voice of your own conscience.

God loves you, and you deserve all the best that God has to offer. You can claim His blessings today by being faithful to Him.

It is a joy that God never abandons His children. He guides faithfully all who listen to His directions.

Corrie ten Boom

— A PRAYER —

Heavenly Father, Your faithfulness is complete and perfect. Great is Your faithfulness. Lord, help me to be faithful to You, and to demonstrate faithfulness and loyalty to my friends. Amen

GIVING THANKS
TO THE GIVER

Is anyone cheerful? He should sing praises.

James 5:13 HCSB

The 100th Psalm reminds us that the entire earth should "Shout for joy to the Lord." As God's children, we are blessed beyond measure, but sometimes, as busy women living in a demanding world, we are slow to count our gifts and even slower to give thanks to the Giver.

Our blessings include life and health, family and friends, freedom and possessions—for starters. And, the gifts we receive from God are multiplied when we share them. May we always give thanks to God for His blessings, and may we always demonstrate our gratitude by sharing our gifts with others.

The 118th Psalm reminds us that, "This is the day which the LORD has made; let us rejoice and be glad in it" (v. 24, NASB). May we celebrate this day and the One who created it.

God is worthy of our praise and is pleased when we come before Him with thanksgiving.

Shirley Dobson

— A PRAYER —

Dear Lord, today, I will join in the celebration of life. I will be a joyful Christian, and I will share my joy with all those who cross my path. You have given me countless blessings, Lord, and today I will thank You by celebrating my life, my faith, and my Savior. Amen

REGULAR, PURPOSEFUL WORSHIP

I rejoiced with those who said to me, "Let us go to the house of the Lord."

Psalm 122:1 HCSB

The Bible teaches that we should worship God in our hearts and in our churches (Acts 20:28). We have clear instructions to "feed the church of God" and to worship our Creator in the presence of fellow believers.

We live in a world that is teeming with temptations and distractions—a world where good and evil struggle in a constant battle to win our minds, our hearts, and our souls. Our challenge, of course, is to ensure that we cast our lot on the side of God. One way that we remain faithful to Him is through the practice of regular, purposeful worship with our families. When we worship the Father faithfully and fervently, we are blessed.

Our churches are meant to be havens where the caste rules of the world do not apply.

Beth Moore

— A PRAYER —

Lord, wherever it is that we worship, You are there. Let me support Your church, let me help build Your church, and let me remember that church is not only a place, it is also a state of mind and a state of grace. Amen

CELEBRATING OTHERS

*And let us be concerned about one another in order to promote love
and good works.*

Hebrews 10:24 HCSB

Do you delight in the victories of others? You should. Each
day provides countless opportunities to encourage others and to
praise their good works. When you do so, you not only spread
seeds of joy and happiness, you also obey the commandments of
God's Holy Word.

Life is a team sport, and all of us need occasional pats on the
back from our teammates. As Christians, we are called upon to
spread the Good News of Christ, and we are also called to spread
a message of encouragement and hope to the world.

Today, let us be cheerful Christians with smiles on our faces
and encouraging words on our lips. By blessing others, we also
bless ourselves, and, at the same time, we do honor to the One
who gave His life for us.

Encouragement starts at home, but it should never end there.

Marie T. Freeman

— A PRAYER —

Dear Lord, let me celebrate the accomplishments of others. Make
me a source of genuine, lasting encouragement to my family and
friends. And let my words and deeds be worthy of Your Son, the
One who gives me strength and salvation, this day and for all
eternity. Amen

FOCUSING ON GOD

Therefore do not worry about tomorrow, for tomorrow will worry about its own things. Sufficient for the day is its own trouble.

Matthew 6:34 NKJV

All of us may find our courage tested by the inevitable disappointments and tragedies of life. After all, ours is a world filled with uncertainty, hardship, sickness, and danger. Old Man Trouble, it seems, is never too far from the front door.

When we focus upon our fears and our doubts, we may find many reasons to lie awake at night and fret about the uncertainties of the coming day. A better strategy, of course, is to focus not upon our fears, but instead upon our God.

God is as near as your next breath, and He is in control. He offers salvation to all His children, including you. God is your shield and your strength; you are His forever. So don't focus your thoughts upon the fears of the day. Instead, trust God's plan and His eternal love for you. And remember: God is good, and He has the last word.

— A PRAYER —

Lord, You are my shepherd. You care for me; You love me; You protect me. With You as my shield, I have no reason to be afraid. But sometimes, Lord, I am afraid. In times of uncertainty, I feel threatened. In times of sorrow, I weep. In times of trouble, I become angry. Help me, Lord, to lean not upon my own incomplete understanding, but upon You. Keep me ever mindful of Your promises, and let me trust You always. You are my shepherd, Lord; and I am Yours forever. Amen

FACING DIFFICULT DAYS

We are pressured in every way but not crushed; we are perplexed but not in despair.

2 Corinthians 4:8 HCSB

All of us face difficult days. Sometimes even the most devout Christian women can become discouraged, and you are no exception. After all, you live in a world where expectations can be high and demands can be even higher.

If you find yourself enduring difficult circumstances, remember that God remains in His heaven. If you become discouraged with the direction of your day or your life, turn your thoughts and prayers to Him. He is a God of possibility, not negativity. He will guide you through your difficulties and beyond them. And then, with a renewed spirit of optimism and hope, you can thank the Giver of all things good for gifts that are simply too numerous to count.

Unparalleled joy and victory come from allowing Christ to do "the hard thing" with us.

Beth Moore

— A PRAYER —

Dear Lord, give me the insight to make wise decisions and the courage to act upon the decisions that I make. Amen

THE COMMANDMENT TO FORGIVE

Be merciful, just as your Father also is merciful.

Luke 6:36 HCSB

Forgiving other people is hard—sometimes very hard. But God tells us that we must forgive others, even when we'd rather not. So, if you're angry with anybody (or if you're upset by something you yourself have done) it's time to forgive . . . now!

Life would be much simpler if you could forgive people "once and for all" and be done with it. Yet forgiveness is seldom that easy. Usually, the decision to forgive is straightforward, but the process of forgiving is more difficult. Forgiveness is a journey that requires effort, time, perseverance, and prayer.

God instructs you to treat other people exactly as you wish to be treated. And since you want to be forgiven for the mistakes that you make, you must be willing to extend forgiveness to other people for the mistakes that they have made. If you can't seem to forgive someone, you should keep asking God to help you until you do. And you can be sure of this: if you keep asking for God's help, He will give it.

— A PRAYER —

Heavenly Father, forgiveness is Your commandment, and I know that I should forgive others just as You have forgiven me. But, genuine forgiveness is difficult. Help me to forgive those who have injured me, and deliver me from the traps of anger and bitterness. Forgiveness is Your way, Lord; let it be mine. Amen

THE ROCK

The Lord is my rock, my fortress and my deliverer; my God is my rock, in whom I take refuge. He is my shield and the horn of my salvation, my stronghold.

Psalm 18:2 NIV

God is the Creator of life, the Sustainer of life, and the Rock upon which righteous lives are built. God is a never-ending source of support for those who trust Him, and He is a never-ending source of wisdom for those who study His Holy Word.

Is God the Rock upon which you've constructed your own life? If so, then you have chosen wisely. Your faith will give you the inner strength you need to rise above the inevitable demands and struggles of your daily life.

Do the demands of this day seem overwhelming? If so, you must rely not only upon your own resources, but more importantly upon the Rock that cannot be shaken. Even if your circumstances are difficult, trust the Father. His promises remain true; His love is eternal; and His goodness endures. And because He is the One who can never be moved, you can stand firm in the knowledge that you are protected by Him now and forever.

Measure the size of the obstacles against the size of God.

Beth Moore

— A PRAYER —

Dear Lord, You are the rock upon which I will build my life. You have given me so much, and I am thankful. I give thanks for Your gifts—and I will share them today and every day. Amen

ACCEPTING HIS LOVE

Praise the Lord, all nations! Glorify Him, all peoples! For great is His faithful love to us; the Lord's faithfulness endures forever. Hallelujah!

Psalm 117 HCSB

The words of 1 John 4:8 teach us that "He who does not love does not know God, for God is love" (NKJV). And because we can be assured that God is love, we can also be assured that God's heart is a loving heart.

God loves you. He loves you more than you can imagine; His affection is deeper than you can fathom. God made you in His own image and gave you salvation through the person of His Son Jesus Christ. And as a result, you have an important decision to make. You must decide what to do about God's love: you can return it . . . or not.

When you accept the love that flows from the heart of God, you are transformed. When you embrace God's love, you feel differently about yourself, your neighbors, your community, your church, and your world.

God's heart is overflowing with love . . . for you. Accept that love. Return that love. And share that love. Today.

When once we are assured that God is good, then there can be nothing left to fear.

Hannah Whitall Smith

— A PRAYER —

Lord, the Bible tells me that You are my loving Father. I thank You for Your love and for Your Son. I will praise You, I will worship You, and I will love You, Dear Lord, today, tomorrow, and forever. Amen

HE IS WITH US ALWAYS

I am not alone, because the Father is with Me.

John 16:32 NKJV

Where is God? God is eternally with us. He is omnipresent. He is, quite literally, everywhere you have ever been and everywhere you will ever go. He is with you night and day; He knows your every thought; He hears your every heartbeat.

Sometimes, in the crush of your daily duties, God may seem far away. Or sometimes, when the disappointments and sorrows of life leave you brokenhearted, God may seem distant, but He is not. When you earnestly seek God, you will find Him because He is here, waiting patiently for you to reach out to Him . . . right here . . . right now.

Make the least of all that goes and the most of all that comes. Don't regret what is past. Cherish what you have. Look forward to all that is to come. And most important of all, rely moment by moment on Jesus Christ.

Gigi Graham Tchividjian

— A PRAYER —

Heavenly Father, help me to feel Your presence in every situation and every circumstance. You are with me, Lord, in times of celebration and in times of sorrow. You are with me when I am strong and when I am weak. You never leave my side even when it seems to me that You are far away. Today and every day, God, let me feel You and acknowledge Your presence so that others, too, might know You through me. Amen

HIS HEALING TOUCH

The Lord says, "Peace, peace to the one who is far or near, and I will heal him."

Isaiah 57:19 HCSB

Are you concerned about your spiritual, physical, or emotional health? If so, there is a timeless source of comfort and assurance that is as near as your next breath. That source of comfort, of course, is God.

God is concerned about every aspect of your life, including your health. And, when you face concerns of any sort—including health-related challenges—God is with you. So trust your medical doctor to do his or her part, and turn to your family and friends for moral, physical, and spiritual support. But don't be afraid to place your ultimate trust in your benevolent Heavenly Father. His healing touch, like His love, endures forever.

Laughter is the language of the young at heart and the antidote to what ails us.

Barbara Johnson

— A PRAYER —

Dear Lord, place Your healing hand upon me. Heal my body and my soul. Let me trust Your promises, Father, and let me turn to You for hope, for restoration, for renewal, and for salvation. Amen

SOMEBODY HELPED

Finally, all of you be of one mind, having compassion for one another; love as brothers, be tenderhearted, be courteous.

1 Peter 3:8 NKJV

When you experience success, it's easy to look squarely into the mirror and proclaim, "I did that!" But it's wrong.

Oprah Winfrey, a woman who knows something about success, correctly observed, "For every one of us who succeeds, it's because there's somebody there to show us the way." Yet most of us are sorely tempted to overestimate our own accomplishments— it's a temptation we should do our level best to resist.

There is no such thing as a self-made man or woman. All of us are made by God and helped by a long list of family and friends, people who have lightened our loads and guided our steps. And if we're wise, we will happily share the credit.

We are never stronger than the moment we admit we are weak.

Beth Moore

— A PRAYER —

Dear Lord, keep me humble. It is the nature of mankind to be prideful, and I am no exception. When I am boastful, keep me mindful that all my gifts come from You. Let me grow beyond my need for earthly praise, Father, and let me look only to You for approval. You are the Giver of all things good; let me give all the glory to You. Amen

SMILE

Jacob said, "For what a relief it is to see your friendly smile. It is like seeing the smile of God!"

Genesis 33:10 NLT

A smile is nourishment for the heart, and laughter is medicine for the soul—but sometimes, amid the stresses of the day, we forget to take our medicine. Instead of viewing our world with a mixture of optimism and humor, we allow worries and distractions to rob us of the joy that God intends for our lives.

Today, as you go about your daily activities, approach life with a smile on your lips and hope in your heart. Look for reasons to laugh and to smile. The world needs every smile it can get, including yours!

As you're rushing through life, take time to stop a moment, look into people's eyes, say something kind, and try to make them laugh!

Barbara Johnson

— A PRAYER —

Dear Lord, You have given me so many reasons to celebrate life. Today, let me be a joyful Christian—quick to smile and quick to laugh. And, let Your love shine in me and through me, this day and forever. Amen

UNCHANGING LAWS

God's Law is more real and lasting than the stars in the sky and the ground at your feet. Long after stars burn out and earth wears out, God's Law will be alive and working.

Matthew 5:18 MSG

God's laws are eternal and unchanging: obedience leads to abundance and joy; disobedience leads to disaster. God has given us a guidebook for righteous living called the Holy Bible. If we trust God's Word and live by it, we are blessed. But, if we choose to ignore God's commandments, the results are as predictable as they are tragic.

When we obey God's Word, we earn for ourselves the abundance and peace that He intends for our lives.

Do you seek God's peace and His blessings? Then obey Him. When you're faced with a difficult choice or a powerful temptation, seek God's counsel and trust the counsel He gives. Invite God into your heart and live according to His commandments. When you do, you will be blessed today and tomorrow and forever.

— A PRAYER —

Heavenly Father, when I turn my thoughts away from You and Your Word, I suffer. But when I obey Your commandments, when I place my faith in You, I am secure. Let me live according to Your commandments. Direct my path far from the temptations and distractions of this world. And, let me discover Your will and follow it, Dear Lord, this day and always. Amen

A HEART AFLAME?

Whatever your hands find to do, do with [all] your strength.

Ecclesiastes 9:10 HCSB

We have every reason to be enthusiastic about life, but sometimes the struggles of daily living may cause us to feel decidedly unenthusiastic. Whenever we feel our energies begin to fade, it's time to slow down, to rest, to count our blessings, and to have a sensible talk with God. When we feel worried or weary, a few moments spent in quiet conversation with the Creator can calm our fears and restore our perspective.

Mary Lou Retton observed, "Heat is required to forge anything. Every great accomplishment is the story of a flaming heart." Is your heart aflame? Are you fully engaged in life—and in love? If so, keep up the good work! But if you feel the passion slowly draining from your life, it's time to refocus your thoughts, your energies, and your prayers . . . now.

Wouldn't it make astounding difference, not only in the quality of the work we do, but also in the satisfaction, even our joy, if we recognized God's gracious gift in every single task?

Elisabeth Elliot

— A PRAYER —

Heavenly Father, thank You for the gift of Your Son Jesus. I will be His faithful, obedient servant, and I will make fundamental changes in my life for Him. I will be a passionate believer, and I will praise You for Your blessings, for Your love, and for Your Son. Amen

PERSEVERANCE AND PURPOSE

And let us not grow weary while doing good, for in due season we shall reap if we do not lose heart.

Galatians 6:9 NKJV

As you continue to seek God's purpose for your life, you will undoubtedly experience your fair share of disappointments, detours, false starts, and failures. When you do, don't become discouraged: God's not finished with you yet.

The old saying is as true today as it was when it was first spoken: "Life is a marathon, not a sprint." That's why wise travelers select a traveling companion who never tires and never falters. That partner, of course, is your Heavenly Father.

Are you tired? Ask God for strength. Are you discouraged? Believe in His promises. Are you defeated? Pray as if everything depended upon God, and work as if everything depended upon you. And finally, have faith that you play an important role in God's great plan for mankind—because you do.

Failure is one of life's most powerful teachers. How we handle our failures determines whether we're going to simply "get by" in life or "press on."

Beth Moore

— A PRAYER —

Lord, when life is difficult, I am tempted to abandon hope in the future. But You are my God, and I can draw strength from You. Let me trust You, Father, in good times and in bad times. Let me persevere—even if my soul is troubled—and let me follow Your Son Jesus Christ this day and forever. Amen

PRAISING THE SAVIOR

At the name of Jesus every knee should bow, of those in heaven, and of those on earth, and of those under the earth, and that every tongue should confess that Jesus Christ is Lord, to the glory of God the Father.

Philippians 2:10-11 NKJV

The words by Fanny Crosby are familiar: "This is my story, this is my song, praising my Savior, all the day long." As believers who have been saved by the blood of a risen Christ, we must do exactly as the song instructs: We must praise our Savior time and time again throughout the day. Worship and praise should be a part of everything we do. Otherwise, we quickly lose perspective as we fall prey to the demands of everyday life.

Do you sincerely desire to be a worthy servant of the One who has given you eternal love and eternal life? Then praise Him for who He is and for what He has done for you. And don't just praise Him on Sunday morning. Praise Him all day long, every day, for as long as you live . . . and then for all eternity.

The time for universal praise is sure to come some day. Let us begin to do our part now.

Hannah Whitall Smith

— A PRAYER —

Heavenly Father, I come to You today with hope in my heart and praise on my lips. I place my trust in You, Dear Lord, knowing that with You as my Protector, I have nothing to fear. I thank You, Lord, for Your grace, for Your love, and for Your Son. Let me follow in Christ's footsteps today and every day that I live. And then, when my work here is done, let me live with You forever. Amen

PRAY WITHOUT CEASING

Is anyone among you suffering? He should pray. Is anyone cheerful? He should sing praises.

James 5:13 HCSB

In his first letter to the Thessalonians, Paul advised members of the new church to "pray without ceasing" (5:16-18). His advice applies to Christians of every generation. When we consult God on an hourly basis, we avail ourselves of His wisdom, His strength, and His love. As Corrie ten Boom observed, "Any concern that is too small to be turned into a prayer is too small to be made into a burden."

Today, instead of turning things over in your mind, turn them over to God in prayer. Instead of worrying about your next decision, ask God to lead the way. Don't limit your prayers to meals or bedtime. Become a woman of constant prayer. God is listening, and He wants to hear from you. Now.

What of the great prayer Jesus taught us to pray? It is for His kingdom and His will, yet we ought not to ask it unless we ourselves are prepared to cooperate.

Elisabeth Elliot

— A PRAYER —

Dear Lord, make me a woman of constant prayer. Your Holy Word commands me to pray without ceasing. In all things great and small, at all times, whether happy or sad, let me seek Your wisdom and Your strength in prayer. Amen

WHAT TO DO?

You have already heard about this hope in the message of truth, the gospel that has come to you. It is bearing fruit and growing all over the world, just as it has among you since the day you heard it and recognized God's grace in the truth.

Colossians 1:5-6 HCSB

"What on earth does God intend for me to do with my life?" It's an easy question to ask but, for many of us, a difficult question to answer. Why? Because God's purposes aren't always clear to us. Sometimes we wander aimlessly in a wilderness of our own making. And sometimes, we struggle mightily against God in an unsuccessful attempt to find success and happiness through our own means, not His.

Sometimes, God's intentions will be clear to you; other times, God's plan will seem uncertain at best. But even on those difficult days when you are unsure which way to turn, you must never lose sight of these overriding facts: God created you for a reason; He has important work for you to do; and He's waiting patiently for you to do it. And the next step is up to you.

The Creator has made us each one of a kind. There is nobody else exactly like us, and there never will be. Each of us is his special creation and is alive for a distinctive purpose.

Luci Swindoll

— A PRAYER —

Heavenly Father, give me a servant's heart. When I lose sight of Your purpose for my life, give me a passion for my daily responsibilities, and when I have completed my work, let all the honor and glory be Yours. Amen

THE HEART OF A SERVANT

The generous soul will be made rich, and he who waters will also be watered himself.

Proverbs 11:25 NKJV

You are a wondrous creation treasured by God. How will you respond? Will you consider each day a glorious opportunity to celebrate life and improve your little corner of the world? Hopefully so because your corner of the world, like so many other corners of the world, can use all the help it can get.

Nicole Johnson observed, "We only live once, and if we do it well, once is enough." Her words apply to you. You can make a difference, a big difference in the quality of your own life and lives of your neighbors, your family, and your friends.

You make the world a better place whenever you find a need and fill it. And in these difficult days, the needs are great—but so are your abilities to meet those needs.

Through our service to others, God wants to influence our world for Him.

Vonette Bright

— A PRAYER —

Lord, You have given me the gift of life. Let me treasure it, and let me use it for Your service and for Your glory. Amen

THE JOURNEY TOWARD SPIRITUAL MATURITY

For this reason also, since the day we heard this, we haven't stopped praying for you. We are asking that you may be filled with the knowledge of His will in all wisdom and spiritual understanding.

Colossians 1:9 HCSB

As Christians, we can and should continue to grow in the love and the knowledge of our Savior as long as we live. Norman Vincent Peale had simple advice for believers of all ages: "Ask the God who made you to keep remaking you." That advice, of course, is perfectly sound, but too often ignored.

In those quiet moments when we open our hearts to God, the Creator who made us keeps remaking us. He gives us direction, perspective, wisdom, and courage. And, the appropriate moment to accept His spiritual gifts is always this one.

You are either becoming more like Christ every day or you're becoming less like Him. There is no neutral position in the Lord.

Stormie Omartian

— A PRAYER —

Dear Lord, when I open myself to You, I am blessed. Let me accept Your love and Your wisdom, Father. Show me Your way, and deliver me from the painful mistakes that I make when I stray from Your commandments. Let me live according to Your Word, and let me grow in my faith every day that I live. Amen

YOUR GOOD WORKS

Even so faith, if it has no works, it is dead.

James 2:17 NASB

The central message of James' letter is the need for believers to act upon their beliefs. James' instruction is clear: "faith without works is dead." We are saved by our faith in Christ, but salvation does not signal the end of our earthly responsibilities; it marks the true beginning of our work for the Lord.

If your faith in God is strong, you will find yourself drawn toward God's work. You will serve Him, not just with words or prayers, but also with deeds. Because of your faith, you will feel compelled to do God's work—to do it gladly, faithfully, joyfully, and consistently.

Today, redouble your efforts to do God's bidding here on earth. Never have the needs—or the opportunities—been greater.

God provides the ingredients for our daily bread but expects us to do the baking. With our own hands!

Barbara Johnson

— A PRAYER —

Lord, direct my path far from the temptations and distractions of the world. Make me a worthy example to my family and friends. And, let my kind words and my good deeds serve as a testimony to the changes You have made in my life. Let me praise You, Father, by following in the footsteps of Your Son, and let others see Him through me. Amen

ACCEPTANCE AND PEACE

Come to terms with God and be at peace; in this way good will come to you.

Job 22:21 HCSB

All of us experience adversity and pain. As human beings with limited understanding, we can never fully understand the will of our Father in heaven. But as believers in a benevolent God, we must always trust His providence.

Are you embittered by a personal tragedy that you did not deserve and cannot understand? If so, it's time to make peace with life. It's time to forgive others, and, if necessary, to forgive yourself. It's time to accept the unchangeable past, to embrace the priceless present, and to have faith in the promise of tomorrow. It's time to trust God completely. And it's time to reclaim the peace—His peace—that can and should be yours.

Faith is the willingness to receive whatever he wants to give, or the willingness not to have what he does not want to give.

Elisabeth Elliot

— A PRAYER —

Dear Lord, when I obey Your commandments, and when I trust the promises of Your Son, I experience love, peace, and abundance. Direct my path far from the temptations and distractions of this world. And, let me discover Your will and follow it, Lord, this day and always. Amen

BEYOND PANIC

When my anxious thoughts multiply within me, Your consolations delight my soul.

Psalm 94:19 NASB

We live in a world that seems to invite panic. Everywhere we turn, or so it seems, we are confronted with disturbing images that seem to cry out. "All is lost." But with God, there is always hope.

God calls us to live above and beyond anxiety. God calls us to live by faith, not by fear. He instructs us to trust Him completely, this day and forever. But sometimes, trusting God is difficult, especially when we become caught up in the incessant demands of an anxious world.

When you feel anxious—and you will—return your thoughts to God's love. Then, take your concerns to Him in prayer and, to the best of your ability, leave them there. Whatever "it" is, God is big enough to handle it. Let Him . . . now!

He treats us as sons, and all he asks in return is that we shall treat Him as a Father whom we can trust without anxiety. We must take the son's place of dependence and trust, and we must let Him keep the father's place of care and responsibility.

Hannah Whitall Smith

— A PRAYER —

Lord, when I am tempted to lose faith in the future, touch my heart with Your enduring love. And, keep me mindful, Lord, that nothing, absolutely nothing, will happen this day that You and I cannot handle together. Amen

BEYOND BLAME

All bitterness, anger and wrath, insult and slander must be removed from you, along with all wickedness. And be kind and compassionate to one another, forgiving one another, just as God also forgave you in Christ.

Ephesians 4:31-32 HCSB

To blame others for our own problems is the height of futility. Yet blaming others is a favorite human pastime. Why? Because blaming is much easier than fixing, and criticizing others is so much easier than improving ourselves. So instead of solving our problems legitimately (by doing the work required to solve them) we are inclined to fret, to blame, and to criticize, while doing precious little else. When we do, our problems, quite predictably, remain unsolved.

Have you acquired the bad habit of blaming others for problems that you could or should solve yourself? If so, you are not only disobeying God's Word, you are also wasting your own precious time. So, instead of looking for someone to blame, look for something to fix, and then get busy fixing it. As you consider your own situation, remember this: God has a way of helping those who help themselves, but He doesn't spend much time helping those who don't.

— A PRAYER —

Dear Lord, free me from the poison of bitterness and the futility of blame. Let me turn away from destructive emotions so that I may know the perfect peace and spiritual abundance that can be mine through Your Son, and when I discover His peace, let me share it with praise on my lips and love in my heart. Amen

THE GIFT OF CHEERFULNESS

A miserable heart means a miserable life; a cheerful heart fills the day with a song.

Proverbs 15:15 MSG

Cheerfulness is a gift that we give to others and to ourselves. And, as believers who have been saved by a risen Christ, why shouldn't we be cheerful? The answer, of course, is that we have every reason to honor our Savior with joy in our hearts, smiles on our faces, and words of celebration on our lips.

Few things in life are more sad, or, for that matter, more absurd, than grumpy Christians. Christ promises us lives of abundance and joy if we accept His love and His grace. Yet sometimes, even the most righteous among us are beset by fits of ill temper and frustration. During these moments, we may not feel like turning our thoughts and prayers to Christ, but if we seek to gain perspective and peace, that's precisely what we must do.

Are you a cheerful Christian? You should be! And what is the best way to attain the joy that is rightfully yours? By giving Christ what is rightfully His: your heart, your soul, and your life.

— A PRAYER —

Dear Lord, Your Word reminds me that this is the day that You have created; let me rejoice in it. Today, let me choose an attitude of cheerfulness and celebration. Let me be a joyful Christian, Lord, quick to smile and slow to anger. And, let me share Your goodness with all whom I meet so that Your love might shine in me and through me. Amen

THREATENED BY THE STORMS OF LIFE

Immediately Jesus spoke to them. "Have courage! It is I. Don't be afraid."

Matthew 14:27 HCSB

A storm rose quickly on the Sea of Galilee, and the disciples were afraid. Although they had seen Jesus perform many miracles, the disciples feared for their lives, so they turned to their Savior, and He calmed the waters and the wind.

Sometimes, we, like the disciples, feel threatened by the inevitable storms of life. And when we are fearful, we, too, can turn to Christ for courage and for comfort.

The next time you're afraid, remember that the One who calmed the wind and the waves is also your personal Savior. And remember that the ultimate battle has already been won at Calvary. We, as believers, can live courageously in the promises of our Lord . . . and we should.

With each new experience of letting God be in control, we gain courage and reinforcement for daring to do it again and again.

Gloria Gaither

— A PRAYER —

Lord, sometimes I face challenges that leave me breathless. When I am fearful, let me lean upon You. Keep me ever mindful, Lord, that You are my God, my strength, and my shield. With You by my side, I have nothing to fear. And, with Your Son Jesus as my Savior, I have received the priceless gift of eternal life. Help me to be a grateful and courageous servant this day and every day. Amen

YOUR GREAT EXPECTATIONS

When dreams come true, there is life and joy.

Proverbs 13:12 NLT

Do you expect your future to be bright? Are you willing to dream king-sized dreams . . . and are you willing to work diligently to make those dreams happen? Hopefully so—after all, God promises that we can do "all things" through Him. Yet most of us, even the most devout among us, live far below our potential. We take half measures; we dream small dreams; we waste precious time and energy on the distractions of the world. But God has other plans for us.

Our Creator intends that we live faithfully, hopefully, courageously, and abundantly. He knows that we are capable of so much more; and He wants us to do the things we're capable of doing; and He wants us to begin doing those things today.

Always stay connected to people and seek out things that bring you joy. Dream with abandon. Pray confidently.

Barbara Johnson

— A PRAYER —

Dear Lord, let me raise my hopes and my dreams, my worries and my fears to You. Let me be a worthy example to family and friends, showing them the importance and the power of prayer. Let me take everything to You in prayer, Lord, and when I do, let me trust in Your answers. Amen

WHAT KIND OF EXAMPLE?

You are the light that gives light to the world . . . . In the same way, you should be a light for other people. Live so that they will see the good things you do and will praise your Father in heaven.

Matthew 5:14, 16 NCV

Whether we like it or not, all of us are examples. The question is not whether we will be examples to our families and friends; the question is simply what kind of examples will we be.

What kind of example are you? Are you the kind of woman whose life serves as a powerful example of righteousness? Are you a woman whose behavior serves as a positive role model for young people? Are you the kind of woman whose actions, day in and day out, are based upon integrity, fidelity, and a love for the Lord? If so, you are not only blessed by God, you are also a powerful force for good in a world that desperately needs positive influences such as yours.

D. L. Moody advised, "A man ought to live so that everybody knows he is a Christian, and most of all, his family ought to know." And that's sound advice because our families and friends are watching . . . and so, for that matter, is God.

One of the best ways to witness to family, friends, and neighbors is to let them see the difference Jesus has made in your life.

Anne Graham Lotz

— A PRAYER —

Lord, I am aware that my behavior will influence others. Let my influence be positive. Let me follow in the footsteps of Your Son, and let others see Him through me. Amen

IS CHRIST THE FOCUS?

I do not consider myself to have taken hold of it. But one thing I do: forgetting what is behind and reaching forward to what is ahead, I pursue as my goal the prize promised by God's heavenly call in Christ Jesus.

Philippians 3:13-14 HCSB

Is Christ the focus of your life? Are you fired with enthusiasm for Him? Are you an energized Christian who allows God's Son to reign over every aspect of your day? Make no mistake: that's exactly what God intends for you to do.

God has given you the gift of eternal life through His Son. In response to God's priceless gift, you are instructed to focus your thoughts, your prayers, and your energies upon God and His only begotten Son. To do so, you must resist the subtle yet powerful temptation to become a "spiritual dabbler."

A person who dabbles in the Christian faith is unwilling to place God in His rightful place: above all other things. Resist that temptation; make God the cornerstone and the touchstone of your life. When you do, He will give you all the strength and wisdom you need to live victoriously for Him.

Whatever we focus on determines what we become.

E. Stanley Jones

— A PRAYER —

Dear Lord, help me to face this day with a spirit of optimism and thanksgiving. And let me focus my thoughts on You and Your incomparable gifts. Amen

FINDING FULFILLMENT

Until now you have not asked for anything in my name. Ask and you will receive, so that your joy will be the fullest possible joy.

John 16:24 NCV

Everywhere we turn, or so it seems, the world promises fulfillment, contentment, and happiness. But the contentment that the world offers is fleeting and incomplete. Thankfully, the fulfillment that God offers is all encompassing and everlasting.

Happiness depends less upon our circumstances than our thoughts. When we turn our thoughts to God, to His gifts, and to His glorious creation, we experience the joy that God intends for His children. But, when we focus on the negative aspects of life— or when we disobey God's commandments—we cause ourselves needless suffering.

Sometimes, amid the inevitable hustle and bustle of life-here-on-earth, we can forfeit—albeit temporarily—the joy of Christ as we wrestle with the challenges of daily living. Yet God's Word is clear: fulfillment through Christ is available to all who seek it and claim it. Count yourself among that number. Then claim the joy, the fulfillment, and the spiritual abundance that the Shepherd offers His sheep.

— A PRAYER —

Dear Lord, when I turn my thoughts and prayers to You, I feel the peace and fulfillment that You intend for my life. But sometimes, when I am distracted by the busyness of the day or the demands of the moment, fulfillment seems far away. You are the Giver of all things good, and You give me peace when I draw close to You. Let me trust Your will, let me follow Your commands, and let me accept Your peace, today and forever. Amen

HIS STRENGTH

The Lord is my light and my salvation; whom shall I fear? The Lord is the strength of my life; of whom shall I be afraid?

Psalm 27:1 NKJV

Have you made God the cornerstone of your life, or is He relegated to a few hours on Sunday morning? Have you genuinely allowed God to reign over every corner of your heart, or have you attempted to place Him in a spiritual compartment? The answer to these questions will determine the direction of your day and your life.

God loves you. In times of trouble, He will comfort you; in times of sorrow, He will dry your tears. When you are weak or sorrowful, God is as near as your next breath. He stands at the door of your heart and waits. Welcome Him in and allow Him to rule. And then, accept the peace and the strength and the protection and the abundance that only God can give.

In my weakness, I have learned, like Moses, to lean hard on God. The weaker I am, the harder I lean on Him. The harder I lean, the stronger I discover Him to be. The stronger I discover God to be, the more resolute I am in this job He's given me to do.

Joni Eareckson Tada

— A PRAYER —

Dear Lord, as I face the challenges of this day, You protect me. I thank You, Father, for Your love and for Your strength. I will lean upon You today and forever. Amen

YOUR HOPE, YOUR CONFIDENCE

Lord, I turn my hope to You. My God, I trust in You.

Psalm 25:1-2 HCSB

The hope that the world offers is fleeting and imperfect. The hope that God offers is unchanging, unshakable, and unending. It is no wonder, then, that when we seek security from worldly sources, our hopes are often dashed. Thankfully, God has no such record of failure.

Where will you place your hopes today? Will you entrust your future to man or to God? Will you seek solace exclusively from fallible human beings, or will you place your hopes, first and foremost, in the trusting hands of your Creator? The decision is yours, and you must live with the results of the choice you make.

For thoughtful believers, hope begins with God. Period. So today, as you embark upon the next stage of your life's journey, consider the words of the Psalmist: "You are my hope; O Lord GOD, You are my confidence" (71:5 NASB). Then, place your trust in the One who cannot be shaken.

Love is the seed of all hope. It is the enticement to trust, to risk, to try, and to go on.

Gloria Gaither

— A PRAYER —

Dear Lord, make me a woman who places her hopes in you. If I become discouraged, let me turn to You. If I grow weak, let me seek strength in You. Today and every day, I will trust You, Father, so that my heart will be filled with faith, and with hope, and with love for You. Amen

LOOK FOR THE JOY

You will show me the path of life; in Your presence is fullness of joy; at Your right hand are pleasures forevermore.

Psalm 16:11 NKJV

Barbara Johnson says, "You have to look for the joy. Look for the light of God that is hitting your life, and you will find sparkles you didn't know were there."

Have you experienced that kind of joy? Hopefully so, because it's not enough to hear someone else talk about being joyful—you must actually experience that kind of joy in order to understand it.

Should you expect to be a joy-filled woman 24 hours a day, seven days a week, from this moment on? No. But you can (and should) experience pockets of joy frequently—that's the kind of joy-filled life that a woman like you deserves to live.

I wanted the deepest part of me to vibrate with that ancient yet familiar longing, that desire for something that would fill and overflow my soul.

Joni Eareckson Tada

— A PRAYER —

Lord, You have told me to give thanks always and to rejoice in Your marvelous creation. Let me be a joyful Christian, Lord, and let me focus my thoughts upon Your blessings and Your love. Help me make this day and every day a cause for celebration as I share the Good News of Your Son Jesus. Amen

AND THE GREATEST OF THESE

Love is patient; love is kind. Love does not envy; is not boastful; is not conceited; does not act improperly; is not selfish; is not provoked; does not keep a record of wrongs; finds no joy in unrighteousness, but rejoices in the truth; bears all things, believes all things, hopes all things, endures all things.

1 Corinthians 13:4-7 HCSB

The beautiful words of 1st Corinthians 13 remind us that love is God's commandment: "But now abide faith, hope, love, these three; but the greatest of these is love" (v. 13, NASB). Faith is important, of course. So, too, is hope. But, love is more important still. Christ showed His love for us on the cross, and, as Christians, we are called upon to return Christ's love by sharing it. Today, let us spread Christ's love to families, friends, and strangers by word and by deed.

When we do little acts of kindness that make life more bearable for someone else, we are walking in love as the Bible commands us.

Barbara Johnson

— A PRAYER —

Dear God, let me share Your love with the world. Make me a woman of compassion. Help me to recognize the needs of others. Let me forgive those who have hurt me, just as You have forgiven me. And let the love of Your Son shine in me and through me today, tomorrow, and throughout all eternity. Amen

Old Testament: Isaiah 49-51

New Testament: 2 Thessalonians 3

CLAIM THE INNER PEACE

Peace I leave with you. My peace I give to you. I do not give to you as the world gives. Your heart must not be troubled or fearful.

John 14:27 HCSB

Are you at peace with the direction of your life? Or are you still rushing after the illusion of "peace and happiness" that our world promises but cannot deliver? The answer to this simple question will determine, to a surprising extent, the direction and the quality of your day and your life.

Joyce Meyer observes, "We need to be at peace with our past, content with our present, and sure about our future, knowing they are all in God's hands."

Today, as a gift to yourself, to your family, and to your friends, claim the inner peace that is your spiritual birthright. It is offered freely; it is yours for the asking. So ask. And then share.

In the center of a hurricane there is absolute quiet and peace. There is no safer place than in the center of the will of God.

Corrie ten Boom

— A PRAYER —

Dear Lord, the peace that the world offers is fleeting, but You offer a peace that is perfect and eternal. Let me take my concerns and burdens to You, Father, and let me feel the spiritual abundance that You offer through the person of Your Son, the Prince of Peace. Amen

WHOSE EXPECTATIONS?

The person who knows my commandments and keeps them, that's who loves me. And the person who loves me will be loved by my Father, and I will love him and make myself plain to him.

John 14:21 MSG

Here's a quick quiz: Whose expectations are you trying to meet?

A. Your friends' expectations

B. Society's expectations

C. God's expectations

If you're a Christian, the correct answer is C., but if you're overly concerned with either A. or B., you're not alone. Plenty of people invest too much energy trying to meet society's expectations and too little energy trying to please God. It's a common behavior, but it's also a very big mistake.

A better strategy, of course, is to try to please God first. To do so, you must prioritize your day according to God's commandments, and you must seek His will and His wisdom in all matters.

Are you having trouble choosing between God's priorities and society's priorities? If so, turn the concerns over to God—prayerfully, earnestly, and often. Then, listen for His answer . . . and trust the answer He gives.

— A PRAYER —

Lord, You know my heart, and you're concerned with the "inner me." Today, I will worry less about what other people think . . . and I'll worry more about what You think. Amen

THE ANTIDOTE TO FEAR

I sought the Lord, and He heard me, and delivered me from all my fears.

Psalm 34:4 NKJV

Considered by some to be the most popular cowgirl of time, she starred with cowboy husband Roy Rogers, and she wrote their theme song "Happy Trails." She was Dale Evans, and she said, "I have found the perfect antidote for fear. Whenever it sticks up its ugly face, I clobber it with prayer."

The Psalmist, we read, "In my distress I prayed to the LORD, and the LORD answered me and rescued me" (118:5). And He'll do the same for you. So if you've been beset by the inevitable disappointments and fears that grip us all from time to time, pray for courage and keep praying. When you do, like Dale Evans and Roy Rogers, you'll see plenty of clear skies and lots of happy trails.

A prayerful heart and an obedient heart will learn, very slowly and not without sorrow, to stake everything on God Himself.

Elisabeth Elliot

— A PRAYER —

I pray to You, my Heavenly Father, because You desire it and because I need it. Prayer not only changes things, it changes me. Help me, Lord, never to face the demands of the day without first spending time with You. Amen

LIVING ON PURPOSE

For it is God who is working among you both the willing and the working for His good purpose.

Philippians 2:13 HCSB

Life is best lived on purpose. And purpose, like everything else in the universe, begins with God. Whether you realize it or not, God has a plan for your life, a divine calling, a direction in which He is leading you. When you welcome God into your heart and establish a genuine relationship with Him, He will begin, in time, to make His purposes known.

Sometimes, God's intentions will be clear to you; other times, God's plan will seem uncertain at best. But even on those difficult days when you are unsure which way to turn, you must never lose sight of these overriding facts: God created you for a reason; He has important work for you to do; and He's waiting patiently for you to do it.

Only God's chosen task for you will ultimately satisfy. Do not wait until it is too late to realize the privilege of serving Him in His chosen position for you.

Beth Moore

— A PRAYER —

Dear Lord, I know that You have a purpose for my life, and I will seek that purpose today and every day that I live. Let my actions be pleasing to You, and let me share Your Good News with a world that so desperately needs Your healing hand and the salvation of Your Son. Amen

HIS ANSWER TO OUR GUILT

If My people who are called by My name will humble themselves, and pray and seek My face, and turn from their wicked ways, then I will hear from heaven, and will forgive their sin and heal their land.

2 Chronicles 7:14 NKJV

All of us have sinned. Sometimes our sins result from our own stubborn rebellion against God's commandments. And sometimes, we are swept up in events that are beyond our abilities to control. Under either set of circumstances, we may experience intense feelings of guilt. But God has an answer for the guilt that we feel. That answer, of course, is His forgiveness. When we confess our wrongdoings and repent from them, we are forgiven by the One who created us.

Are you troubled by feelings of guilt or regret? If so, you must repent from your misdeeds, and you must ask God for His forgiveness. When you do so, He will forgive you completely and without reservation. Then, you must forgive yourself just as God has forgiven you: thoroughly and unconditionally.

When true repentance comes, God will not hesitate for a moment to forgive, cast the sins in the sea of forgetfulness, and put the child on the road to restoration.

Beth Moore

— A PRAYER —

Dear Lord, sometimes I make mistakes and fall short of Your commandments. You have forgiven me, Father; let me forgive myself. When I disobey You, give me a repentant heart. And, whatever my circumstances, keep me mindful that I am Yours today, tomorrow, and forever. Amen

HE WANTS YOUR ATTENTION

Let us lay aside every weight and the sin that so easily ensnares us, and run with endurance the race that lies before us, keeping our eyes on Jesus, the source and perfecter of our faith.

Hebrews 12:1-2 HCSB

Is yours a life of moderation or accumulation? Are you more interested in the possessions you can acquire or in the person you can become? The answers to these questions will determine the direction of your day and, in time, the direction of your life.

Ours is a highly complicated society, a place where people and corporations vie for your attention, for your time, and for your dollars. Don't let them succeed in complicating your life! Keep your eyes focused instead upon God.

If your material possessions are somehow distancing you from God, discard them. If your outside interests leave you too little time for your family or your Creator, slow down the merry-go-round or, better yet, get off the merry-go-round completely. Remember: God wants your full attention, and He wants it today, so don't let anybody or anything get in His way.

Nobody is going to simplify your life for you. You've got to simplify things for yourself.

Marie T. Freeman

— A PRAYER —

Thank You Lord, for the perfect example of how to live, Your Son, Jesus Christ. Help me follow Your voice, Father, not the multitude of voices demanding my attention. And, let me meet Your expectations for my life by serving and loving those whom You have placed along my path. Amen

GOD'S PLAN, OUR RESPONSIBILITIES

His master said to him, "Well done, good and faithful slave! You were faithful over a few things; I will put you in charge of many things. Enter your master's joy!"

Matthew 25:21 HCSB

God has promised us this: when we do our duties in small matters, He will give us additional responsibilities. Sometimes, those responsibilities come when God changes the course of our lives so that we may better serve Him. Sometimes, our rewards come in the form of temporary setbacks that lead, in turn, to greater victories. Sometimes, God rewards us by answering "no" to our prayers so that He can say "yes" to a far grander request that we, with our limited understanding, would never have thought to ask for.

If you seek to be God's servant in great matters, be faithful, be patient, and be dutiful in smaller matters. Then step back and watch as God surprises you with the spectacular creativity of His infinite wisdom and His perfect plan.

As faithful stewards of what we have, ought we not to give earnest thought to our staggering surplus?

Elisabeth Elliot

— A PRAYER —

Dear Lord, make me a faithful steward of my possessions. I trust, Father, that You will provide for me now and throughout eternity. And I will obey Your commandment that I give sacrificially to the needs of Your Church. Thank You, Lord, for Your gifts. Use my tithe as a blessing to others so that Your will might be done today and forever. Amen

SHARING YOUR TESTIMONY

And I say to you, everyone who confesses Me before men, the Son of Man will confess him also before the angels of God.

Luke 12:8 NASB

In his second letter to Timothy, Paul offers a message to believers of every generation when he writes, "God has not given us a spirit of timidity" (1:7 NASB). Paul's meaning is crystal clear: When sharing our testimonies, we, as Christians, must be courageous, forthright, and unashamed.

We live in a world that desperately needs the healing message of Christ Jesus. Every believer, each in his or her own way, bears a personal responsibility for sharing that message. If you are a believer in Christ, you know how He has touched your heart and changed your life. Now it's your turn to share the Good News with others. And remember: today is the perfect time to share your testimony because tomorrow may quite simply be too late.

There is nothing anybody else can do that can stop God from using us . . . We can turn everything into a testimony.

Corrie ten Boom

— A PRAYER —

Dear Lord, You sent Your Son Jesus to die on a cross for me. Jesus endured indignity, suffering, and death so that I might live. Because He lives, I, too, have Your promise of eternal life. Let me share this Good News, Lord, with a world that so desperately needs Your healing hand and the salvation of Your Son. Today, let me share the message of Jesus Christ through my words and my deeds. Amen

EACH DAY A GIFT

Teach us to number our days carefully so that we may develop wisdom in our hearts.

Psalm 90:12 HCSB

This day is a gift from God. How will you use it? Will you celebrate God's gifts and obey His commandments? Will you share words of encouragement and hope with all who cross your path? Will you share the Good News of the risen Christ? Will you trust in the Father and praise His glorious handiwork? The answer to these questions will determine, to a surprising extent, the direction and the quality of your day.

The familiar words of Psalm 118:24 remind us of a profound yet simple truth: "This is the day which the LORD hath made; we will rejoice and be glad in it" (KJV). For Christian believers, every day begins and ends with God and His Son. Christ came to this earth to give us abundant life and eternal salvation. We give thanks to our Maker when we treasure each day and use it to the fullest.

Today, may we give thanks for this day and for the One who created it.

— A PRAYER —

Help me, Father, to learn from the past but not live in it. And, help me to plan for the future but not to worry about it. This is the day that You have given me, Lord. Let me use it according to Your master plan, and let me give thanks for Your blessings. Enable me to live each moment to the fullest, totally involved in Your will. Amen

THE SOURCE OF STRENGTH

Have you not known? Have you not heard? The everlasting God, the Lord, the Creator of the ends of the earth, neither faints nor is weary. His understanding is unsearchable. He gives power to the weak, and to those who have no might He increases strength.

Isaiah 40:28-29 NKJV

God is a never-ending source of strength and courage if we call upon Him. When we are weary, He gives us strength. When we see no hope, God reminds us of His promises. When we grieve, God wipes away our tears.

Do you feel overwhelmed by today's responsibilities? Do you feel pressured by the ever-increasing demands of your life? Then turn your concerns and your prayers over to God. He knows your needs, and He has promised to meet those needs. Whatever your circumstances, God will protect you and care for you . . . if you let Him. Invite Him into your heart and allow Him to renew your spirit. When you trust Him and Him alone, He will never fail you.

God conquers only what we yield to Him. Yet, when He does, and when our surrender is complete, He fills us with a new strength that we could never have known by ourselves. His conquest is our victory!

Shirley Dobson

— A PRAYER —

Lord, sometimes life is difficult. Sometimes, I am worried, weary, or heartbroken. But, when I lift my eyes to You, Father, You strengthen me. When I am weak, You lift me up. Today, I turn to You, Lord, for my strength, for my hope, and my salvation. Amen

TAKING YOUR WORRIES TO GOD

Cast your burden on the Lord, and He shall sustain you; He shall never permit the righteous to be moved.

Psalm 55:22 NKJV

Because life is sometimes difficult, and because we have understandable fears about the uncertainty of the future, we worry. At times, we may find ourselves fretting over the countless details of everyday life. We may worry about our relationships, our finances, our health, or any number of potential problems, some large and some small.

If you're a "worrier" by nature, it's probably time to rethink the way that you think! Perhaps you've formed the unfortunate habit of focusing too intently on negative aspects of life while spending too little time counting your blessings. If so, take your worries to God . . . and leave them there. When you do, you'll learn to worry a little less and to trust God a little more—and that's as it should be because God is trustworthy, you are protected, and your future can be intensely bright.

Anxiety may be natural and normal for the world, but it is not to be part of a believer's lifestyle.

Kay Arthur

— A PRAYER —

Forgive me, Lord, when I worry. Worry reflects a lack of trust in Your ability to meet my every need. Help me to work, Lord, and not to worry. And, keep me mindful, Father, that nothing, absolutely nothing, will happen this day that You and I cannot handle together. Amen

ACTIONS SPEAK LOUDER

Who is wise and understanding among you? He should show his works by good conduct with wisdom's gentleness.

James 3:13 HCSB

The old saying is both familiar and true: actions speak louder than words. And as believers, we must beware: our actions should always give credence to the changes that Christ can make in the lives of those who walk with Him.

God calls upon each of us to act in accordance with His will and with respect for His commandments. If we are to be responsible believers, we must realize that it is never enough simply to hear the instructions of God; we must also live by them. And it is never enough to wait idly by while others do God's work here on earth; we, too, must act. Doing God's work is a responsibility that each of us must bear, and when we do, our loving Heavenly Father rewards our efforts with a bountiful harvest.

We spend our lives dreaming of the future, not realizing that a little of it slips away every day.

Barbara Johnson

— A PRAYER —

Dear Lord, I have heard Your Word, and I have felt Your presence in my heart; let me act accordingly. Let my words and deeds serve as a testimony to the changes You have made in my life. Let me praise You, Father, by following in the footsteps of Your Son, and let others see Him through me. Amen

WHERE TO TAKE YOUR TROUBLES

Be anxious for nothing, but in everything by prayer and supplication, with thanksgiving, let your requests be made known to God.

Philippians 4:6 NKJV

Sometimes, the world seems to shift beneath our feet. From time to time, all of us face adversity, discouragement, or disappointment. And, throughout life, we must all endure life-changing personal losses that leave us anxiously struggling for breath. When we do, God stands ready to protect us.

The Bible instructs us to, "Be strong and courageous, and do the work. Don't be afraid or discouraged, for the Lord God, my God, is with you. He won't leave you or forsake you" (1 Chronicles 28:20 HCSB). When we are troubled, we must call upon God, and in time He will heal us.

Are you anxious? Take those anxieties to God. Are you troubled? Take your troubles to Him. Does your future seem uncertain? Place your trust in the One who is forever faithful.

We must lay our questions, frustrations, anxieties, and impotence at the feet of God and wait for His answer. And then receiving it, we must live by faith.

Kay Arthur

— A PRAYER —

Father, sometimes troubles and distractions preoccupy thoughts and trouble my soul. When I am anxious, Lord, let me turn my prayers to You. When I am worried, give me faith in You. Let me live courageously, Dear God, knowing that You love me and that You will protect me, today and forever. Amen

HIS COMPASSION

For You, Lord, bless the righteous one; You surround him with favor like a shield.

Psalm 5:12 HCSB

Psalm 145 makes this promise: "The LORD is gracious and compassionate, slow to anger and rich in love. The LORD is good to all; he has compassion on all he has made" (vv. 8-9 NIV). As God's children, we are blessed beyond measure, but sometimes, as busy women in a demanding world, we are slow to count our gifts and even slower to give thanks to the Giver. Our blessings include life and health, family and friends, freedom and possessions—for starters. And, the gifts we receive from God are multiplied when we share them with others. May we always give thanks to God for our blessings, and may we always demonstrate our gratitude by sharing them.

Do we not continually pass by blessings innumerable without notice, and instead fix our eyes on what we feel to be our trials and our losses, and think and talk about these until our whole horizon is filled with them, and we almost begin to think we have no blessings at all?

Hannah Whitall Smith

— A PRAYER —

Lord, let me be a woman who counts her blessings, and let me be Your faithful servant as I give praise to the Giver of all things good. You have richly blessed my life, Lord. Let me, in turn, be a blessing to all those who cross my path, and may the glory be Yours forever. Amen

RECEIVING HIS JOY

I have spoken these things to you so that My joy may be in you and your joy may be complete.

John 15:11 HCSB

Few things in life are more sad, or, for that matter, more absurd, than a grumpy Christian. Christ promises us lives of abundance and joy, but He does not force His joy upon us. We must claim His joy for ourselves, and when we do, Jesus, in turn, fills our spirits with His power and His love.

How can we receive from Christ the joy that is rightfully ours? By giving Him what is rightfully His: our hearts and our souls.

When we earnestly commit ourselves to the Savior of mankind, when we place Jesus at the center of our lives and trust Him as our personal Savior, He will transform us, not just for today, but for all eternity. Then we, as God's children, can share Christ's joy and His message with a world that needs both.

Father and Mother lived on the edge of poverty, and yet their contentment was not dependent upon their surroundings. Their relationship to each other and to the Lord gave them strength and happiness.

Corrie ten Boom

— A PRAYER —

Dear Lord, You have given me so many reasons to celebrate. Today, let me choose an attitude of cheerfulness. Let me be a joyful Christian, Lord, quick to smile and slow to anger. And, let me share Your goodness with all whom I meet so that Your love might shine in me and through me. Amen

WHEN LIFE IS DIFFICULT

Be strong and courageous. Do not be terrified; do not be discouraged, for the LORD your God will be with you wherever you go.

Joshua 1:9 NIV

Life-here-on-earth can be difficult and discouraging at times. During our darkest moments, God offers us strength and courage if we turn our hearts and our prayers to Him.

As believing Christians, we have every reason to live courageously. After all, the ultimate battle has already been fought and won on the cross at Calvary. But sometimes, because we are imperfect human beings who possess imperfect faith, we fall prey to fear and doubt. The answer to our fears, of course, is God.

The next time you find your courage tested to the limit, remember that God is as near as your next breath. He is your shield and your strength; He is your protector and your deliverer. Call upon Him in your hour of need and then be comforted. Whatever your challenge, whatever your trouble, God can handle it . . . and will!

What is courage? It is the ability to be strong in trust, in conviction, in obedience. To be courageous is to step out in faith—to trust and obey, no matter what.

Kay Arthur

— A PRAYER —

Dear Lord, fill me with Your Spirit and help me face my challenges with courage and determination. Keep me mindful, Father, that You are with me always—and with You by my side, I have nothing to fear. Amen

MEETING THE OBLIGATIONS

Work hard and cheerfully at whatever you do, as though you were working for the Lord rather than for people.

Colossians 3:23 NLT

Nobody needs to tell you the obvious: You have lots of responsibilities—obligations to yourself, to your family, to your community, and to your God. And which of these duties should take priority? The answer can be found in Matthew 6:33: "But seek first the kingdom of God and His righteousness, and all these things will be provided for you" (HCSB).

When you "seek first the kingdom of God," all your other obligations have a way of falling into place. When you obey God's Word and seek His will, your many responsibilities don't seem quite so burdensome.

So do yourself and your loved ones a favor: take all your duties seriously, especially your duties to God. When you do, you'll discover that pleasing your Father in heaven isn't just the right thing to do; it's also the best way to live.

Discipleship usually brings us into the necessity of choice between duty and desire.

Elisabeth Elliot

— A PRAYER —

Dear Lord, today and every day, let me recognize my responsibilities, and let me fulfill them. And keep me mindful that absolutely no responsibility is greater than my obligation to follow in the footsteps of Your Son. Amen

SHARING THE GOOD NEWS

I will also make You a light of the nations so that My salvation may reach to the end of the earth.

Isaiah 49:6 NASB

After His resurrection, Jesus addressed His disciples:

But the eleven disciples proceeded to Galilee, to the mountain which Jesus had designated. When they saw Him, they worshiped Him; but some were doubtful. And Jesus came up and spoke to them, saying, "All authority has been given to Me in heaven and on earth. Go therefore and make disciples of all the nations, baptizing them in the name of the Father and the Son and the Holy Spirit, teaching them to observe all that I commanded you; and lo, I am with you always, even to the end of the age" (Matthew 28:16–20 NASB).

Christ's great commission applies to Christians of every generation, including our own. Jesus commanded His disciples to become fishers of men. We must do like them, and we must do so now. Tomorrow may be too late.

— A PRAYER —

Heavenly Father, every man and woman, every boy and girl is Your child. You desire that all Your children know Jesus as their Lord and Savior. Father, let me be part of Your Great Commission. Let me give, let me pray, and let me go out into this world so that I might be a fisher of men . . . for You. Amen

THE JOY OF SERVING GOD

Shepherd the flock of God which is among you.

1 Peter 5:2 NKJV

Martha and Mary both loved Jesus, but they showed their love in different ways. Mary sat at the Master's feet, taking in every word. Martha, meanwhile, busied herself with preparations for the meal to come. When Martha asked Jesus if He was concerned about Mary's failure to help, Jesus replied, "Mary has chosen better" (Luke 10:42 NIV). The implication is clear: as believers, we must spend time with Jesus before we spend time for Him. But, once we have placed Christ where He belongs—at the center of our hearts—we must go about the business of serving the One who has saved us.

How can we serve Christ? By sharing His message and by serving those in need. As followers of Jesus, we must make ourselves humble servants to our families, to our neighbors, and to the world. We must help the helpless, love the unloved, protect the vulnerable, and care for the infirm. When we do, our lives will be blessed by the One who sacrificed His life for us.

God has lots of folks who intend to go to work for him "some day." What He needs is more people who are willing to work for Him today.

Marie T. Freeman

— A PRAYER —

Dear Lord, when Jesus humbled Himself and became a servant, He also became an example for me. Make me a faithful steward of my gifts, and let me be a humble servant to my loved ones, to my friends, and to those in need. Amen

WE ARE ALL ROLE MODELS

Be an example to the believers in word, in conduct, in love, in spirit, in faith, in purity.

1 Timothy 4:12 NKJV

Whether we like it or not, all of us are role models. Our friends and family members watch our actions and, as followers of Christ, we are obliged to act accordingly.

What kind of example are you? Are you the kind of woman whose life serves as a genuine example of righteousness? Are you a woman whose behavior serves as a positive role model for young people? Are you the kind of woman whose actions, day in and day out, are based upon kindness, faithfulness, and a love for the Lord? If so, you are not only blessed by God, you are also a powerful force for good in a world that desperately needs positive influences such as yours.

Corrie ten Boom advised, "Don't worry about what you do not understand. Worry about what you do understand in the Bible but do not live by." And that's sound advice because our families and friends are watching . . . and so, for that matter, is God.

Our walk counts far more than our talk, always!

George Mueller

— A PRAYER —

Lord, I want to be Your faithful servant. Guide my thoughts, my words, and my actions. Let me live each day with an unshakable faith in You, Father, trusting You in every circumstance. And, let me be an example of faithful living so that I might be a worthy ambassador for You. Amen

FOLLOW HIM

If anyone serves Me, let him follow Me; and where I am, there My servant will be also. If anyone serves Me, him My Father will honor.

John 12:26 NKJV

Jesus walks with you. Are you walking with Him? Hopefully, you will choose to walk with Him today and every day of your life.

Jesus loved you so much that He endured unspeakable humiliation and suffering for you. How will you respond to Christ's sacrifice? Will you take up His cross and follow Him (Luke 9:23), or will you choose another path? When you place your hopes squarely at the foot of the cross, when you place Jesus squarely at the center of your life, you will be blessed. If you seek to be a worthy disciple of Jesus, you must acknowledge that He never comes "next." He is always first.

Do you hope to fulfill God's purpose for your life? Do you seek a life of abundance and peace? Do you intend to be a Christian, not just in name, but in deed? Then follow Christ. Follow Him by picking up His cross today and every day that you live. When you do, you will quickly discover that Christ's love has the power to change everything, including you.

As we live moment by moment under the control of the Spirit, His character, which is the character of Jesus, becomes evident to those around us.

Anne Graham Lotz

— A PRAYER —

Dear Jesus, my life has been changed forever by Your love and sacrifice. Today I will praise You, I will honor You, and I will walk with You. Amen

TAKING TIME TO ENJOY

Until now you have asked for nothing in My name. Ask and you will receive, that your joy may be complete.

John 16:24 HCSB

Are you a woman who takes time each day to really enjoy life? Hopefully so. After all, you are the recipient of a precious gift—the gift of life. And because God has seen fit to give you this gift, it is incumbent upon you to use it and to enjoy it. But sometimes, amid the inevitable pressures of everyday living, really enjoying life may seem almost impossible. It is not.

For most of us, fun is as much a function of attitude as it is a function of environment. So whether you're standing victorious atop one of life's mountains or trudging through one of life's valleys, enjoy yourself. You deserve to have fun today, and God wants you to have fun today . . . so what on earth are you waiting for?

Whence comes this idea that if what we are doing is fun, it can't be God's will? The God who made giraffes, a baby's fingernails, a puppy's tail, a crooknecked squash, the bobwhite's call, and a young girl's giggle, has a sense of humor. Make no mistake about that.

Catherine Marshall

— A PRAYER —

Dear Lord, laughter is Your gift to me; help me to enjoy it. Today and every day, put a smile on my face, and help me to share that smile with my family and friends. This is the day that You have made, Lord. Let me enjoy it . . . and let me laugh. Amen

HE WILL INSTRUCT YOU

You will show me the path of life; in Your presence is fullness of joy; at Your right hand are pleasures forevermore.

Psalm 16:11 NKJV

God has made this promise to you: He will instruct you in the way you should go. God is always willing to teach, and you should always be willing to learn . . . but sometimes, you will be tempted to ignore God's instruction. Don't do it—instead of ignoring God, start praying about your situation . . . and start listening!

When we sincerely offer heartfelt prayers to our Heavenly Father, He will give direction and meaning to our lives—but He won't force us to follow Him. To the contrary, God has given us the free will to follow His commandments . . . or not. When we stray from God's commandments, we invite bitter consequences. But, when we follow His commandments—and when we genuinely and humbly seek His instruction—God touches our hearts and leads us on the path of His choosing.

Will you trust God to teach you "in the way you should go"? Prayerfully, you will, because to do otherwise is not only the opposite of wisdom; it is also the prelude to disaster.

When Jesus drives something home to you through His Word, don't try to evade it.

Oswald Chambers

— A PRAYER —

Dear Lord, You are the source of all wisdom. I will study Your Word, and I will seek Your will. Today, I will stand upon the truth that You reveal, and I will share Your wisdom with the world. Amen

GOD'S TIMING

Wait for the Lord; be courageous and let your heart be strong. Wait for the Lord.

Psalm 27:14 HCSB

We should learn to trust God's timing, but we are sorely tempted to do otherwise. Why? Because we human beings are usually anxious for things to happen sooner rather than later. But, God knows better.

God has created a world that unfolds according to His own timetable, not ours . . . thank goodness! We mortals might make a terrible mess of things. God does not. God's plan does not always happen in the way that we would like or at the time of our own choosing. Our task is to wait patiently and never lose hope.

In the words of Elisabeth Elliot, "We must learn to move according to the timetable of the Timeless One, and to be at peace." That's advice worth following today, tomorrow, and every day of your life.

When we read of the great Biblical leaders, we see that it was not uncommon for God to ask them to wait, not just a day or two, but for years, until God was ready for them to act.

Gloria Gaither

— A PRAYER —

Dear Lord, Your timing is seldom my timing, but Your timing is always right for me. You are my Father, and You have a plan for my life that is grander than I can imagine. When I am impatient, remind me that You are never early or late. You are always on time, Lord, so let me trust in You . . . always. Amen

WHEN HOPE SLIPS AWAY

Hope deferred makes the heart sick.

Proverbs 13:12 NKJV

Have you ever felt hope for the future slipping away? If so, you have temporarily lost sight of the hope that we, as believers, must place in the promises of our Heavenly Father. If you are feeling discouraged, worried, or worse, remember the words of Psalm 31: "Be of good courage, and He shall strengthen your heart."

Because we are saved by a risen Christ, we can have hope for the future, no matter how desperate our circumstances may seem. After all, God has promised that we are His throughout eternity. And, He has told us that we must place our hopes in Him.

Of course, we will face disappointments and failures, but these are only temporary defeats. Of course, this world can be a place of trials and tribulations, but we are secure. God has promised us peace, joy, and eternal life. And God keeps His promises today, tomorrow, and forever.

Earth's best is only a dim reflection and a preliminary rendering of the glory that will one day be revealed.

Joni Eareckson Tada

— A PRAYER —

Dear Lord, You are my sovereign God. Your Son defeated death; He overcame the world; He gives me life abundant. Your Holy Spirit comforts and guides me. Let me celebrate all Your gifts, and make me a hope-filled Christian today and every day that I live. Amen

SHARE HIS JOY

The Lord reigns; let the earth rejoice.

Psalm 97:1 NKJV

The Lord intends that believers should share His love with His joy in their hearts. Yet sometimes, amid the inevitable hustle and bustle of life-here-on-earth, we can forfeit—albeit temporarily—God's joy as we wrestle with the challenges of daily living.

Joni Eareckson Tada spoke for Christian women of every generation when she observed, "I wanted the deepest part of me to vibrate with that ancient yet familiar longing, that desire for something that would fill and overflow my soul."

If, today, your heart is heavy, open the door of your soul to Christ. He will give you peace and joy. And if you already have the joy of Christ in your heart, share it freely, just as Christ freely shared His joy with you.

According to Jesus, it is God's will that His children be filled with the joy of life.

Catherine Marshall

— A PRAYER —

Lord, make me a joyous Christian. Because of my salvation through Your Son, I have every reason to celebrate life. Let me share the joyful news of Jesus Christ, and let my life be a testimony to His love and to His grace. Amen

GOD ABOVE POSSESSIONS

No one can be a slave of two masters, since either he will hate one and love the other, or be devoted to one and despise the other. You cannot be slaves of God and of money.

Matthew 6:24 HCSB

In our modern society, we need money to live. But as Christians, we must never make the acquisition of money the central focus of our lives. Money is a tool, but it should never overwhelm our sensibilities. The focus of life must be squarely on things spiritual, not things material.

Whenever we place our love for material possessions above our love for God—or when we yield to the countless other temptations of everyday living—we find ourselves engaged in a struggle between good and evil. Let us respond to this struggle by freeing ourselves from that subtle yet powerful temptation: the temptation to love the world more than we love God.

It's sobering to contemplate how much time, effort, sacrifice, compromise, and attention we give to acquiring and increasing our supply of something that is totally insignificant in eternity.

Anne Graham Lotz

— A PRAYER —

Dear Lord, keep me mindful that material possessions cannot bring me joy—my joy comes from You. I will share that joy with family, with friends, and with neighbors, this day and every day. Amen

GENUINE PEACE

These things I have spoken to you, that in Me you may have peace. In the world you will have tribulation; but be of good cheer, I have overcome the world.

John 16:33 NKJV

Have you found the genuine peace that can be yours through Jesus Christ? Or are you still rushing after the illusion of "peace and happiness" that the world promises but cannot deliver? The beautiful words of John 14:27 remind us that Jesus offers us peace, not as the world gives, but as He alone gives. Our challenge is to accept Christ's peace into our hearts and then, as best we can, to share His peace with our neighbors.

Today, as a gift to yourself, to your family, and to your friends, claim the inner peace that is your spiritual birthright: the peace of Jesus Christ. It is offered freely; it has been paid for in full; it is yours for the asking. So ask. And then share.

— A PRAYER —

Dear Lord, when I turn my thoughts and prayers to You, I feel the peace that You intend for my life. But sometimes, Lord, I distance myself from You; sometimes, I am distracted by the busyness of the day or the demands of the moment. When I am worried or anxious, Father, turn my thoughts back to You. You are the Giver of all things good, and You give me peace when I draw close to You. Help me to trust Your will, to follow Your commands, and to accept Your peace, today and forever. Amen

HOW WILL YOU WORSHIP?

For it is written, "You shall worship the Lord your God, and Him only you shall serve."

Matthew 4:10 NKJV

All of mankind is engaged in the practice of worship. Some choose to worship God and, as a result, reap the joy that He intends for His children. Others distance themselves from God by worshiping such things as earthly possessions or personal gratification . . . and when they do so, they suffer.

Today, as one way of worshiping God, make every aspect of your life a cause for celebration and praise. Praise God for the blessings and opportunities that He has given you, and live according to the beautiful words found in the 5th chapter of 1 Thessalonians: "Rejoice evermore. Pray without ceasing. In every thing give thanks: for this is the will of God in Christ Jesus concerning you" (vv. 16-18 KJV).

God deserves your worship, your prayers, your praise, and your thanks. And you deserve the joy that is yours when you worship Him with your prayers, with your deeds, and with your life.

Worship is about rekindling an ashen heart into a blazing fire.

Liz Curtis Higgs

— A PRAYER —

Dear Lord, today I will worship You with my thoughts, my deeds, my words, and my prayers. Amen

WALKING WITH GOD

How happy is everyone who fears the Lord, who walks in His ways!

Psalm 128:1 HCSB

Are you tired? Discouraged? Fearful? Be comforted. Take a walk with God. Jesus called upon believers to walk with Him, and He promised them that He would teach them how to live freely and lightly (Matthew 11:28-30). Are you worried or anxious? Be confident in God's power. He will never desert you. Do you see no hope for the future? Be courageous and call upon God. He will protect you and then use you according to His purposes. Are you grieving? Know that God hears your suffering. He will comfort you and, in time, He will dry your tears. Are you confused? Listen to the quiet voice of your Heavenly Father. He is not a God of confusion. Talk with Him; listen to Him; follow His commandments. He is steadfast, and He is your Protector . . . forever.

Walk in the daylight of God's will because then you will be safe; you will not stumble.

Anne Graham Lotz

— A PRAYER —

Dear Lord, each day I need to walk with You. Your presence provides me security and comfort. As we walk together, Lord, may Your presence be reflected in my life, and may Your love dwell within my heart. Amen

GOD IS THE GIVER

My purpose is to give life in all its fullness.

John 10:10 HCSB

The familiar words of John 10:10 should serve as a daily reminder: Christ came to this earth so that we might experience His abundance, His love, and His gift of eternal life. But Christ does not force Himself upon us; we must claim His gifts for ourselves.

Every woman knows that some days are so busy and so hurried that abundance seems a distant promise. It is not. Every day, we can claim the spiritual abundance that God promises for our lives . . . and we should.

Hannah Whitall Smith spoke for believers of every generation when she observed, "God is the giver, and we are the receivers. And His richest gifts are bestowed not upon those who do the greatest things, but upon those who accept His abundance and His grace."

Christ is, indeed, the Giver. Will you accept His gifts today?

God's riches are beyond anything we could ask or even dare to imagine! If my life gets gooey and stale, I have no excuse.

Barbara Johnson

— A PRAYER —

Dear Lord, as I take the next steps on my life's journey, let me take them with You. Whatever this day may bring, I thank You for the opportunity to live abundantly. Let me use the tools and talents You have given me, Father, and let me lean upon You, today and forever. Amen

THE LESSONS OF TOUGH TIMES

No discipline seems pleasant at the time, but painful. Later on, however, it produces a harvest of righteousness and peace for those who have been trained by it.

Hebrews 12:11 NIV

The times that try your soul are also the times that build your character. During the darker days of life, you can learn lessons that are impossible to learn during sunny, happier days. Times of adversity can—and should—be times of intense spiritual and personal growth. But God will not force you to learn the lessons of adversity. You must learn them for yourself.

The next time Old Man Trouble knocks on your door, re-member that he has lessons to teach. So turn away Mr. Trouble as quickly as you can, but as you're doing so, don't forget to learn his lessons. And remember: the trouble with trouble isn't just the trouble it causes; it's also the trouble we cause ourselves if we ig-nore the things that trouble has to teach. Got that? Then please don't forget it!

What a comfort to know that God is present there in your life, available to meet every situation with you, that you are never left to face any problem alone.

Vonette Bright

— A PRAYER —

Deal Lord, in these difficult days, let me trust the wisdom that I find in Your Holy Word. I seek wisdom, Lord, not as the world gives, but as You give. Lead me in Your ways so that, in time, my wisdom might glorify Your kingdom and Your Son. Amen

OBEYING GOD

. . . so that you may walk worthy of the Lord, fully pleasing to Him, bearing fruit in every good work and growing in the knowledge of God.

Colossians 1:10 HCSB

Life presents us with decisions, decisions that can bring us closer to God . . . or not. When we obey God's command, we are blessed. But, when we turn our backs upon the Creator by disobeying Him, we bring needless suffering upon ourselves and our families.

Do you seek God's peace and His blessings? Then obey Him. When you're faced with a difficult choice or a powerful temptation, seek God's counsel and trust the counsel He gives. Invite God into your heart and live according to His commandments. When you do, you will be blessed today, tomorrow, and forever.

Although God causes all things to work together for good for His children, He still holds us accountable for our behavior.

Kay Arthur

— A PRAYER —

Dear Lord, today and every day, let my actions be consistent with my beliefs. And let me live a life that is worthy of Your love, Your grace, and Your Son. Amen

WHEN GRIEF VISITS

Nevertheless God, who comforts the downcast, comforted us . . . .

2 Corinthians 7:6 NKJV

Grief visits all of us who live long and love deeply. When we lose a loved one, or when we experience any other profound loss, darkness overwhelms us for a while, and it seems as if we cannot summon the strength to face another day—but, with God's help, we can.

Thankfully, God promises that He is "close to the broken-hearted" (Psalm 34:18 NIV). In times of intense sadness, we can turn to Him, and we can turn to close friends and family. When we do, we can be comforted . . . and in time we will be healed.

Concentration camp survivor Corrie ten Boom noted, "There is no pit so deep that God's love is not deeper still." Let us remember those words and live by them . . . especially when the days seem dark.

Researchers have been learning that people who cry frequently enjoy better health overall.

Barbara Johnson

— A PRAYER —

Heavenly Father, Your Word promises that You will not give us more than we can bear; You have promised to lift us out of our grief and despair. Today, Lord, I pray for those who mourn, and I thank You for sustaining all of us in our days of sorrow. May we trust You always and praise You forever. Amen

BEING UNDERSTOOD

Dear friends, if God loved us in this way, we also must love one another.

1 John 4:11 HCSB

What a blessing it is when our friends and loved ones genuinely seek to understand who we are and what we think. Just as we seek to be understood by others, so, too, should we seek to understand the hopes and dreams of our family members and friends.

We live in a busy world, a place where it is all too easy to overlook the needs of others, but God's Word instructs us to do otherwise. In the Gospel of Matthew, Jesus declares, "In everything, therefore, treat people the same way you want them to treat you, for this is the Law and the Prophets" (Matthew 7:12 NASB).

Today, as you consider all the things that Christ has done in your life, honor Him by being a little kinder than necessary. Honor Christ by slowing down long enough to notice the trials and tribulations of your neighbors. Honor Christ by giving the gift of understanding to friends and to family members alike. As a believer who has been eternally blessed by a loving Savior, you should do no less.

— A PRAYER —

Dear Lord, give me the patience and the insight to understand my family and my friends. Give me wisdom to speak the right words to them, and give me the courage to do the right things for them, today and every day. Amen

HIS ABUNDANCE

I have come that they may have life, and that they may have it more abundantly.

John 10:10 NKJV

The Bible gives us hope—as Christians we can enjoy lives filled with abundance.

But what, exactly, did Jesus mean when, in John 10:10, He promised "life . . . more abundantly"? Was He referring to material possessions or financial wealth? Hardly. Jesus offers a different kind of abundance: a spiritual richness that extends beyond the temporal boundaries of this world.

Is material abundance part of God's plan for our lives? Perhaps. But in every circumstance of life, during times of wealth or times of want, God will provide us what we need if we trust Him (Matthew 6). May we, as believers, claim the riches of Christ Jesus every day that we live, and may we share His blessings with all who cross our path.

If you want purpose and meaning and satisfaction and fulfillment and peace and hope and joy and abundant life that lasts forever, look to Jesus.

Anne Graham Lotz

— A PRAYER —

Heavenly Father, You have promised an abundant life through Your Son Jesus. Thank You, Lord, for Your abundance. Guide me according to Your will, so that I might be a worthy servant in all that I say and do, this day and every day. Amen

THE TAPESTRY OF LIFE

Let not your heart be troubled; you believe in God, believe also in Me. In My Father's house are many mansions; if it were not so, I would have told you. I go to prepare a place for you. And if I go and prepare a place for you, I will come again and receive you to Myself; that where I am, there you may be also.

John 14:1-3 NKJV

Life is a tapestry of good days and difficult days, with good days predominating. During the good days, we are tempted to take our blessings for granted (a temptation that we must resist with all our might). But, during life's difficult days, we discover precisely what we're made of. And more importantly, we discover what our faith is made of.

Has your faith been put to the test yet? If so, then you know that with God's help, you can endure life's darker days. But if you have not yet faced the inevitable trials and tragedies of life-here-on-earth, don't worry: you will. And when your faith is put to the test, rest assured that God is perfectly willing—and always ready—to give you strength for the struggle.

Why should I ever resist any delay or disappointment, any affliction or oppression or humiliation, when I know God will use it in my life to make me like Jesus and to prepare me for heaven?

Kay Arthur

— A PRAYER —

Dear Lord, when the day is difficult, give me perspective and faith. When I am weak, give me strength. Let me trust in Your promises, Father, and let me live with the assurance that You are with me not only today, but also throughout all eternity. Amen

ASKING HIM FOR STRENGTH

Keep asking, and it will be given to you. Keep searching, and you will find. Keep knocking, and the door will be opened to you. For everyone who asks receives, and the one who searches finds, and to the one who knocks, the door will be opened.

Matthew 7:7-8 HCSB

Are you a woman in need of renewal? Ask God to strengthen you. Are you troubled? Take your concerns to Him in prayer. Are you discouraged? Seek the comfort of God's promises. Do you feel trapped in a life that lacks fulfillment and joy? Ask God where He wants you to go, and then go there. In all things great and small, seek the transforming power of God's grace. He hears your prayers, and He will answer.

When you ask God to do something, don't ask timidly; put your whole heart into it.

Marie T. Freeman

— A PRAYER —

Dear Lord, I will turn to You for strength. When my responsibilities seem overwhelming, I will trust You to give me courage and perspective. Today and every day, I will look to You as the ultimate source of my hope, my strength, my peace, and my salvation. Amen

MANAGING CHANGE

The wise see danger ahead and avoid it, but fools keep going and get into trouble.

Proverbs 27:12 NCV

There is no doubt. Your world is changing constantly. So today's question is this: How will you manage all those changes? Will you do your best and trust God with the rest, or will you spend fruitless hours worrying about things you can't control, while doing precious little else? The answer to these simple questions will help determine the direction and quality of your life.

The best way to confront change is head-on . . . and with God by your side. The same God who created the universe will protect you if you ask Him, so ask Him—and then serve Him with willing hands and a trusting heart. When you do, you may rest assured that while the world changes moment by moment, God's love endures—unfathomable and unchanging—forever.

Live for today, but hold your hands open to tomorrow. Anticipate the future and its changes with joy. There is a seed of God's love in every event, every circumstance, every unpleasant situation in which you may find yourself.

Barbara Johnson

— A PRAYER —

Dear Lord, our world is constantly changing. When I face the inevitable transitions of life, I will turn to You for strength and assurance. Thank You, Father, for love that is unchanging and everlasting. Amen

COMFORTING THOSE IN NEED

When it is in your power, don't withhold good from the one to whom it is due.

Proverbs 3:27 HCSB

We live in a world that is, on occasion, a frightening place. Sometimes, we sustain life-altering losses that are so profound and so tragic that it seems we could never recover. But, with God's help and with the help of encouraging family members and friends, we can recover.

In times of need, God's Word is clear: as believers, we must offer comfort to those in need by sharing not only our courage but also our faith. In times of adversity, we are wise to remember the words of Jesus, who, when He walked on the waters, reassured His disciples, saying, "Take courage! It is I. Don't be afraid" (Matthew 14:27 NIV). Then, with Christ on His throne—and with trusted friends and loving family members at our sides—we can face our fears with courage and with faith.

— A PRAYER —

Dear Lord, this world can be a difficult place, a place full of suffering and tears. Let me give comfort to those in need, and let me share Your love with those who grieve. When I encounter events that I cannot understand, Lord, keep me ever mindful of Your infinite wisdom and love. When I meet those who mourn, guide my speech. And when I, too, become discouraged, turn my thoughts to Your love and to Your promises. Amen

GOD REWARDS DISCIPLINE

Apply yourself to instruction and listen to words of knowledge.

Proverbs 23:12 HCSB

God's Word reminds us again and again that our Creator expects us to lead disciplined lives. God doesn't reward laziness, misbehavior, or apathy. To the contrary, He expects believers to behave with dignity and discipline.

We live in a world in which leisure is glorified and indifference is often glamorized. But God has other plans. He did not create us for lives of mediocrity; He created us for far greater things.

Life's greatest rewards seldom fall into our laps; to the contrary, our greatest accomplishments usually require lots of work, which is perfectly fine with God. After all, He knows that we're up to the task, and He has big plans for us; may we, as disciplined believers, always be worthy of those plans.

The goal of any discipline is to result in greater freedom. Gal. 5:1

Anonymous

— A PRAYER —

Heavenly Father, make me a woman who understands the need to live a disciplined life. Let me teach others by the faithfulness of my conduct, and let me follow Your will and Your Word, today and every day. Amen

HOPE IS CONTAGIOUS

A word fitly spoken is like apples of gold in pictures of silver.

Proverbs 25:11 KJV

Hope, like other human emotions, is contagious. If you associate with hope-filled, enthusiastic people, their enthusiasm will have a tendency to lift your spirits. But if you find yourself spending too much time in the company of naysayers, pessimists, or cynics, your thoughts, like theirs, will tend to be negative.

Are you a hopeful, optimistic Christian? And do you associate with like-minded people? If so, then you're availing yourself of a priceless gift: the encouragement of fellow believers. But, if you find yourself focusing on the negative aspects of life, perhaps it is time to search out a few new friends.

As a faithful follower of the man from Galilee, you have every reason to be hopeful. So today, look for reasons to celebrate God's endless blessings. And while you're at it, look for people who will join with you in the celebration. You'll be better for their company, and they'll be better for yours.

Sometimes one little spark of kindness is all it takes to reignite the light of hope in a heart that's blinded by pain.

Barbara Johnson

— A PRAYER —

Dear Lord, make a source of genuine, lasting encouragement to my family and friends. And, let my words and deeds be worthy of Your Son, the One who gives me strength and salvation. Today, Father, I will celebrate Your blessings, and I will share your Good News with those who cross my path. Amen

WHEN YOUR COURAGE IS TESTED

Be strong and courageous, all you who put your hope in the Lord.

Psalm 31:24 HCSB

Even the most dedicated Christian woman may find her courage tested by the inevitable disappointments and tragedies of life. After all, we live in a world filled with uncertainty, hardship, sickness, and danger. Old Man Trouble, it seems, is never too far from the front door.

When we focus upon our fears and our doubts, we may find many reasons to lie awake at night and fret about the uncertainties of the coming day. A better strategy, of course, is to focus not upon our fears, but instead upon our God.

God is as near as your next breath, and He is in control. He offers salvation to all His children, including you. God is your shield and your strength; you are His forever. So don't focus your thoughts upon the fears of the day. Instead, trust God's plan and His eternal love for you. And remember: whatever the size of your challenge, God is bigger.

God may say "Wait," but He never says, "Worry."

Anonymous

— A PRAYER —

Father, even when I walk through the valley of the shadow of death, I will fear no evil because You are with me. Thank You, Lord, for Your perfect love, a love that casts out fear and gives me strength and courage to meet the challenges of this world. Amen

GOD CAN HELP US FORGIVE

I will lift up my eyes to the hills. From whence comes my help? My help comes from the Lord, Who made heaven and earth.

Psalm 121:1-2 NKJV

There's no doubt about it: forgiveness is difficult. Being frail, fallible, imperfect human beings, we are quick to anger, quick to blame, slow to forgive, and even slower to forget. Yet as Christians, we are commanded to forgive others, just as we, too, have been forgiven. So even when forgiveness is difficult, we must ask God to help us move beyond the spiritual stumbling blocks of bitterness and hate.

If, in your heart, you hold bitterness against even a single person, forgive. If there exists even one person, alive or dead, whom you have not forgiven, follow God's commandment and His will for your life: forgive. If you are embittered against yourself for some past mistake or shortcoming, forgive. Then, to the best of your abilities, forget. And move on. Bitterness and regret are not part of God's plan for your life. Forgiveness is.

How often should you forgive the other person? Only as many times as you want God to forgive you!

Marie T. Freeman

— A PRAYER —

Heavenly Father, sometimes I am tempted to strike out at those who have hurt me. Keep me mindful that forgiveness is Your commandment. You have forgiven me, Lord; let me show my thankfulness to You by offering forgiveness to others. And, when I do, may others see Your love reflected through my words and deeds. Amen

WHEN WE CANNOT UNDERSTAND

For My thoughts are not your thoughts, nor are your ways My ways, says the LORD. "For as the heavens are higher than the earth, so are My ways higher than your ways, and My thoughts than your thoughts."

Isaiah 55:8-9 NKJV

Try though we might, we simply cannot understand God. We can see His handiwork; we can feel His presence; we can worship His Son; but as mere mortals, we lack the capacity to comprehend a being of infinite power and infinite love. Someday, we will understand Him completely, but until then, we must trust Him completely.

The journey through life leads us over many peaks and through many valleys. When we reach the mountaintops, we find it easy to praise God, to trust Him, and to give thanks. But, when we trudge through the dark valleys of bitterness and despair, trusting God is more difficult.

When our courage is tested to the limit, we must lean upon God's promises. And we must remember that God rules both mountaintops and valleys—with limitless wisdom and unchanging love—now and forever.

— A PRAYER —

Dear Lord, today I will trust You more completely. I will lean upon Your understanding, not mine. And I will trust You to guide my steps along a path of Your choosing. Amen

WE BELONG TO HIM

For He is gracious and compassionate, slow to anger, rich in faithful love.

Joel 2:13 HCSB

The line from the children's song is reassuring and familiar: "Little ones to Him belong. We are weak but He is strong." That message applies to kids of all ages: we are all indeed weak, but we worship a mighty God who meets our needs and answers our prayers.

When we sincerely call upon Him, God is a never-ending source of strength and courage. When we are weary, He gives us strength. When we see no hope, God reminds us of His promises. When we grieve, God wipes away our tears. Whatever our circumstances, God will protect us and care for us . . . if we let Him.

The Bible promises that you can do all things through the power of our risen Savior, Jesus Christ. Your challenge, then, is clear: you must place Christ where He belongs, at the very center of your life. When you do, you will discover that, yes, Jesus loves you and that, yes, He will give you direction and strength if you ask it in His name.

— A PRAYER —

Thank You, Lord, for Your love. Your love is boundless, infinite, and eternal. Today, let me pause and reflect upon Your love for me, and let me share that love with all those who cross my path. And, as an expression of my love for You, Father, let me share the saving message of Your Son with a world in desperate need of His peace. Amen

SETTING ASIDE
QUIET MOMENTS

The Lord is with you when you are with Him. If you seek Him, He will be found by you.

2 Chronicles 15:2 HCSB

Since God is everywhere, we are free to sense His presence whenever we take the time to quiet our souls and turn our prayers to Him. But sometimes, amid the incessant demands of everyday life, we turn our thoughts far from God; when we do, we suffer.

Do you set aside quiet moments each day to offer praise to your Creator? As a woman who has received the gift of God's grace, you most certainly should. Silence is a gift that you give to yourself and to God. During these moments of stillness, you will often sense the infinite love and power of your Creator—and He, in turn, will speak directly to your heart.

The familiar words of Psalm 46:10 remind us to "Be still, and know that I am God." When we do so, we encounter the awesome presence of our loving Heavenly Father, and we are comforted in the knowledge that God is not just near. He is here.

In the sanctuary, we discover beauty: the beauty of His presence.

Kay Arthur

— A PRAYER —

Heavenly Father, You never leave or forsake me. You are always with me, protecting me and encouraging me. Whatever this day may bring, I thank You for Your love and Your strength. Let me lean upon You, Father, this day and forever. Amen

HEAVEN IS HOME

For our citizenship is in heaven, from which also we eagerly wait for a Savior, the Lord Jesus Christ.

Philippians 3:20 NASB

Sometimes the troubles of this old world are easier to tolerate when we remind ourselves that heaven is our true home. An old hymn contains the words, "This world is not my home; I'm just passing through." Thank goodness!

This crazy world can be a place of trouble and danger. Thankfully, God has offered you a permanent home in heaven, a place of unimaginable glory, a place that your Heavenly Father has already prepared for you,

In John 16:33, Jesus tells us He has overcome the troubles of this world. We should trust Him, and we should obey His commandments. When we do, we can withstand any problem, knowing that our troubles are temporary, but that heaven is not.

The home you've always wanted, the home you continue to long for with all your heart, is the home God is preparing for you!

Anne Graham Lotz

— A PRAYER —

I know, Lord, that this world is not my home; I am only here for a brief while. And, You have given me the priceless gift of eternal life through Your Son Jesus. Keep the hope of heaven fresh in my heart, and, while I am in this world, help me to pass through it with faith in my heart and praise on my lips . . . for You. Amen

IMITATING CHRIST

For I have given you an example that you also should do just as I have done for you.

John 13:15 HCSB

Each day, we make countless decisions that can bring us closer to God . . . or not. And if we turn our backs upon God by disobeying Him, we must suffer because of our disobedience.

Do you seek to walk in the footsteps of the One from Galilee, or will you choose another path? If you sincerely seek God's peace and His blessings, then you must strive to imitate God's Son.

Thomas Brooks spoke for believers of every generation when he observed, "Christ is the sun, and all the watches of our lives should be set by the dial of his motion." Christ, indeed, is the ultimate Savior of mankind and the personal Savior of those who believe in Him. As His servants, we should walk in His footsteps as we share His love and His message with a world that needs both.

Study the Bible and observe how the persons behaved and how God dealt with them. There is explicit teaching on every condition of life.

Corrie ten Boom

— A PRAYER —

Dear Lord, in weak moments, I seek to build myself up by placing myself ahead of others. But Your commandment, Father, is that I become a humble servant to those who need my encouragement, my help, and my love. Create in me a servant's heart. And, let be a woman who follows in the footsteps of Your Son Jesus who taught us by example that to be great in Your eyes, Lord, is to serve others humbly, faithfully, and lovingly. Amen

THE GLORIOUS GIFT OF LIFE

Seek the Lord and live.

Amos 5:6 NKJV

Life is a glorious gift from God. Treat it that way. This day, like every other, is filled to the brim with opportunities, challenges, and choices. But, no choice that you make is more important than the choice you make concerning God. Today, you will either place Him at the center of your life—or not—and the consequences of that choice have implications that are both temporal and eternal.

Sometimes, without our even realizing it, we gradually drift away from the One we need most. Thankfully, God never drifts away from us. He remains always present, always steadfast, always loving.

As you begin this day, place God and His Son where they belong: in your head, in your prayers, on your lips, and in your heart. And then, with God as your guide and companion, let the journey begin . . .

You have a glorious future in Christ! Live every moment in His power and love.

Vonette Bright

— A PRAYER —

Lord, You have created this glorious universe, and You have created me. Let me use my life to Your glory, and let me dedicate my life to Your Son. Amen

OBEDIENCE AND PEACE

Abundant peace belongs to those who love Your instruction; nothing makes them stumble.

Psalm 119:165 HCSB

If we trust God's Word and live by it, we are blessed. But, if we choose to ignore God's commandments, the results are as predictable as they are tragic.

Do you seek God's peace and His blessings? Then obey Him. When you're faced with a difficult choice or a powerful temptation, seek God's counsel and trust the counsel He gives. Invite God into your heart and live according to His commandments. When you do, you will be blessed today, tomorrow, and forever.

Obedience invites Christ to show his incomparable strength in our mortal weakness.

Beth Moore

— A PRAYER —

Dear Lord, when I am tempted to disobey Your commandments, correct my errors and guide my path. Make me a faithful steward of my talents, my opportunities, and my possessions so that Your kingdom may be glorified, now and forever. Amen

ACCEPTING THE PAST

One thing I do, forgetting those things which are behind and reaching forward to those things which are ahead, I press toward the goal for the prize of the upward call of God in Christ Jesus.

Philippians 3:13-14 NKJV

When you find the courage to accept the past by forgiving all those who have injured you (including yourself), you can then look to the future with a sense of optimism and hope.

Because we are saved by a risen Christ, we can have hope for the future, no matter how troublesome our circumstances may seem. After all, God has promised that we are His throughout eternity. And, He has told us that we must place our hopes in Him.

Of course, we will face disappointments and failures while we are here on earth, but these are only temporary defeats. Of course, this world can be a place of trials and tribulations, but we are secure. God has promised us peace, joy, and eternal life. And God keeps His promises today, tomorrow, and forever.

Shake the dust from your past, and move forward in His promises.

Kay Arthur

— A PRAYER —

Heavenly Father, free me from anger, resentment, and envy. When I am bitter, I cannot feel the peace that You intend for my life. Keep me mindful that forgiveness is Your commandment, and help me accept the past, treasure the present, and trust the future . . . to You. Amen

HE PERSEVERED AND SO MUST WE

If you falter in times of trouble, how small is your strength!

Proverbs 24:10 NIV

In a world filled with roadblocks and stumbling blocks, we need strength, courage, and perseverance. And, as an example of perfect perseverance, we need look no further than our Savior, Jesus Christ.

Jesus finished what He began. Despite the torture He endured, despite the shame of the cross, Jesus was steadfast in His faithfulness to God. We, too, must remain faithful, especially during times of hardship.

Perhaps you are in a hurry for God to reveal His plans for your life. If so, be forewarned: God operates on His own timetable, not yours. Sometimes, God may answer your prayers with silence, and when He does, you must patiently persevere. In times of trouble, you must remain steadfast and trust in the merciful goodness of your Heavenly Father. Whatever your problem, He can handle it. Your job is to keep persevering until He does.

God never gives up on you, so don't you ever give up on Him.

Marie T. Freeman

— A PRAYER —

Dear Lord, life is not a sprint, but a marathon. When the pace of my life becomes frantic, slow me down and give me perspective. Keep me steady and sure. When I become weary, let me persevere so that, in Your time, I might finish my work here on earth, and that You might then say, "Well done my good and faithful servant." Amen

WORSHIP EVERY DAY

I will praise You every day; I will honor Your name forever and ever.

Psalm 145:2 HCSB

Too many of us, even well-intentioned believers, tend to "compartmentalize" our waking hours into a few familiar categories: work, rest, play, family time, and worship. As creatures of habit, we may find ourselves praising God only at particular times of the day or the week. But praise for our Creator should never be reserved for mealtimes or bedtimes or church. Instead, we should praise God all day, every day, to the greatest extent we can, with thanksgiving in our hearts, and with a song on our lips.

Worship and praise should be woven into the fabric of everything we do; they should not be relegated to a weekly three-hour visit to church on Sunday morning. So today, find a little more time to lift your prayers to God, and thank Him for all that He has done. His gifts are beyond understanding, and His love endures forever.

Most of the verses written about praise in God's Word were voiced by people faced with crushing heartaches, injustice, treachery, slander, and scores of other difficult situations.

Joni Eareckson Tada

— A PRAYER —

Heavenly Father, today and every day I will praise You. I come to You with hope in my heart and words of thanksgiving on my lips. Let me follow in Christ's footsteps, and let my thoughts, my prayers, my words, and my deeds praise You now and forever. Amen

HE DESERVES YOUR BEST

For every tree is known by its own fruit.

Luke 6:44 NKJV

God deserves your best. Is He getting it? Do you make an appointment with your Heavenly Father each day? Do you carve out moments when He receives your undivided attention? Or is your devotion to Him fleeting, distracted, and sporadic?

When you acquire the habit of focusing your heart and mind squarely upon God's intentions for your life, He will guide your steps and bless your endeavors. But if you allow distractions to take priority over your relationship with God, they will—and you will pay a price for your mistaken priorities.

Today, focus upon God's Word and upon His will for your life. When you do, you'll be amazed at how quickly everything else comes into focus, too.

Sin is largely a matter of mistaken priorities. Any sin in us that is cherished, hidden, and not confessed will cut the nerve center of our faith.

Catherine Marshall

— A PRAYER —

Lord, let Your priorities be my priorities. Let Your will be my will. Let Your Word be my guide, and let me grow in faith and in wisdom this day and every day. Amen

GETTING PAST THE REGRETS

But as God has distributed to each one, as the Lord has called each one, so let him walk.

1 Corinthians 7:17 NKJV

Bitterness can destroy you if you let it . . . so don't let it!

If you are caught up in intense feelings of anger or regret, you know all too well the destructive power of these emotions. How can you rid yourself of these feelings? First, you must prayerfully ask God to free you from these feelings. Then, you must learn to catch yourself whenever thoughts of bitterness begin to attack you. Your challenge is this: You must learn to resist negative thoughts before they hijack your emotions.

Barbara Johnson has this sound advice: "It is better to forgive and forget than to resent and remember." And she's right—it's better to forget than regret.

Self blame over the past leads to depression in the present and poor decisions for the future.

Barbara Johnson

— A PRAYER —

Heavenly Father, free me from regret, resentment, and anger. When I am bitter, I cannot feel the peace that You intend for my life. Keep me mindful that forgiveness is Your commandment, and help me accept the past, treasure the present, and trust the future to You. Amen

HIS LOVE ENDURES

But the love of the Lord remains forever with those who fear him. His salvation extends to the children's children of those who are faithful to his covenant, of those who obey his commandments!

Psalm 103:17-18 NLT

Are you anxious about situations that you cannot control? Take your anxieties to God. Are you troubled by changes that threaten to disrupt your life? Take your troubles to Him. Does your corner of the world seem to be shaking beneath your feet? Seek protection from the One who cannot be moved.

The same God who created the universe will protect you if you ask Him . . . so ask Him . . . and then serve Him with willing hands and a trusting heart. Rest assured that the world may change moment by moment, but God's love—a love that is unfathomable and unchanging—endures forever.

Conditions are always changing; therefore, I must not be dependent upon conditions. What matters supremely is my soul and my relationship to God.

Corrie ten Boom

— A PRAYER —

Lord, You sent Your Son to live as a man on this earth, and You know what it means to be completely human. You understand my worries and my fears, Lord, and You forgive me when I am weak. When my faith begins to wane, help me, Lord, to trust You more. Then, with Your Holy Word on my lips and with the love of Your Son in my heart, let me live courageously, faithfully, prayerfully, and thankfully today and every day. Amen

WHEN YOUR COURAGE IS TESTED

Do not be afraid. Stand still, and see the salvation of the Lord, which He will accomplish for you today.

Exodus 14:13 NKJV

Jesus has won the victory, so all Christians should live courageously, including you. If you have been touched by the transforming hand of God's Son, then you have every reason to be confident about your future here on earth and your future in heaven. But even if you are a faithful believer, you may find yourself discouraged by the inevitable disappointments and tragedies that are the inevitable price of life here on earth.

If your courage is being tested today, lean upon God's promises. Trust His Son. Remember that God is always near and that He is your protector and your deliverer. When you are worried, anxious, or afraid, call upon Him and accept the touch of His comforting hand. Remember that God rules both mountaintops and valleys—with limitless wisdom and love—now and forever.

Just as courage is faith in good, so discouragement is faith in evil, and, while courage opens the door to good, discouragement opens it to evil.

Hannah Whitall Smith

— A PRAYER —

Dear Lord, give me confidence and courage for the coming day. When I am fearful, let me feel Your strength. Let me always trust in Your promises, Lord, and let me draw strength from those promises and from Your unending love. Amen

DISCIPLINE MATTERS

I discipline my body and bring it under strict control, so that after preaching to others, I myself will not be disqualified.

1 Corinthians 9:27 HCSB

God's Word is clear: as believers, we are called to lead lives of discipline, diligence, moderation, and maturity. But the world often tempts us to behave otherwise. Everywhere we turn, or so it seems, we are faced with powerful temptations to behave in undisciplined, ungodly ways.

We live in a world in which leisure is glorified and misbehavior is glamorized. But God has other plans. He did not create us for lives of mischief or mediocrity; He created us for far greater things.

Life's greatest rewards seldom fall into our laps; to the contrary, God rewards diligence and righteousness just as certainly as He punishes laziness and sin. As believers in a just God, we should behave accordingly.

— A PRAYER —

Dear Lord, Your Holy Word tells us that You expect Your children to be diligent and disciplined. You have told us that the fields are ripe and the workers are few. Lead me to Your fields, Lord, and make me a disciplined worker in the service of Your Son, Christ Jesus. When I am weary, give me strength. When I am discouraged, give me hope. Make me a disciplined, courageous, industrious servant for Your Kingdom today and forever. Amen

STRENGTH FOR TODAY

But those who wait on the LORD shall renew their strength; they shall mount up with wings like eagles, they shall run and not be weary, they shall walk and not faint.

Isaiah 40:31 NKJV

All of us have moments when we feel drained. All of us suffer through difficult days, trying times, and perplexing periods of our lives. Thankfully, God stands ready and willing to give us comfort and strength if we turn to Him.

Burning the candle at both ends is tempting but potentially destructive. Instead, we should place first things first by saying no to the things that we simply don't have the time or the energy to do. As we establish our priorities, we should turn to God and to His Holy Word for guidance.

If you're a woman with too many demands and too few hours in which to meet them, don't fret. Instead, focus upon God and upon His love for you. Then, ask Him for the wisdom to prioritize your life and the strength to fulfill your responsibilities. God will give you the energy to do the most important things on today's to-do list . . . if you ask Him. So ask Him.

— A PRAYER —

Lord, let me find my strength in You. When I am weary, give me rest. When I feel overwhelmed, let me look to You for my priorities. Let Your power be my power, Lord, and let Your way be my way, today and forever. Amen

BEYOND FEAR

But He said to them, "Why are you fearful, O you of little faith?"
Then He arose and rebuked the winds and the sea, and there was a
great calm.

Matthew 8:26 NKJV

A frightening storm rose quickly on the Sea of Galilee, and the disciples were afraid. Because of their limited faith, they feared for their lives. When they turned to Jesus, He calmed the waters and He rebuked His disciples for their lack of faith in Him.

On occasion, we, like the disciples, are frightened by the inevitable storms of life. Why are we afraid? Because we, like the disciples, possess imperfect faith.

When we genuinely accept God's promises as absolute truth, when we trust Him with life-here-on-earth and life eternal, we have little to fear. Faith in God is the antidote to worry. Faith in God is the foundation of courage and the source of power. Today, let us trust God more completely and, by doing so, move beyond our fears to a place of abundance, assurance, and peace.

Only believe, don't fear. Our Master, Jesus, always watches over us, and no matter what the persecution, Jesus will surely overcome it.

Lottie Moon

— A PRAYER —

Heavenly Father, when I am fearful, keep me mindful that You are my protector and my salvation. Give me strength, Lord, to face the challenges of this day as I gain my courage from You. Amen

DISOBEDIENCE INVITES DISASTER

The one who conceals his sins will not prosper, but whoever confesses and renounces them will find mercy.

Proverbs 28:13 HCSB

As creatures of free will, we may disobey God whenever we choose, but when we do so, we put ourselves and our loved ones in peril. Why? Because disobedience invites disaster. We cannot sin against God without consequence. We cannot live outside His will without injury. We cannot distance ourselves from God without hardening our hearts. We cannot yield to the ever-tempting distractions of our world and, at the same time, enjoy God's peace.

Sometimes, in a futile attempt to justify our behaviors, we make a distinction between "big" sins and "little" ones. To do so is a mistake of "big" proportions. Sins of all shapes and sizes have the power to do us great harm. And in a world where sin is big business, that's certainly a sobering thought.

Christians see sin for what it is: willful rebellion against the rulership of God in their lives. And in turning from their sin, they have embraced God's only means of dealing with sin: Jesus.

Kay Arthur

— A PRAYER —

Dear Lord, I am an imperfect human being. When I have sinned, let me repent from my wrongdoings, and let me seek forgiveness— first from You, then from others, and finally from myself. Amen

DEFINING SUCCESS

If you do not stand firm in your faith, then you will not stand at all.

Isaiah 7:9 HCSB

How do you define success? Do you define it as the accumulation of material possessions or the adulation of your neighbors? If so, you need to reorder your priorities. Genuine success has little to do with fame or fortune; it has everything to do with God's gift of love and His promise of salvation.

If you have accepted Christ as your personal Savior, you are already a success in the eyes of God, but there is still more that you can do. Your task—as a believer who has been touched by God's grace—is to accept the spiritual abundance and peace that He offers through the person of His Son. Then, you can share the healing message of God's love and His abundance with a world that desperately needs both. When you do, you have reached the pinnacle of success.

Success isn't the key. Faithfulness is.

Joni Eareckson Tada

— A PRAYER —

Dear Lord, let Your priorities be my priorities. Let Your will be my will. Let Your Word be my guide, and keep me mindful that genuine success is a result, not of the world's approval, but of Your approval. Amen

GIVING THANKS TO THE CREATOR

In everything give thanks; for this is the will of God in Christ Jesus for you.

1 Thessalonians 5:18 NKJV

Psalm 145 makes this promise: "The LORD is gracious and compassionate, slow to anger and rich in love. The LORD is good to all; he has compassion on all he has made" (vv. 8-9 NIV).

Most of us have been blessed beyond measure, but sometimes, as busy women living in a demanding world, we are sometimes slow to count our gifts and even slower to give thanks to the Giver. Our blessings include life and health, family and friends, freedom and possessions—for starters. And those blessings are multiplied when we share them with others.

As the old saying goes, "When we drink the water, we should remember the spring." May we, who have been so richly blessed, give thanks for our gifts—and may we demonstrate our gratitude by sharing them.

God is in control, and therefore in everything I can give thanks, not because of the situation, but because of the One who directs and rules over it.

Kay Arthur

— A PRAYER —

Lord, let me be a woman of gratitude. You have given me much; when I think of Your grace and goodness, I am humbled and thankful. Today, let me praise You not just through my words but also through my deeds . . . and may all the glory be Yours. Amen

EXPECTING THE BEST

Let us hold fast the confession of our hope without wavering, for He who promised is faithful.

Hebrews 10:23 NKJV

What do you expect from the day ahead? Are you expecting God to do wonderful things, or are you living beneath a cloud of apprehension and doubt? The familiar words of Psalm 118:24 remind us of a profound yet simple truth: "This is the day which the LORD hath made; we will rejoice and be glad in it" (KJV).

For Christian believers, every day begins and ends with God and His Son. Christ came to this earth to give us abundant life and eternal salvation. We give thanks to our Maker when we treasure each day and use it to the fullest. Today, let us give thanks for the gift of life and for the One who created it. And then, let's use this day—a precious gift from the Father above—to serve our Savior and to share His Good News with all who cross our paths.

Each day, each moment is so pregnant with eternity that if we "tune in" to it, we can hardly contain the joy.

Gloria Gaither

— A PRAYER —

Lord, You have given me another day of life; let me celebrate this day, and let me use it according to Your plan. I praise You, Father, for my life and for the friends and family members who make it rich. Enable me to live each moment to the fullest as I give thanks for Your creation, for Your love, and for Your Son. Amen

ON MISTAKES AND OPPORTUNITIES

Before I was afflicted I went astray, but now I keep Your word.

Psalm 119:67 HCSB

Have you experienced a recent setback? If so, look for the lesson that God is trying to teach you. Instead of complaining about life's sad state of affairs, learn what needs to be learned, change what needs to be changed, and move on. View failure as an opportunity to reassess God's will for your life. And while you're at it, consider life's inevitable disappointments to be powerful opportunities to learn more—more about yourself, more about your circumstances, and more about your world.

Life can be difficult at times. And everybody (including you) makes mistakes. Your job is to make them only once. And how can you do that? By learning the lessons of tough times sooner rather than later, that's how.

Mistakes offer the possibility for redemption and a new start in God's kingdom. No matter what you're guilty of, God can restore your innocence.

Barbara Johnson

— A PRAYER —

Lord, I know that I am imperfect and that I fail You in many ways. Thank You for Your forgiveness and for Your unconditional love. Show me the error of my ways, Lord, that I might confess my wrongdoing and correct my mistakes. And, let me grow each day in wisdom, in faith, and in my love for You. Amen

CLOSE TO THE BROKENHEARTED

For I am the Lord who heals you.

Exodus 15:26 HCSB

In time, tragedy visits all those who live long and love deeply. When our friends or family members encounter life-shattering events, we struggle to find words that might offer them comfort and support. But finding the right words can be difficult, if not impossible. Sometimes, all that we can do is to be with our loved ones and to pray for them, trusting that God will do the rest.

Thankfully, God promises that He is "close to the brokenhearted" (Psalm 34:18 NIV). In times of intense sadness, we must turn to Him, and we must encourage our friends and family members to do likewise. When we do so, our Father comforts us and, in time, He heals us.

Those who mourn are those who have allowed themselves to feel real feelings because they care about other people.

Barbara Johnson

— A PRAYER —

You have promised, Lord, that You will not give me any more than I can bear. You have promised to lift me out of my grief and despair. You have promised to put a new song on my lips. I thank You, Lord, for sustaining me in my day of sorrow. Restore me, and heal me, and use me as You will. Amen

PRAY ALWAYS

Watch therefore, and pray always that you may be counted worthy.

Luke 21:36 NKJV

Jesus made it clear to His disciples: they should pray always. And so should we. Genuine, heartfelt prayer changes things and it changes us. When we lift our hearts to our Father in heaven, we open ourselves to a never-ending source of divine wisdom and infinite love.

Do you have questions that you simply can't answer? Ask for the guidance of your Father in heaven. Do you sincerely seek the gift of everlasting love and eternal life? Accept the grace of God's only begotten Son. Whatever your need, no matter how great or small, pray about it. Instead of waiting for mealtimes or bedtimes, follow the instruction of your Savior: pray always and never lose heart. And remember: God is not just near; He is here, and He's ready to talk with you. Now!

Allow your dreams a place in your prayers and plans. God-given dreams can help you move into the future He is preparing for you.

Barbara Johnson

— A PRAYER —

Dear Lord, when I pray, let me feel Your presence. When I worship You, let me feel Your love. In the quiet moments of the day, I will open my heart to You, Almighty God. And I know that You are with me always and that You will always hear my prayers. Amen

FORGIVENESS IS A CHOICE

Above all, love each other deeply, because love covers a multitude of sins.

1 Peter 4:8 NIV

Forgiveness is a choice. We can either choose to forgive those who have injured us, or not. When we obey God by offering forgiveness to His children, we are blessed. But when we allow bitterness and resentment to poison our hearts, we are tortured by our own shortsightedness.

Do you harbor resentment against anyone? If so, you are faced with an important decision: whether or not to forgive the person who has hurt you. God's instructions are clear: He commands you to forgive. God doesn't suggest that you forgive or request that you forgive; He commands it. Period.

To forgive or not to forgive: that is the question. The answer should be obvious. The time to forgive is now because tomorrow may be too late . . . for you.

— A PRAYER —

Lord, forgiveness is Your commandment, and I know that I need to forgive others just as You have forgiven me. But genuine, lasting forgiveness is difficult. Help me to forgive those who have injured me, and deliver me from the traps of anger and bitterness. Keep me mindful, Father, that I am never fully liberated until I have been freed from the prison of hatred—and that You offer me that freedom through Your Son, Christ Jesus. Amen

BEYOND CONFUSION

Trust in the Lord with all your heart, and do not rely on your own understanding; think about Him in all your ways, and He will guide you on the right paths.

Proverbs 3:5-6 HCSB

The Bible contains promises, made by God, upon which we, as believers, can and must depend. But sometimes, especially when we find ourselves caught in the inevitable entanglements of life, we fail to trust God completely.

Are you tired? Discouraged? Fearful? Be comforted and trust the promises that God has made to you. Are you worried or anxious? Be confident in God's power. Do you see a difficult future ahead? Be courageous and call upon God. He will protect you and then use you according to His purposes. Are you confused? Listen to the quiet voice of your Heavenly Father. He is not a God of confusion. Talk with Him; listen to Him; trust Him, and trust His promises.

Are you serious about wanting God's guidance to become a personal reality in your life? The first step is to tell God that you know you can't manage your own life; that you need his help.

Catherine Marshall

— A PRAYER —

Dear Lord, thank You for Your constant presence and Your constant love. I draw near to You this day with the confidence that You are ready to guide me. Help me walk closely with You, Father, and help me share Your Good News with all who cross my path. Amen

WHAT NOW, LORD?

For we are His making, created in Christ Jesus for good works, which God prepared ahead of time so that we should walk in them.

Ephesians 2:10 HCSB

God has things He wants you to do and places He wants you to go. The most important decision of your life is, of course, your commitment to accept Jesus Christ as your personal Lord and Savior. And, once your eternal destiny is secured, you will undoubtedly ask yourself the question "What now, Lord?" If you earnestly seek God's will for your life, you will find it . . . in time.

As you prayerfully consider God's path for your life, you should study His Word and be ever watchful for His signs. You should associate with fellow believers who will encourage your spiritual growth, and you should listen to that inner voice that speaks to you in the quiet moments of your daily devotionals.

Rest assured: God is here, and He intends to use you in wonderful, unexpected ways. He desires to lead you along a path of His choosing. Your challenge is to watch, to listen . . . and to follow.

God never calls without enabling us. In other words, if he calls you to do something, he makes it possible for you to do it.

Luci Swindoll

— A PRAYER —

Dear Lord, I seek to live a meaningful life; I will turn to You to find that meaning. I will study Your Word, I will obey Your commandments, I will trust Your providence, and I will honor Your Son. Give me Your blessings, Father, and lead me along a path that is pleasing to You, today, tomorrow, and forever. Amen

A RIGHTEOUS LIFE

But seek first the kingdom of God and His righteousness, and all these things shall be added to you.

Matthew 6:33 NKJV

A righteous life has many components: faith, honesty, generosity, love, kindness, humility, gratitude, and worship, to name but a few. If we seek to follow the steps of our Savior, Jesus Christ, we must seek to live according to His commandments. In short, we must, to the best of our abilities, live according to the principles contained in God's Holy Word.

The Holy Bible contains thorough instructions which, if followed, lead to fulfillment, righteousness, and salvation. But, if we choose to ignore God's commandments, the results are as predictable as they are tragic. Let us follow God's commandments, and let us conduct our lives in such a way that we might be shining examples for those who have not yet found Christ.

He doesn't need an abundance of words. He doesn't need a dissertation about your life. He just wants your attention. He wants your heart.

Kathy Troccoli

— A PRAYER —

Lord, You are a righteous and Holy God, and You have called me to be a righteous woman. When I fall short, forgive me and renew a spirit of holiness within me. Lead me, Lord, along Your path, and guide me far from the temptations of this world. Let Your Holy Word guide my actions, and let Your love reside in my heart, this day and every day. Amen

YOUR RESPONSE TO HIS LOVE

For God so loved the world, that He gave His only begotten Son, that whoever believes in Him shall not perish, but have eternal life.

John 3:16 NASB

God's love for you is deeper and more profound than you can fathom. And now, precisely because you are a wondrous creation treasured by God, a question presents itself: What will you do in response to God's love? Will you ignore it or embrace it? Will you return it or neglect it? The decision, of course, is yours and yours alone.

When you embrace God's love, you are forever changed. When you embrace God's love, you feel differently about yourself, your neighbors, and your world. When you embrace God's love, you share His message and you obey His commandments.

When you accept the Father's grace and share His love, you are blessed here on earth and throughout all eternity. Accept His love today.

Everything I possess of any worth is a direct product of God's love.

Beth Moore

— A PRAYER —

Thank You, Dear God, for Your love. You are my loving Father. I thank You for Your love and for Your Son. I will praise You; I will worship You; and, I will love You today, tomorrow, and forever. Amen

FILLED BY THE SPIRIT

I will put my Spirit in you and you will live....

Ezekiel 37:14 NIV

Are you burdened by the pressures of everyday living? If so, it's time to take the pressure off. How can you do so? By allowing the Holy Spirit to fill you and do His work in your life.

When you are filled with the Holy Spirit, your words and deeds will reflect a love and devotion to Christ. When you are filled with the Holy Spirit, the steps of your life's journey are guided by the Lord. When you allow God's Spirit to work in you and through you, you will be energized and transformed.

Today, allow yourself to be filled with the Spirit of God. And then stand back in amazement as God begins to work miracles in your own life and in the lives of those you love.

The Holy Spirit testifies of Jesus. So when you are filled with the Holy Spirit you speak about our Lord and really live to His honor.

Corrie ten Boom

— A PRAYER —

Dear Lord, You are my sovereign God. Your Son defeated death; Your Holy Spirit comforts and guides me. Let me celebrate all Your gifts, Father, and let me be a hope-filled Christian today and every day. Amen

A HEALTHY FEAR

The fear of man brings a snare, but whoever trusts in the Lord shall be safe.

Proverbs 29:25 NKJV

Are you a woman who possesses a healthy, fearful respect for God's power? Hopefully so. After all, God's Word teaches that the fear of the Lord is the beginning of knowledge (Proverbs 1:7).

When we fear the Creator—and when we honor Him by obeying His commandments—we receive God's approval and His blessings. But, when we ignore Him or disobey His commandments, we invite disastrous consequences.

God's hand shapes the universe, and it shapes our lives. God maintains absolute sovereignty over His creation, and His power is beyond comprehension. As believers, we must cultivate a sincere respect for God's awesome power. The fear of the Lord is, indeed, the beginning of knowledge. So today, as you face the realities of everyday life, remember this: until you acquire a healthy, respectful fear of God's power, your education is incomplete, and so is your faith.

The Holy Spirit will not come to us in his fullness until we see and assent to his priority—his passion for ministry.

Catherine Marshall

— A PRAYER —

Dear Lord, let my greatest fear be the fear of displeasing You. I will strive, Father, to obey Your commandments and seek Your will this day and every day of my life. Amen

NOTES AND FAVORITE SCRIPTURE

NOTES AND FAVORITE SCRIPTURE

NOTES AND FAVORITE SCRIPTURE

NOTES AND FAVORITE SCRIPTURE

NOTES AND FAVORITE SCRIPTURE

NOTES AND FAVORITE SCRIPTURE

NOTES AND FAVORITE SCRIPTURE

NOTES AND FAVORITE SCRIPTURE

NOTES AND FAVORITE SCRIPTURE

NOTES AND FAVORITE SCRIPTURE

NOTES AND FAVORITE SCRIPTURE